PUNISHMENT AND CIVILIZATION

PUNISHMENT AND CIVILIZATION

Penal Tolerance and Intolerance in Modern Society

John Pratt

SAGE Publications
London • Thousand Oaks • New Delhi

SAGE Publications Ltd
6 Bonhill Street
London EC2A 4PU

SAGE Publications Inc
2455 Teller Road
Thousand Oaks, California 91320

SAGE Publications India Pvt Ltd
32, M-Block Market
Greater Kailash - I
New Delhi 110 048

British Library Cataloguing in Publication data

A catalogue record for this book is available
from the British Library

ISBN 0 7619 6209 3
ISBN 0 7619 6210 7 (pbk)

Library of Congress Control Number: 2002102282

Typeset by SIVA Math Setters, Chennai, India
Printed in Great Britain by Athenaeum Press, Gateshead

For Isabella

We have the idea that the civilization we are talking about – ours – is in itself something great and beautiful; something too which is nobler, more comfortable, and better, both morally and materially speaking, than anything outside it – savagery, barbarity, or semi-civilization ... we are confident that such civilization, in which we participate, in which we propagate, benefit from and popularize, bestows on us all a certain value, prestige and dignity.

Lucien Febvre (1930)

Contents

Acknowledgements

It would not have been possible for me to write a book of this scope without the receipt of a Marsden Award from the Royal Society of New Zealand. I am thus most grateful to John Morrow, who, as Assistant Vice-Chancellor (Research) at Victoria University of Wellington, encouraged me to apply for one of these awards, and to the administrative support I subsequently received from VicLink for its duration.

As usual, I received wonderful library support while undertaking this research: from Victoria University, the National Library of New Zealand, the International Documents Room at the Parliamentary Library, Wellington, John Myrtle at the Australian Institute of Criminology, the British Library and the Department of Corrections libraries of New South Wales, Victoria, New York State and Georgia. I have been able to employ excellent research assistants during the course of this research and I would like to thank them for their help: Karlene Hazlewood, Bronwyn Morrison and Anne Holland.

I would also like to thank the group of people who at various times gave me encouragement, references, ideas, provided me with introductions and directions when I seemed lost, commented on drafts, and so on. These are, in no particular order, Mark Finnane, Ian Culpitt, Jonathan Simon, Pat O'Malley, Mick Cavadino, Mark Brown, Malcolm Feiner, Neal Shover, Alison Liebling, Kathy Daly, Ken Polk, Robert van Krieken, Kevin Stenson, Roger Hood, Sarah Anderson, Allan Brodie and colleagues at English Heritage, Willem de Lint, Paul Morris, Nils Christie, Richard Sparks, Gary Wickham, Carolyn Strange, Joe Sim, Martha Myers, Bill Tyler, Andrea Napier, Eric Dunning, the Stephenson family, Stephen Mennell and David Pearson.

The book was completed while I was a Visiting Fellow at the Key Centre for Ethics, Justice, Law and Governance at Griffith University, Brisbane, and I would like to thank all for their hospitality. I would also like to thank the editors and referees of the following journals for their helpful comments and suggestions on papers which helped me to develop the ideas now set out in this book: *Social and Legal Studies, British*

Journal of Sociology, British Journal of Criminology, Punishment and Society, and *Theoretical Criminology*. Photographs are reproduced with the permission of English Heritage.

Finally, I would like to thank my daughter Isabella and my dogs, first Kate then her successor Suzie who did their best to keep me civilized while I explored the civilizing process.

List of Figures

1

Introduction

When asked to comment on the possibility of vigilante attacks in reaction to his decision to release two juvenile murderers after eight years detention, British Home Secretary David Blunkett replied: 'We are not in the Mid West in the mid-nineteenth century, we are in Britain in the twenty-first century and we will deal with things effectively and we will deal with them in a civilized manner'.[1]

By making this link between punishment and civilization, the Home Secretary was following what has become quite a well trodden path, for the standards associated with the term 'civilization' have often been invoked to either justify or condemn a society's penal arrangements.[2] In so doing, this concept helps to set the possibilities of punishing, at least in those societies which like to think of themselves as belonging to the civilized world. But what does 'civilization' actually mean? The *Oxford English Dictionary* (1992: 144) defines it as 'a stage in the evolution of organized society'; and the verb 'to civilize' as 'to cause to improve from a savage or primitive stage of human society to a more developed one'. Commonsensically, then, there is not only a cultural quality to the concept of civilization, but there is a teleological one as well. Hence its usual association today with organized/developed/Western societies: and its non-association with different social formations which are seen, almost by definition, as being at an earlier stage of social development by virtue of not possessing these attributes and identifiers of the civilized world.

And, as was inferred by Home Secretary Blunkett, one of these has become the way a society punishes its offenders. Punishment in the civilized world would not take the form of arbitrary, indefinite detention associated with the notorious gulags of the former Eastern bloc;[3] nor would it involve the public executions, floggings, maimings, and so on associated with the Third World and Islamic societies. Instead, it would be expected to demonstrate such features as the possession of a penal system that was overseen by an enlightened bureaucratic rationalism, precluding any recourse to vigilantism and citizen involvement, since through this organ of government, the state itself would have monopolistic control of the power to punish; and precluding punishments to the human body, relying instead on imprisonment or community-based sanctions. Instead of destroying or brutalizing offenders, punishment in the civilized world was intended to be dispensed with a kind of productive frugality, reforming and rehabilitating criminals. The more a society punished its offenders in these ways, the more it would be thought of as 'civilized' – advanced, socially just, and so on: 'civilization' thus helps to set the cultural parameters of punishment. In addition to its teleological associations, it is as if there is now some innate, essentialist quality to our understandings of the term which is also the exclusive property of those Western societies that identify themselves in this way. Unaware of the term's shifting etymological history,

> by the early part of the twentieth century, [civilization] was used by people in Western societies to refer to a completed process. They increasingly saw themselves as the vanguard of a particular form of personality make-up which they felt compelled to disseminate and thereby advance to all those individuals/societies thought to be uncivilized. (Fletcher, 1997: 8)

At the same time, however, it is as if the very possession of this standard becomes a form of protection for us: so long as our social arrangements sit within its boundaries, then all the darkness associated with the uncivilized regions beyond its boundaries cannot dim our own light.

However, there is another way of understanding the term 'civilization'. Here, it becomes much less comforting, much more disturbing; here, its invocation provides us with no guarantees against darkness and barbarism: indeed, here, the very qualities that we have come to associate with the term 'civilization' – technological proficiency, bureaucratic rationalism, scientific expertise, and so on – are themselves capable of turning off its light; leading us instead into the commission of monstrous incivilities, conduct that we would think had no place in the civilized world. This was the argument most dramatically set out in Zygmund Bauman's *Modernity and the Holocaust* in explaining the barbarities of Nazi Germany:

> civilized manners showed an outstanding ability to cohabit, peacefully and harmoniously with mass murder ... Those mechanisms needed the civilized code of behaviour to co-ordinate criminal actions in such a way that they seldom clashed with the self-righteousness of the perpetrators ... Most bystanders reacted as civilized norms advise and prompt us to react to things unsightly and barbaric; they turned their eyes the other way. (1989: 110)

It was followed by Nils Christie's *Crime Control as Industry* which argued that the growth of mass imprisonment in the civilized world today, exemplified by the United States, is a 'natural outgrowth of our type of society, not an exception to it' (1993: 177).

To a certain extent, this book – a history of punishment in the English-speaking parts of the civilized world from the early nineteenth century to the present time – follows in the distinguished footsteps of these authors but it also takes significant departures from them. My purpose is to examine how the characteristics of a framework of punishment that came to assume qualities that were 'civilized' was established and set in place in these societies during the course of the nineteenth century and for much of the twentieth. I am not saying, however, that such penal arrangements were in themselves civilized in the common sense under-standing of the term. On the contrary, punishment in the civilized world, notwithstanding its differing economy and scale of suffering to that found in the Eastern bloc and Third World, became largely anonymous, remote, encircled by the growing power of the bureaucratic forces pre-siding over it which then shaped, defined and made it understandable; and where, *precisely because of this framework,* which differentiated it from the uncivilized world, brutalities and privations could go largely unchecked or unheeded by a public that preferred not to be involved in such matters. Having said this, there was no necessary stability or per-manence to these arrangements. As has been the case in penal develop-ment from the 1970s in most of these societies, the boundaries of legally sanctioned punishment seem to have been pushed significantly outwards, setting new limits to its possibilities, invoking new strategies that up to that time seemed to have no place in the penal arrangements of the civi-lized world, as they then were, but which have now become acceptable and tolerable.

Norbert Elias and the Civilizing Process

Why is it the case, though, that it is possible to discern such patterns of development taking place across the civilized world over the course of the last two centuries? Why is it that the commitment to being civilized can lend itself to such uncivilized eventualities? To answer such questions, we must move from common-sense understandings of the term 'civi-lization', and instead, consider its use as a sociological construct, as set out in the work of Norbert Elias (1939).[4] For him, what we understand as 'civilization' today is not some innate quality that Western societies possess as of right, but instead the current state of play in a long-term historical *process,* representing the contingent outcome of socio-cultural and psychic change over several centuries. This brought with it two major consequences. First, the central state gradually began to assume much more authority and control over the lives of its citizens, to the point where it came to have a monopoly regarding the raising of taxes, the use of legitimate force and, by inference at least, since Elias himself across the whole corpus of his work said next to nothing about punishment, the imposition of legal sanctions to address disputes. Second, citizens in these societies came to internalize restraints, controls and inhibitions on their conduct, as their values and actions came to be framed around increased sensibility to the suffering of others and the privatization of disturbing events (Elias, 1939; Garland, 1990: 216–25). Elias based his claims on his wide examination of literature, memoirs, artworks, engravings and, most famously, books of etiquette from the Middle Ages through to the nineteenth century. Through these last sources in particular, he was able to trace the long-term developmental changes to a range of features essential to the conduct of everyday life – toilet habits, eating, washing, preparation of food, and so on.

The origins of these sensitivities were to be found in the courtier societies of the late Middle Ages. Over the course of several centuries the mannered society of the court and the forms of civilized behaviour that were demonstrated there began to work their way down and across society at large, establishing, in very general terms, new standards of behaviour, sensitivities and etiquette, and a narrowing of the social distance between rulers and the ruled, so that the habits and practices of both gradually became more interchangeable. Over the last two centuries, the pace of these changes seems to have accelerated, and, with the increased democratization of modern societies, the elite groups who set standards and help to formulate opinion have become both more extensive and diverse, thereby helping to cement the civilizing process across wider areas of the modern social fabric, and at the same time incorporating significant sections of the middle and working classes into democratic systems of rule ('functional democratization'). Indeed, this trend towards 'diminishing social contrasts, but increasing varieties' is for Elias another key identifier of the civilizing process gaining momentum (Mennell, 1992).

However, the cultural changes for which his work is probably best known are only one feature of the civilizing process. 'Culture' is not some free-floating entity, determining values and standards as it sees fit. As Stephen Mennell (1995: 9) has put it, 'regimes of emotion management form and change hand in hand with changes in social organization'. Cultural values must be understood as interacting with, rather than existing independently of, three other features necessary for the civilizing process to take effect. The first of these relates to social structural change. The increasing authority of the state meant that, when disputes arose, citizens would look increasingly to it to resolve such matters for them, rather than attempt to do this themselves. Equally, the growth of European nation–states and the very formation of firm and defensible territorial boundaries were likely to bring a concomitant rise in feelings of responsibility towards and identification with fellow citizens. It would make possible the formation of 'interdependencies' that would become both wider and more firmly cemented with the heterogeneous division of labour in modern society and the attendant shift from rural to urban life. One's significant others, for whom some kind of reciprocity/obligation was owed became more extensive and necessitated restrictions on impulsive behaviour and aggression while simultaneously fostering the converse: foresight and self-restraint.

The second of these relates to changes in social habitus. Elias coined this term to refer to people's 'social character or personality make-up' (Mennell, 1990: 207). That is to say, it was as if, with the advancement of the civilizing process, these moves towards greater foresight and self-restraint would become, as it were, 'second nature'. As these internalized controls on an individual's behaviour became more automatic and pervasive, more and more a taken for granted aspect of cultural life which thereby again raised the threshold of sensitivity and embarrassment, they eventually helped to produce the ideal of the fully rational, reflective and responsible citizen of the civilized world in the nineteenth and twentieth centuries: one who would be sickened by the sight of suffering and, with their own emotions under control, one who respected the authority of the state to resolve disputes on their behalf.

The third is what Elias referred to as 'modes of knowledge' – human belief systems and ways of understanding the world. We thus find, particularly over the last two centuries, less and less reliance on extra human forces such as Nature, Fate and Luck. Instead, with the growth of scientific knowledge, the world became more calculable and understandable. By the same token, this produced belief systems that were no longer organized around myth and fantasy, but instead were much more objective and neutral, based on professional, specialized expertise of varying kinds.

From society to society, the interactive sequences of the civilizing process were likely to be varied, were likely to travel at a different pace and take off at different tangents according to the predominance of what he referred to as 'local centrifugal forces' (for example, population levels, and geographical boundaries), a point he makes clear in his *magnum opus* and elsewhere (Elias, 1996). Thus, if the civilizing process can be seen as taking on a very general form, it can also produce differing, localized manifestations. The same is true of its effects on the different social groupings and interdependencies, or, to use another of Elias' terms, 'figurations'.[5] At both macro and micro levels of social formation, innumerable, dynamic, interchanging and intercrossing civilizing processes have taken place, reflecting the struggle for power between the different groups in any particular figuration: or, again using Eliasian concepts, reflecting the 'established – outsider' relations created by power differentials within it (Elias and Scotson, 1965). The greater the social distance between these groups in any particular figuration, the more predominant would be the world-view of the established, and the more power, within the specifics of the figuration, it would have – with the converse being applied to the outsider group. Indeed, the position of the established is reinforced by the sense of 'group charisma' which comes with their position as an established group. Furthermore, the greater the distance between the two, so the established would come to characterize the outsiders on the basis of myth and fantasy – 'real' knowledge of the outsiders being increasingly minimized.

The civilizing process is thus not formulaic and there is no inevitability to it. Indeed, its fragile and contingent nature could – and has been – interrupted at any time by phenomena such as war, catastrophe, dramatic social change and the like.[6] Under such circumstances, the civilizing process would, as it were, be 'put into reverse' and 'decivilizing forces' would shape social and individual development – the duration and intensity of which being dependent on their own particular strengths and the local stability or instability of the civilizing process. In such situations, 'the armour of civilized conduct crumbles very rapidly', with a concomitant fragmentation of centralized governmental authority and a decline in human capacity for rational action (see Elias, 1994; Fletcher, 1997: 82), making possible the re-emergence of conduct and values more appropriate to previous eras.

From this exegesis, it is necessary to consider some necessary modifications to and defences of Elias' thesis if it is to provide the theoretical backcloth to this book. First, probably one of the most usual criticisms of his work is that, given the history of the uncivilized events of the twentieth century, culminating in the Holocaust itself, his own theory must necessarily fail. However, such criticisms are based on a fundamental misunderstanding of what Elias attempts to do: the term 'civilization', by and large, is not used normatively but as an explanation of the social *process* at work in European societies which then made possible certain forms of conduct which were recognized as being 'civilized' by contemporary standards.[7] *These forms of conduct do not of necessity bring about civilized consequences.* In these respects, the civilizing process itself can be seen as responsible for some of the greatest barbarities of the twentieth century, a point Elias himself makes clear in his later work on the Holocaust (Elias, 1996), in similar fashion to Bauman, notwithstanding the latter's own criticisms of his work.[8] As such, the Holocaust itself could not take place without the harnessing of all the forces of organization and rationalized state planning associated with the civilized world:

> that the camps were able to slaughter on such a huge scale depended on a vast social organization, most people involved in which squeezed no triggers, turned no taps, perhaps saw no camps and set eyes upon few victims. They sat, like Adolf Eichmann, in a highly controlled manner at desks, working out railway timetables. (Mennell, 1992: 249)

Nonetheless, in Elias' (1939) original work, the civilizing process is left at a point around the early nineteenth century – and it therefore does not really capture the significance of features quite specific to social development in the civilized world in the last two centuries – which also seem integrally linked to the twentieth-century barbarities to be found there. That is to say, the central state monopolistic control and regulation of various features of everyday life ultimately led to bureaucratization. The bureaucratization of the activities necessary for the Holocaust not only turned them into organizational routines (whereby nobody could claim ultimate responsibility for what happened) but at the same time drew an effective administrative veil across these most disturbing of all disturbing events: for a good time, at least, 'nobody knew what was going on'.

But nobody knew what was going on because nobody cared what was going on. In the contemporary civilized world, self-restraint seems to turn very easily into moral indifference, when it combines with the range of other anonymizing, anomic factors present in such societies: the loss of community, employment in the large bureaucratic organizations themselves, where one is removed from ultimate responsibility for any distasteful features of its work, remoteness of extended family, and so on. In effect, conduct which we might otherwise find extremely offensive does not trouble us unduly, so long as it is hidden from our view: we are detached from it and thus feel no sense of responsibility or ownership for it. As Bauman writes:

> A civilized society ... is understood as a state from which most of the natural ugliness and morbidity, as well as most of the immanent human propensity to cruelty and violence, have been at least eliminated or suppressed. The popular image of civilized society is more than anything else that of the absence of violence, of a gentle, polite, safe society. (1989: 96)

This is despite what it then allows to happen 'behind the scenes'. For much of the nineteenth and twentieth centuries, I maintain in this book, the contours of penal development in the civilized world followed this route. A system of punishment was established which on the face of it conformed to these values and expectations, and which covered over its more distasteful, debasing features.

However, there is another tendency at work in the civilized world today: the fear of 'Others'. Of course, in any society there has been fear and suspicion of those who seem different, who demonstrate 'otherness'. However, in the twentieth century especially, these tendencies seem to have been built into the construction of the social arrangements of the civilized world: suspicion of 'others' and indifference to depriving them in various ways of full citizenship is exaggerated by the modernist tendency towards the formation of homogenous nation–states. In addition, the reliance on more abstract forms of communication by way of which we discover the world (Giddens, 1990) means that our evidence for the threats posed by such others is likely to be based on television and newspaper accounts rather than our personal experience of them. In all these ways, the boundaries of normal, everyday, self-identifying existence which the scientific know-how and expertise associated with the civilizing process help us to construct are also likely to be challenged on a regular basis by those whose 'otherness' threatens to breach these boundaries. Today, this fear of others can take the form of what Bauman refers to as,

> heterophobia, this is a focussed manifestation of a still wider phenomenon of anxiety aroused by the feeling that one has no control over the situation, and that thus one can neither influence its development, nor foresee the consequences of one's actions ... heterophobia is a fairly common phenomenon at all times and more common still in an age of modernity, when occasions for the 'no control' experience become more frequent, and their interpretation in terms of the obtrusive interference by an alien human group becomes more plausible. (1989: 64)

For Bauman, then, it seems to be the characteristics of civilization itself, one of which is the tendency towards heterophobia, that make the Holocaust a possibility. In contrast, Elias maintains in his later work that it was the combination of the technological and bureaucratic proficiency of the civilizing process and the hatred of Jews brought on by decivilizing influences that in combination made it possible. *There had to be a fusion of both the civilizing process and decivilizing counter-trends.* The heterophobic sentiments in Bauman's work are seen by Elias as the product of group-specific decivilizing influences at work in Germany in the early twentieth century, a product of the way in which these influences broke down tolerance and self-restraint, allowed myth and fantasy to take a hold of popular consciousness, factors which might otherwise have kept their seething hatred under control and internalized (Elias, 1996; Fletcher, 1997). In these respects, if heterophobia can exist in the civilized world, it is as an aberrational feature of it: instead, the values of self-restraint and the internalization of the emotions are its more usual features – leading to what Bauman refers to as 'moral indifference', and keeping our fear of others in control and in check. The subsequent 'jump' from this kind of habitus to one which can embrace and express heterophobia would seem to require some significant decivilizing interruption to make this possible: something which quite dramatically reverses the tradition of restraint, reserve and forbearance.

The position I take in this book is that the civilizing process itself can bring about most uncivilized consequences. The technology and bureaucracy associated with it lead to the framework of punishment that came to be set in place across most of the civilized world around 1970. This alone, though, will not then lead to gulag-type possibilities in the West (*contra* Christie), or other penal developments that we have seen since and which were hitherto associated with uncivilized societies. For such features to come into existence, the forces associated with the civilizing process must be harnessed to the seething, heterophobic tendencies that Bauman refers to: the former provide the engine of punishment, the latter give it its direction. Such distinctions are extremely important, since they lead to very different possibilities. Whereas for Christie, setting free human values and sentiments is seen as having the ability to act as a counterweight to today's gulag tendencies, as if they contain within them some essentialized goodness that has the potential to undermine dark bureaucratic forces, for me the very act of doing so may not only make gulag possibilities more likely but may even lead to new twists in the spiral of penal control beyond this, since we would also be setting free all those 'human propensities for cruelty and violence'. (Bauman, 1989: 96).

The use of the term 'decivilizing' relates to my second point. This particular concept (rather undeveloped in *The Civilizing Process* itself) does not involve some wholesale 'turning the clock back', even if it does make possible the reintroduction of sanctions from previous eras, as I maintain later on in this book. First, the specific intensity and duration of any such 'spurt' is going to be dependent, like the pace of development of the civilizing process itself, on local contingencies. And, second, the effectivity of the civilizing process as a whole seems most unlikely to be swept aside by such forces. Indeed, in the civilized world today, the long-standing trends towards bureaucratization not only in themselves provide an important bulwark against large-scale collapse of the existing social order, but their own momentum is likely to carry them forward, thus further localizing the effects of any decivilizing influences. Under such circumstances it becomes possible to see civilizing and de-civilizing trends operating together with varying degrees of intensity: a continuity of the bureaucratic rationalism associated with the former, running alongside the emotive penal sentiments associated with the latter – thus providing the possibility for the peculiar combination of 'volatile and contradictory punishment' (O'Malley, 1999) that we currently find in existence at the present time.

The third point I wish to discuss relates to the issue of sensitivities themselves: in the civilizing process tradition, these feelings are seen as taking the form of a dislike of disturbing events (usually those which are considered unseemly or brutal) and sympathy for the suffering of others. I do not think these feelings apply in equal measure to all aspects of the civilized world. A desire to have some disturbing events hidden away is greater than for others; sympathy for the suffering of some will be greater than that for others. When we apply these sensitivities to penal development, then it seems clear that the dislike of disturbing events, as the public execution came to be understood in the nineteenth century for the increasingly important middle-class elites and opinion formers, and the antipathy in the twentieth century of nearly all social classes to the presence of a prison as a neighbour has always been a much stronger force than sympathy for the suffering of criminals through the way they have been punished. Indeed, throughout this period, sympathy for the suffering of animals through ill treatment seems to have been far greater, certainly in England.[9] These elite sensitivities to suffering did indeed come to play a part in the eventual abolition of the death penalty and, particularly in the post-war period from around 1950 to 1970, were influential in the development of a kind of scientific humanitarianism which then had a significant influence on penal development. On the part of the general public, however, I do not really think there was ever much sympathy, by and large, except when they got to hear about periodic scandals indicating that the parameters of 'the civilized' had been breached in some way. Then there might be some sympathy and concern. By and large, however, the cold, remorseless deprivation that punishment could inflict in the civilized world – especially if it involved going to prison – did not much trouble the public. If this sanction was certainly enough to decay the human spirit, it was not enough to destroy the human body – and there were thus few grounds for concern: it seemed to produce no ostensible suffering or brutality. If there was any, this took place behind the scenes – no one need know or worry about it. For me, recognition of this unequal distribution of sensitivities does not weaken the civilizing process thesis, it just provides another necessary qualification to it.

Methods

What follows is not the penal history of one particular society, but what can happen in a given society when the forces of the civilizing process combine in a particular way, and what can happen when they begin to unravel. In these respects, it has been necessary to draw on sources from as wide a field as possible and practical to establish the generality of this cultural framework: England, New Zealand, Australia, the United States and Canada. The first two are sole jurisdiction countries; for the rest, purposive sampling techniques selected states, provinces, etc. that represented the extremes of modern development. As regards Australia, in addition to all appropriate commonwealth documentation, the annual prison reports, etc. from New South Wales and Victoria (the one a former prison colony with an historically high prison population, the other with a history of free settlement and a low prison population) have been read; similarly as regards Canada, in relation to Ontario and British Columbia, both of which followed differing patterns of settlement during different eras. From the United States, the same data has been accessed from two states in the North (New York) and the South (Georgia), again representing extremes in social and penal organization in that country.

English penal development provides my main empirical focus, however. Data from the other societies is used to affirm the generality of English trends and the analytical claims that can be made of this, as well as demonstrating and theorizing differences between the respective jurisdictions. I chose to focus on England for the following reasons. It remains the country I am most familiar with, and it has an excellent and accessible record-keeping penal bureaucracy; in addition, from the early nineteenth century, we find wide-ranging commentary on penal affairs. Furthermore, England has provided a greater source for penal development in Australia and New Zealand than the United States (even if the position does not seem so clear in Canada); besides which, it presents an entirety in itself – unlike the United States, where there have been very differing developmental processes at work from North to South (Hindus, 1980). While England thus features predominantly in this book, it is hoped that these other societies will be able to identify themselves to a greater or lesser extent with the themes that emerge.

How, though, might it be possible to undertake such a history of punishment? The way I have done this is to make use of a wide range of historical documentation including penal commentaries, official reports, memoirs, literature and photographs. While all appropriate penal documentation has been read, greatest use has been made of annual prison reports[10] – around 1300 from across these societies and jurisdictions in all. These are the most regular sources of documentation (a testament, perhaps, to the order and efficiency of modern penal bureaucracies) being produced from the nineteenth century onwards, with, usually, the only interruptions to their sequence coming about during periods of significant departmental reorganization or wartime exigencies. It was originally intended to include annual probation reports as well but these have been produced on a much more irregular basis (for New South Wales and Victoria, for example, only from the 1950s), sometimes not at all, and sometimes incorporated in the annual prison reports. As it would thus not be possible to obtain long-standing continuity in most of these jurisdictions, nor provide points of comparison, it was decided not to pursue the probation reports. Much of the documentation is, then, to do with prison development. Here, as with the use Elias made of his 'manners books', it becomes possible to trace in what the penal authorities determined to be appropriate standards of health, personal hygiene, diet – what were thought to be, in effect, the necessary features of prison life itself. By the same token, discontinuities from these standards, or the emergence of new penal norms that discourses of punishment reveal can then be interpreted as indicators of new values that order its development and administration.

Is it possible, however, to rely on such 'official documentation' to understand prison history and the general attitudes to punishment that it reveals? For the purposes of this project, this was an essential component.

For good or bad, it has been official discourse of this nature which has mainly determined 'the reality' of what prison is like and how the public at large have come to 'know' about this institution and the life contained within it – even if it ultimately produces a reality which obviously reflects the expectations and interests of the prison authorities. Of course, when we read the large collection of prisoner memoirs and biographies available to us, a very different reality of prison life emerges.[11] But what these differences between official and unofficial discourse point to is the need to theorize the way in which the reality of prison life came to be largely represented by the official accounts, and how these alternative versions of 'the truth' were covered over or ignored.

Finally, here, to ensure specificity within the project itself, and recognizing the practical limitations to it, it was designed to focus on adult male penality. Juveniles have been excluded since, in the modern world, their penal arrangements have always been more innovative and thereby less entrenched in terms of reflecting core cultural values and more peripheral to mainstream penal thought. Women have not been included since the project attempts to examine the punishment of male offenders in an innovative, exploratory way: my view as well, is that women (and juveniles for that matter) are likely to have been subject to the same penal effects, but often very different ones as well, due to differing cultural attitudes and tolerances towards their particular punishment, which need to be given a specificity of their own. I have had to impose limits on my scholarship and these are the choices I have made, notwithstanding the criticisms that might now be made of them.

Punishment and Civilization

In the first part of this book I examine how the particular understanding of punishment in the civilized world came to take effect, during a period that spans the early nineteenth century through to the 1970s. This involved, first, a shift away from public to private punishment and the eventual demise of punishment to the human body (Chapter 2). It was then followed by the way in which the same effects of the civilizing process led to the large-scale removal of prisons and prisoners from the mainstream of the civilized world: the civilized prison became the invisible prison (Chapter 3). As a further point of differentiation from uncivilized punishment, formal accounts of penal development make frequent reference to the amelioration of its sanctions (using changing attitudes to prison diet, clothing and personal hygiene to illustrate this point, Chapter 4), expressed in the form of a sanitized, objective language of punishment, stripped of unchecked emotion (Chapter 5). This is not to say that the claims made by the authorities led to punishment that was 'civilized': a century and a half of prisoner biographies disputes these claims (Chapter 6). However, that it was the authorities in their formal, sanitized accounts who came to be seen as 'telling the truth' about prison, was in itself the product of two forces specific to the social conditions of the nineteenth and twentieth centuries: on the one hand, bureaucratization (whereby alternative truth claims to those of the authorities would come to be silenced or denied) and, on the other, indifference to what took place in the penal realm on the part of the general public (Chapter 7). It was through this coalescence of wide-ranging social forces and emotions that it became possible to establish a framework of punishment that was recognized as civilized. From the 1970s onwards, however, such understandings of what punishment should be like, fragment and unravel, as the penal effects of the civilizing process begin to break down (Chapter 8). From thereon, new possibilities of punishing in the civilized world emerge: one route is capable of taking us towards Western-style gulags; another to a stage of penal development that lies beyond this, as if the growth of imprisonment in the civilized world today is not sufficient to soak up the intensity of hostile, punitive public sensibilities that have been unleashed (Chapter 9). What thus follows is not a history of how punishment became more – or less – civilized over the course of the nineteenth and twentieth centuries; instead it is a history of how punishment came to take a form that indicated it was 'civilized', and the consequences of such an identification.

Notes

---

1 The comments were made after the decision to release Robert Thompson and John Venables who, at the age of ten, murdered two-year-old James Bulger (*The Weekly Telegraph*, 27 June–3 July 2001: 4).

2 In addition to the most well-known links that have been made between punishment and civilization by Churchill (*Hansard*, col. 1354, 20 July 1910) and Dostoyevsky (1860), it has also been made by commentators as diverse as the Irish political prisoner Michael Davitt (1886), Sir Evelyn Ruggles-Brise (1921), former Head of the English Prison Commission, and Her Majesty's Chief Inspector of Prisons (*Report of the Chief Inspector of Prisons*, 1993).

3 This was an acronym for the central administrative department of the Soviet security service.

4 Norbert Elias (1897–1990) was born in Germany and died in Amsterdam. He became a sociologist in the German Weimar Republic, but, as a Jew, he had to flee the country after Hitler came to power in 1933 (although both his

parents remained in Germany, only to die in the Holocaust). After 1945, he taught in England, Africa and Europe, only really achieving fame in the eighth decade of his life. While his *magnum opus* was published in German in 1939, it was not translated into English until 1969, and only then did his work begin to stimulate wide interest.

5 Elias (1939, 1984: 214) uses the analogy of the dance to explain this concept:

> The image of the mobile figurations of interdependent people on a dance floor perhaps makes it easier to imagine states, cities, families and also capitalist, communist and feudal systems as figurations. Like every other social figuration, a dance figuration is relatively independent of the specific individuals forming it here and now, but not of individuals as such ... Just as the small dance figurations change – becoming now slower, now quicker – so too, gradually or more suddenly, do the large figurations which we call societies.

6 As becomes clear in Chapter 2, in relation to the death penalty debates post-1945, war, in certain circumstances, can also lead to a civilizing spurt.

7 As Fletcher (1997: 45) puts the matter, 'There is some residual ambiguity surrounding the concept of civilization used by Elias. It is not completely clear whether the normative aspect of the term features in his work – he does not consistently place "civilization" in inverted commas to indicate a normative valuation'.

8 See Bauman (1989: 12).

9 See, for example, Strutt (1830), Walvin (1978), Cunningham (1980), Thomas (1983).

10 The annual reports for England and Wales begin in 1835; those for New Zealand in 1880, Georgia 1854, New York State 1848 (there is also a separate series for the State Commission on Prisons from 1897), Ontario 1879, British Columbia 1881, the Canadian Federal Reports 1880, New South Wales 1874, Victoria 1872.

11 Here again I have drawn exclusively on English prisoner biographies: for a variety of reasons, most of which seem beyond the scope of this project, English sources seem to vastly outweigh those from the corresponding countries. I am not minimizing the significance of prisoner biographies in other societies in bringing about penal reform and even broader social change (see, for example, in relation to the United States, Burns, 1932; Jackson, 1971).

2

Carnival, Execution and Civilization

> This morning the Fenian convict, Michael Barrett, expiated his great crime on the scaffold, in the presence of a vast concourse of people. The crowd was, to a large extent, composed of a better class of persons than usually assemble at executions there, and the prevailing behavior was in accordance ... Instead of being conducted to the press room to be pinioned, the convict was pinioned in his cell in the presence of the Under-Sheriffs, and there conducted by a way entirely private and unusual to the scaffold. This he mounted with a firm step, accompanied by his priest and ... the executioner. The moment he appeared upon the drop a kind of cheer broke from the crowd, which swayed about with the wildest excitement ... [the priest] continued to utter words of consolation to the doomed man, whose responses were indented by the motion of the lips, concealed though the mouth was by the cap which had been drawn over the features. The drop at length fell, and piercing shrieks from women in the crowd rent the air for a moment, and that indescribable hum peculiar to such occasions broke upon the ear. The convict, who had great muscular strength, appeared to die slowly. (*The Times*, 26 May 1868: 12)

This was the last occasion that a legal public execution was witnessed in England.[1] The end of public executions in that country, as elsewhere, proved to be a defining moment in the development of punishment in the civilized world. First, in terms of the way in which punishment as a whole – but most graphically here the death penalty – would from now be screened off from public view and administered in private. Second, the way in which the shift from public to private executions which followed the death of Barrett in England was another step on what proved to be a rather longer route towards the complete prohibition on punishments to the body in the civilized world, finally coming to an end around 1970. Barrett's execution thus had a dual significance, intersecting as it did these separate lines of penal development, which I want to trace in this chapter.

Close down the Carnival

In London, up to 1783, the execution march from Newgate prison to Tyburn gallows lasted about two hours, to the accoutrement of tolling bells and all the paraphernalia of spectacle and crowd participation along the way. Thereafter, executions were held outside the prison, marking the end of the long tradition of the execution march. Around the same time, a trend that involves both restricting the savagery and further confining the spectacle of the execution begins. The last occasion when beheading the corpse of the condemned was part of the execution process was in 1820; in 1832 gibbeting was abolished, as was the hanging of bodies in chains in 1834. Family members and friends were by now excluded from the scaffold, which had come to be draped in black, in a bid to give some decorum and solemnity to the proceedings. By 1845 public attendance at the condemned sermon on 'execution eve' came to a halt. Henceforth, the condemned would only be visited by a minister of religion, by their relatives and friends and legal advisers. As we see from the above, by the time of Barrett's execution, some of its preliminaries were being conducted in private.

Not only this, but the execution spectacle itself, by this time, was being performed with growing infrequency. Gatrell (1994) calculates that there were between 6000 and 7000 executions in England between 1770 and 1830 but between 1837 and 1868 there were just 347. By the second half of the nineteenth century the availability of the death penalty had also been significantly restricted. It had been abolished for such offences as forgery, coining, sheep and horse stealing, house breaking, theft of post office letters and sacrilege; after 1861, it was available, for all intents and purposes, only for the offence of murder.

Alongside this more restricted and prescribed death penalty, various other elements of the carnivalesque array of public punishments available around the end of the eighteenth century began to be subjected to similar curtailments. Already, public whipping posts were falling into disuse (Beattie, 1986), although whipping continued as a public sanction for men until 1862.[2] The pillory, it seems, was hardly used after 1815 and was finally abolished in 1837. The ducking stool was last used in 1817 and, although the stocks had a greater longevity, this sanction seems to have fallen into disuse after 1860. There was also a decline in the more informal modes of justice and punishment that then existed over this period. *The Times* (27 March 1869: 5) reported that duelling – a highly ritualized mode of dispute resolution between members of the upper classes, activated when it was thought that 'Honour' had been impugned – 'has of late years fallen into disuse ... with punch and port wine and drinking songs ... it bears witness to the influence of society – that is to the public opinion of the higher classes'. Lower down the social order, we find the demise of the chari-vari, skimmity rides, skimmingtons and other forms of highly theatrical local community actions against particular individuals that involved shaming or humiliating them (often for adultery or some other breach of morals).[3]

What was it, though, that had brought about these shifts from public to private punishment? What I want to give particular attention to here is the role played by changing sensibilities to the carnival that the public execution had become, from the late eighteenth century through to the mid-nineteenth. There are two dimensions to this. The first relates to a growing sympathy for those on the scaffold who had to endure being sent to their death amidst all the ribaldry of the crowd. We see a recognition of the sufferings of the condemned being more readily appreciated in the crowd reaction to the execution of Dr Dodd in 1777 for forgery, himself a well-known society clergyman who had turned to crime to help himself out of financial embarrassment. A contemporary account stated that 'every visage expressed sadness; it appeared, indeed, a day of universal calamity ... tens of thousands of hats, which formed a black mass as the coach advanced were taken off simultaneously ... the [crowd's] silence added to the awfulness of the scene' (Radzinowicz, 1948: 460). Particular individuals, then, who had been condemned, were capable of swinging the mood of the crowd, as result of their personal circumstances, away from celebration and towards sympathy and sadness.

Again, sympathies for those waiting death might be particularly pronounced when this penalty seemed an excessive reaction to the crime that had been committed:

> When mankind beheld the life of a fellow creature sacrificed for a petty theft, or trifling injury or fraud, their feelings at once revolted, they sympathized with the sufferer in his dying moments, and ascribing his punishment to the effect of superior power alone, they too often inwardly loaded both laws and judges with execrations. (*Hansard*, 1822, ns, vol. 7 col. 794)

Or, again, especially bloody executions might now be capable of arousing distaste rather than jubilation. Wakefield wrote of one man who had tried to cheat execution by (unsuccessfully) attempting suicide: he was afterwards,

> carried from the press yard to the scaffold, and in the struggle of death blood flowed from his wounds, which became visible to the crowd. This shocking scene was known and commented upon by a great part of the population of London ... respectable shopkeepers in the neighbourhood of the scene of execution were heard to say that worse than murder had been committed. (1832: 91–2)

From the early nineteenth century, what becomes increasingly evident amongst an emerging middle-class intelligentsia and penal reform groups is the growth of their distaste for such 'spectacles of suffering'

(Spierenburg, 1984), which seemed in breach of what should be the standards of correct conduct in the civilized world. As John Stuart Mill wrote:

> One of the effects of civilization ... is that the spectacle, and even the very idea of pain, is kept more and more out of the sight of those classes who enjoy in their fullness the benefits of civilization ... it is in avoiding the presence not only of actual pain, but of whatever suggests offensive or disagreeable ideas, that a great part of refinement consists. (1836: 130–1)

In a bid to have public executions – one of the most glaring breaches of the civilized code of norms and conduct that was being produced by Mill and others – abolished, the Society for the Diffusion of Knowledge Upon the Punishment of Death and the Improvement in Prison Discipline was established in 1808, founded and chaired by William Allen. For him, the purpose of punishment should not be to terrorize or humiliate, by means of the scaffold, but instead to 'reform the guilty and to restore [criminals] as useful members of the community ... [this] is a triumph of humanity and marks a state rising in the scale of civilization' (Allen, 1847: 129). By the same token, the public execution, then available as a punishment across the criminal spectrum, and providing the opportunity for crowd celebration rather than any more instructive utilitarian purpose, seemed to belong to a penality that was out of place with such standards. Indeed, James Stuart Mill (1811: 153) had earlier written that executions were 'occasions of excessive hardness of heart, of indecent merriment at the place of execution or at best a state of carelessness and indifference attributable only to the most abject ignorance and brutality'. Discomfort at such sights led 37 citizens of Aylesbury who lived near or opposite the County Hall to petition the Grand Jury assembled for the Lenten assizes in 1809 to complain about its decision to move executions to the front of that building. Under the old procedures it had taken ten minutes, they wrote, to move the condemned out of town to be hanged and no resident was inconvenienced 'by the melancholy procession for more than one fourth of that time' (Laqueur, 1989: 313). But the new procedure 'will exhibit before our doors and windows, for upwards of an hour, a spectacle at which Human Nature must shudder'.

By now, those expressing opposition to public executions were thought to represent a 'refinement in character which represented the essence of an advanced civilization. The "sensibility" so created consisted of that delicate perception of the feelings and wishes of others, which enables us to avoid whatever will give them pain' (*Monthly Repository*, McGowen, 1986: 32). For the increasingly influential elites who espoused these sensibilities, public executions were becoming increasingly difficult to witness. The novelist William Thackeray (1840: 156), on going to see a man hanged, found it impossible to witness, protesting that he could 'look no more, but shut my eyes, as the last dreadful act was going on'. Charles Dickens' (Collins, 1962: 238) reaction to watching the execution of the Mannings in 1849 was to write that 'I think it is a most cruel thing to send a man into another scene altogether before an excited mob.' Again, the prison authorities in allowing public attendance at the church service for the condemned on the eve of their execution were now subjected to criticism for their insensitivity. On their prohibition in 1845, such scenes were described as 'a disgrace, not only to the particular locality in which they occurred, but to the whole community, for these reports went abroad and affected the national character' (*Report of the Inspectors of Prisons* [*Home District*] 1845: 5). It was claimed in the *Report from the Select Committee of the House of Lords on Capital Punishment* (1856: 12) that 'these execution carnivals belonged to the rule of morality which was adapted by a less educated age than the present'.

What we thus find by the mid-nineteenth century is an increasingly strong body of influential opinion that was prepared to speak out and condemn the public execution on the grounds that this now seemed repugnant to the values of the civilized world; these values included a prohibition on inflicting any unnecessary suffering on others – which is exactly what was so offensive to these reform-minded individuals about the public execution. As a result of the enlargement of the democratic process that had taken place during the nineteenth century, these sensibilities also found a political constituency which was able to secure the abolition of public executions (Capital Punishment within Prisons Act) in 1868. The legislation was described as being 'in keeping with the spirit of the age' (*The Times*, 14 August 1868: 12). Yet at the same time, a proposal to abolish the death penalty itself was defeated in the House of Commons by 127 votes to 23.

How, then, do we explain the tolerance of this new site of suffering – the private execution? What is clear is that the main body of opposition to public executions at this time, while it included *some* who were opposed to the death penalty in principle and therefore felt revolted by the sufferings of those on the scaffold (whether the execution took place in public or private), was far more repulsed by the macabre, distasteful carnival that was associated with them. For these groups, what carried far greater weight at this time than the sufferings of those about to be executed was *the site* of death, not death itself. As with various other scenes that had, until then, been a regular feature of everyday life – fairs, sporting activities, wakes, hunting, and so on – the crowd disorder and debauchery that were associated with all these public carnivals and theatres of passion seemed increasingly distasteful to a growing body of influential opinion.[4] In these respects, far from possessing any solemnity that should be associated with the taking of another person's life, it was as if the public execution was interchangeable with, or simply an extension of, other sporting or festive occasions. Thus in the early eighteenth century, Manderville had complained that the route to the gallows was 'one continued fair, for whores and rogues of the meaner sort' (1725: 25). The appointed day for London executions was known as 'Tyburn Fair' or 'the Hanging Match' (Radzinowicz, 1948: 171). *The Philanthropist* (1812: 207–8), on the occasion of a group execution, made the point that, for the general public, 'to see five of their fellow creatures hanged was as good as a horse race, a boxing matching or a bull-baiting'. And, as a variety of prints from the late eighteenth century and early nineteenth century reveal (Laqueur, 1989; Gatrell, 1994; O'Connell, 1999), these were occasions when all social classes would be in attendance: there was little by way of class differentiation in crowd participation at that time.

For the most part, the enthusiasm for these carnivals remained undiminished, all the way through to Barrett's execution. During that of Fauntleroy's in 1824, for example, 'every window and roof which could command a view of the horrible spectacle was occupied' (Griffiths, 1884: 240). In fact, right up until their abolition, crowds at public executions became 'bigger over the course of the nineteenth century as executions became rarer and railway travel made getting there easier' (Laqueur, 1989: 352). However, it is also clear that the carnivalesque atmosphere of the public execution begins to attract a sense of disgust – at least among middle-class elites. Later prints concentrate less on the scaffold itself but instead focus more on the revolting antics of the crowd, which, in terms of the dynamics of penal reform, was of rather more concern to middle-class reformers than any sympathies they might have for the condemned (Gatrell, 1994). Thus George Sinclair described to Parliament his experience of travelling near an execution. He claimed to have had to advert his eyes after witnessing a 'sight so painful to humanity' and described the crowd attending the event to be demonstrating 'equally revolting emotions which might be traced in the countenances of all who surrounded [him]' (*Hansard*, 1819, 39, col. 905–6).

Notwithstanding his sympathy for the Mannings as they stood on their execution dais, Dickens was another who was rather more taken up with the ugliness of the execution crowd, than the pitiable figures awaiting death. In his letters and journalism (Dickens, 1841b; Collins, 1962), the gallows were variously described as a 'hideous apparatus of death', with 'its nooses dangling in the light like loathsome garlands', appearing as an 'obscene presence' which should not have been within the sight of public spectators. After one execution he reported that 'even little children were held above the people's heads to see what kind of toy a gallows was, and learn how men were hanged' (1841b: 592). The scene 'swarmed with human life ... It was terrible to see ... the world of eager eyes, all strained upon the scaffold and the beam' (1841b: 592). In *Oliver Twist*, he focused on the vulgarity of the crowd at the execution scene, 'pushing, quarrelling, joking', assembled around 'the black stage, the cross-beam [and] the rope' (1838: 411). Again, the horrors of the execution crowd, not the horrors of the execution itself, feature in

Barnaby Rudge (1841a: 533–5): '[at] Daybreak the murmur of tongues was heard, shutters were thrown open, and blinds drawn up, and those who had slept in rooms over against the prison, where places to see the execution were let at high prices, rose lustily from their beds.' In *A Tale of Two Cities* it is the mawkish insensitivity of the crowd, when Charles Darnay is on trial for his life, that predominates the execution scenes:

> The sort of interest with which this man was stared and breathed at, was not a sort that elevated humanity. Had he stood in peril of a less horrible sentence – had there been a chance of any one of its savage details being spared – by just so much would he have lost in his fascination? The form that was to be doomed to be so shamefully mangled, was the sight; the immortal creature that was to be so butchered and torn asunder, yielded the sensation. Whatever gloss the various spectators put upon the interest, according to their several arts and powers of self-deceit, the interest was, at the root of it, Ogreish. (1859: 223)

For Dickens, on witnessing the execution of the Mannings in 1849, it was the 'dregs of society' who attended public executions:

> Disgust and indignation, or recklessness and indifference, or a morbid tendency to brood over the sight until temptation is engendered by it, are the inevitable consequences of the spectacles ... we have seen that around Capital Punishment there lingers a fascination, urging weak and bad people towards it and imparting an interest to details connected with it, and with malefactors awaiting it or suffering with it, which even good and well disposed people cannot withstand. We know that last-dying speeches and Newgate calendars are the favourite literature of very low intellects. (*The Times*, 14 November 1849: 5)

Yet Dickens was still in favour of executions, if they were to be conducted in private, where the vulgarity and insensitivity he found so distasteful would be expelled. Thus his response to the execution of the Mannings was not to call for the abolition of the death penalty itself but instead the abolition of *public* executions; criminals could thus still be executed – but now in more dignified, solemn settings. Indeed, the quiet dignity in contemporary accounts of those about to die stood in contrast to the raucous, undignified disorder of the crowd. As regards this particular execution, *The Times* itself (14 November 1849: 3) reported that,

> the scene in the chapel before the process of pinioning commenced, and again the final farewell between the guilty couple ere the drop fell, were singular illustrations of the truth that there is no human being, however fallen, in whom some sparks of feeling and earthly sympathy do not linger ... the fatal procession was at once formed, and in a slow and solemn manner moved forward and towards the drop, with the prison bell tolling and everything around contributing to the severe and sober character of the spectacle.

Here, then, were all the ingredients for an execution to suit the values of the mid-nineteenth century civilized world. It was the opportunity for a melodramatic theatre, which involved solemnity, sobriety, repentance and dignity. What then spoilt this earnest Victorian morality play were the crowd scenes beyond the scaffold itself: 'for days past Horsemonger Lane and its immediate neighbourhood had presented the appearance of a great fair, so large were the crowds of people constantly collected there, and so intense the state of excitement in which all present appeared to be' (*The Times*, 14 November).

It again seems to have been concerns about similar crowd scenes at the execution of Hatto in 1854 that then provided the momentum to establish the Select Committee on the Death Penalty.[5] Much of the evidence that the Committee heard took the form of complaints against the crowds attending these occasions, rather than any objection to capital punishment *per se*. The findings of the Committee confirmed that, rather than a solemn event, conducted on the basis of a kind of dignified majesty, as a life was dispatched, the public execution was a popular entertainment, eagerly awaited by the local populace: 'there is a great proportion of the individuals who attend executions who regard the day more as a kind of holiday, and in many cases the remainder of the day is spent at the beerhouse in idleness and debauchery' (*Report from the Select Committee of the House of Lords on Capital Punishment*, 1856: 22). When called upon to give his evidence to the Committee, Inspector Kittle again confirmed the way in which the execution had become analogous to any other sporting or festive occasion:

> The crowd looks on executions much as they would look upon any other exhibition for which there is nothing to pay to see. I think that they look upon it as they would a prize fight, or any other exhibition of a like nature ... [the crowd] seem to amuse and rather enjoy themselves previous to the sight which they come to see. (*Report from the Select Committee*, 1856: 878)

For *The Times* (17 July 1856: 4), now campaigning for the abolition of public executions (but not the death penalty itself), these spectacles were 'regarded as a show ... all kinds of levity, jeering, laughing, hooting, whistling while the man is coming up, while he is yet suffering – while he is struggling and his body is writhing are going on with obscene expression'. It later reported (11 November 1864: 5) on the crowd of the execution of Muller in 1864 as 'made up of young men, but such young men as only such a scene could bring together – sharpers, thieves, gamblers, betting men, the outsiders of the boxing ring, bricklayers labourers, dock workmen, German artisans and sugar bakers'. The execution carnival had come to be regarded as a meeting place only for society's undesirables: more respectable, more restrained and dignified citizens – more *civilized* citizens – would keep away. On this occasion, and as with the Mannings before, Muller himself is shown as displaying dignity and composure:

emerging at length into an open court yard within the precincts of the prison they paused for a few moments, until a door at the further end of the courtyard was unexpectedly opened, and Muller presented himself, attended by a single warder, on the way from his cell to the scaffold. He was pale but quite calm and collected. He walked with a somewhat measured pace, with his hands clasped in front of him and looking upward, with a touching expression of countenance ... Without the slightest touch of bravado his demeanor at this time was quiet and self-possessed in a remarkable degree ... while all about him were visibly touched, not a muscle in his face moved and he showed no sign of emotion.

Immediately after his death, however, *The Times* reporter turned again to the crowd: 'before the slight, slow vibrations of the body had well ended, robbery and violence, loud laughing, fighting and obscene conduct, and still more filthy language reigned round the gallows far and near'.

By now, a case had been established for the abolition of the public execution, but not the death penalty itself – notwithstanding the ability of Muller and others to move at least the more sensitive onlookers. Indeed, such 'nobility' under adverse circumstances can be seen as actually confirming the legitimacy of the execution as a penalty, *when conducted at a more appropriate site* – one from which the insensitive, ill-mannered members of the public would be excluded. Here, then, was the driving force behind the move to have public executions abolished in England: sympathy for the condemned, to a degree, but not of sufficient weight to have the death penalty itself abolished at this time; sufficient only to transfer its site from public to private venues. When conducted in this more appropriate setting, the execution would be in keeping with the values of the civilized world, as they were then, and not in breach of them.

Sanitizing Suffering

After the Capital Punishment within Prison Act became law in England, the way was clear for a new, more sanitized modality of execution to emerge, with none of the outlandish public drama and carnival previously associated with such occasions. *The Times* (9 September 1868: 5) reported the first private execution in London:

There was no uproar, there were no barriers and, above all, there was no wolfish crowd of thieves and prostitutes waiting to see a man die; the catcalls, the bonnettings, the preachings of ministers, whose every word used to be interrupted by obscenity and blasphemy, the wild jumping dances to the chorus of 'Oh my, think I've got to die' were all absent. There was not even a policeman, the windows opposite the gaol were all untenanted ... Death by hanging now means a silent, terrible execution, where the half dozen or dozen spectators have the painful duty of staying by until the man is hanged till he is dead. This is almost all that has to be said about private executions. Yesterday Newgate Street ... was almost empty. A little group of people, not one hundred in all, were standing watching the great gaunt flagstaff at the base of which lay a mass of black – the black flag which was to be hoisted while he was hanging. Beyond this, there was nothing.

What we do not have as yet is a penalty that prohibits all punishments to the human body; and there was still thought to be an obvious need for the drama of punishment, but drama that could make the death penalty all the more sombre and evocative through the silence that now accompanied it, not the drama of spectacle and celebration which had usually accompanied the public execution. What we do have, though, is a penalty that had become an increasingly privatized affair, presided over largely by bureaucratic officials thus making possible the dismantling of the emotive force that the public display of punishment had been able to invoke, and which public participation had been able to convey, and instead making possible its administration by the more rationalistic, efficient forces of modern government. Only the prison authorities and members of the press – those whose job or duty it was to attend – would now participate and observe. It was still intended at this stage that the execution would deliver a message that would reach out beyond the prison walls – but in the form of one that spoke of death with solemnity and dignity. Under the provisions of the 1868 Act, a black flag was to be hoisted at the moment of execution and shown in an elevated and conspicuous part of the prison, and then to be displayed for one hour. In addition, the church bell within the prison was to be tolled for fifteen minutes before and fifteen minutes after the execution itself.

In this way, the drama of execution had been transformed. Hidden behind the prison walls and performed only in the presence of accredited officials, the communicative nature of the death penalty was to be simultaneously reduced and dignified. It would no longer take place in its ribald, carnivalesque form where loss of life had become a reason for celebration and disorder. At the same time, it would only be used sparingly, inflicted on murderers rather than the random collection of criminals whose execution, up to then, had often been due to their own ill luck and poor standing in their local communities (Gatrell, 1994). When practised under such conditions, the death penalty itself was still tolerable. Arguing against a subsequent proposal for its abolition, *The Times* (25 July 1872: 5) reflected that 'it may at least be stated that the countries in which the punishment of death for Murder is maintained are those in which human life is most respected. Where a malicious murder has been committed the public do not feel that the penalty of death is disproportionate to the offence.' Again, sensitivities about the death penalty extended, for the most part, to the manner of its application, not its existence. When conducted with due solemnity and privacy, it still had another important symbolic message to convey: 'justice is the only secure foundation for law and a deep sentiment declares that a man who will-fully takes the life of another has surely forfeited his own' (*The Times*, 25 July 1872). If the public still wanted a close-hand experience of the execution, then for the time being they could visit Newgate Prison to see the shelves of plaster cast criminal heads that were still kept there.[6] Or they could visit the Chamber of Horrors at Madam Tussaud's. This section of her waxworks display had been opened in 1846 and, notwith-standing complaints about its vulgarity by both Thackeray and Dickens, had proved to be immensely popular (Chapman, 1984): initially as a complement or adjunct to the public executions but, after their abolition, as a replacement for them where the general public, who did not share the sensitivities of the elite social groups, could still enjoy some vicarious proximity to scenes of crime and punishment.

At this point, then, an important stage in the development of punish-ment in the civilized world had been reached. A much more solemn, restricted and privatized death penalty could be retained: its administra-tion was now the exclusive property of state officials with the general public, for all intents and purposes, excluded from participation. At the same time, the death penalty in this fashion was now virtually all that was left of the spectacle of punishment that had been in existence at the beginning of the nineteenth century, where the public had not only been able to watch but, to an extent, participate as well. If the demise, by this time, of the more informal community sanctions had been indicative of the growth of state power and its monopolistic control of the regulation of disputes, so the growth of middle-class elites seem to have been largely responsible for the mid-nineteenth century shift in the site of punishment – from public to private – that had now taken place. If the vulgarity of the carnival previously associated with public executions was now out of place in the civilized world, the more sober, sombre private administra-tion of the death penalty that replaced it was not. Restricted for all prac-tical purposes to murder cases only, the death penalty could be retained on this rationalistic, efficient basis: sensitivities would not yet extend to murderers and spare them its consequences. In the aftermath of another heavily defeated attempt to abolish the death penalty in England in 1877 in the House of Commons, *The Times* (14 March 1878: 9) reported that 'the storm which once seemed to be gathering has subsided and has been followed by a great calm. Abolition no longer has a place among the real questions of the day.'

The death penalty itself still had a place in the civilized world but it had now been turned into a bureaucratic accomplishment, not an oppor-tunity for carnival. In these respects, the concern was to maximize its efficiency: to further remove any of the more unseemly aspects of it, such as prolonged suffering or visible death throes. The bureaucratic task was to administer death with the minimum amount of pain and drama. As

Sir Edmund Du Cane, Head of the English Prison Commissioners (1885: 25) explained, 'The mode by which death is brought about is one of much practical importance, in consideration of the universal feeling that all painful scenes and all unnecessary and prolonged suffering to the criminal should be avoided.' Thus, in England, a new technology of death was introduced to allow the final death struggles of the condemned to be screened off from those officials in attendance.[7] *The Times* (5 January 1875: 5) reported the use of this newly sanitized mode of execution as follows:

> For the first time at Newgate a novelty was introduced in executing the extreme sentence of the law. Instead of the convict having, in accordance with immemorial usage, to mount a scaffold, he was simply placed on a sort of trapdoor level with the ground, and below which a deep hole had been excavated ... the drop fell at a given signal, the convict soon ceased to live ... *his sufferings did not appear to be so great as in ordinary cases*; and after the drop fell the crown of the head seemed to be on a level with the ground. (my italics)

The more sanitized the arrangements for administering the death penalty, the more it automatically followed that the sufferings of the condemned would be reduced.

So long as the death penalty remained a culturally tolerable sanction in the civilized world, the central issue would be its sanitization. This was the justification for the introduction of the electric chair in the United States. When it was first used in New York in 1889 it was reported that the condemned's death had been 'completely painless' (*Report of the New York [State] Prison Department*, 1891). In Canada, consideration was given to use of lethal gas rather than hanging during the 1930s, after ghastly mistakes were made in length of rope/body weight calculation necessary to ensure a 'clean' execution (Strange, 2001). In the post-war period death by lethal injection was considered in that country: although it would ensure 'instantaneous and painless' death, with the then available technology it was thought inhumane to ask doctors to perform this task. Again, in post-war Canada, the electric chair was considered 'more humane' than hanging: 'it is the only method of execution where it could be established that unconsciousness was produced instantly and that death was painless' (*Report of the Joint Committee of the Senate and the House of Commons on Capital and Corporal Punishment and Lotteries*, 1954: 839).

If death in this fashion had to be as painless as possible, then any ostentatious qualities the private execution might still possess should also be sanitized and minimized. Thus, in England, the heavily solemnized symbolism still associated with executions was seen as excessive and unnecessarily melodramatic in the early twentieth century. In 1901, the tolling of the prison bell was changed: it now need only occur after the execution was complete and not for the fifteen minutes before and after this – there was no need to unnecessarily dwell on the matter. Similarly, in 1902, the legislation requiring a black flag to be hoisted at each execution was also revoked: no such dramatic insignia were necessary now. In 1925 the reporting of executions was restricted: the press were to be excluded and a simple death notice was posted by the authorities on the prison gate where it had taken place. The public drama of execution, once a carnival that had attracted thousands, had now been reduced to a small piece of paper: the execution itself had become the exclusive property of the authorities, with the public not even allowed some second-hand knowledge of its theatre through newspaper reports. And just as it became more physically restricted and diminished in dramatic effect, so its frequency commenced another sharp decline. Further categories of exemption to the death penalty were introduced to the criminal law. Thus, in 1908, capital punishment was abolished for children under sixteen. In 1922 it was abolished for those convicted of infanticide. In 1931 it was abolished for expectant mothers convicted of murder. In 1932 it was abolished for murderers under eighteen and in 1957, although retained under the provisions of the Homicide Act, it was now to be restricted to 'the worst murderers'. From the mid-1920s through to the mid-1950s, executions became steadily more infrequent. In England, there was a high number of 26 in 1928, but in most years in this period, the number of executions in a year barely reached double figures,[8] reflecting a decline in the use of the death penalty across the civilized world at this time.[9]

Civilization and Death

There came a point, however, when even the relatively unobtrusive use of the death penalty was regarded by a growing body of political opinion and reform pressure groups as breaching the boundaries of acceptable punishment in the civilized world: for them, its presence had become 'a blot upon any civilized nation', as a supporter of abolition stated in an English House of Commons debate (*Hansard* [151] 393, 1 March 1922). Nonetheless, the still more numerous supporters of the death penalty were able to convincingly rely, at that time, on a combination of common-sense assumptions about its deterrent effect and biblical teachings of retribution ('if we are going to have a sane policy which will help towards the safety of our law abiding citizens we must in the worst cases still extract an eye for an eye,' *Hansard* [232] 262, 30 October 1929) to justify its continued (if restricted) place in the penal system. In contrast, the abolitionists were accused of showing excessive sentimentality to murderers, rather than a rational, reasoned argument for their case. Thus *The Times* (6 January 1923: 9), on the Home Secretary's refusal to grant reprieves in the case of a woman and young man who had murdered her husband:

> It is true that the thought of putting to death a boy and a young woman is naturally abhorrent to the civilized mind. But it is also true that executions of this nature are contrary neither to custom nor to the law of the land, and one of the first essentials of civilized society is that the law and its penalties should be enforced in all kinds of murder, unless extenuating circumstances can be proved to exist. In this case there are none.

It was as if the very restricted form of the death penalty that still existed was both tolerable and justified in the existing reasoning processes, and at the same time was sufficiently institutionalized as a response to some murders to ward off any sentiment for those sentenced to death: here, notwithstanding the potential of both the condemned (femininity and youth) to provoke some stirrings of public conscience about its suitability as a sanction under any circumstances in the civilized world.

Post-1945, however, it now seemed to be the retentionists who were relying on 'sentimentalism'. They were increasingly unable to provide scientific, rational argument to establish their case that the death penalty was a deterrent, since a growing body of research evidence demonstrated the opposite effect (see, for example, *Report of the Royal Commission on Capital Punishment*, 1956: 19). It was their own sentiment for a social order which had a legitimate role for the death penalty in its penal framework, and where trite biblical phrases served as reason in support of their retribution arguments, but which itself now seemed to have passed away in the aftermath of war, that seemed out of place. To allow the state to take another's life through the infliction of the death penalty seemed increasingly inappropriate in the era of post-war reconstruction.

Such a sanction, it was thought, with its strong associations with the totalitarian states that the war had been fought against, had no part to play in this new social order. In the 1948 parliamentary debate on the death penalty in England, it was claimed:

> [This] is the one remaining relic in our penal code of the old system of complete repression which was tried against criminals and so badly failed. I want to suggest to this House, as the representative assembly of a country of free men and women, that these instruments have no proper place in the institutions of a free democracy. By their very nature, by their inherent quality, repressive punishments belong to the systems of totalitarian states and not democracies. It was no accident that the chief exponents of violence and severity in the treatment of criminals in other times were the Nazi and Fascist states. (*Hansard* [449] 1014–15, 14 April 1948)

Indeed, the link between 'civilized societies' and the necessary absence of the death penalty to justify that claim now became a central theme in the ongoing debates about its legitimacy. For example, in Canada: 'we as a Dominion have progressed too far in the forefront of world leadership to retain this method from the dark ages'; and 'abolition of the death penalty will make Canada a more enlightened and civilized country' (*Report of the Joint Committee of the Senate and the House of Commons on Capital and Corporal Punishment and Lotteries*, 1954: 833). In England, it was argued that 'If we continue with the death penalty, it will be for revenge, an admission that we are living in the dark ages. We should join together in asking the government to let us join the other civilized countries of the world by abolishing the death penalty' (*Hansard* [235] 503, 9 November 1961). In the United States, *The New York Times* (12 December 1962: 6) wrote that 'capital punishment should be abolished. Legal killing by the state solves no problem ... in our civilized age of some enlightenment it is a practice that brutalizes society, but does not improve it.' And again in the House of Commons in England: 'Abolition would strengthen the forces for our democratic system in the West by showing that it was possible to build up a system of strong government without an all powerful state. Acceptance of capital punishment weakens our case – capital punishment symbolises the spirit of fascism' (*Hansard* [793] 1167, 16 December 1969). There was a new symbolism associated with the death penalty: by being prepared to abolish it, a society could give assurances that it rightfully belonged in the civilized world; by corollary, its continued presence had now become firmly established as a property of the uncivilized world. After 1945, one of the distinguishing features between the civilized and uncivilized world was the way in which it was increasingly regarded as the duty of the former to foster, nurture and cherish life – even, now, the life of a murderer; it was in the latter where the state was prepared to callously toss away and destroy human life, whether this was by use of the death penalty or other means.

The growth of penological expertise in the post-war period not only discredited deterrence and retribution arguments, but increasingly emphasized the importance of treatment and rehabilitation. These, based as they were on the knowledge of experts who now had an increasingly important advisory capacity in the planning and development of state policy, were thought to be more appropriate penal objectives for the civilized world post-1945 than the former two. Even murderers could be included in such a reform programme. In the New South Wales parliamentary debate on capital punishment in 1949, it was claimed that 'psychology and psychiatry have a greater place in deciding what punishments shall be inflicted on offenders. The modern school favours corrective punishment – over the old revenge or deterrence' (*Hansard* [190] 574, 28 May 1949). Again, in the 1955 debate in that state to abolish the death penalty it was argued that 'we do not punish for the sake of punishment. Retribution has long since ceased to have any relevance' (*Hansard* [3rd series 12] 3226, 24 March 1955).

Indeed, the more societies in the civilized world were prepared to abandon retribution and deterrence in favour of these new philosophies of punishment, the more we find the emergence of a sentiment which sought to reduce the blame of offenders for their crimes – even murderers – and shift responsibility for crime onto society as a whole. A vision of the offender as an unwitting victim of society rather than a coherent moral actor begins to emerge – again making punitive sanctions such as the death penalty morally unacceptable, as in subsequent Canadian debates: 'crime and murder are products of our society. The death penalty punishes the fact and does nothing to remove the cause or find a cure' (*Hansard* [1967–1968] 616, 12 December 1967); 'society has to share some of the blame for these crimes [of murder]. Offenders often come from conditions permitted by society – poverty, disadvantage and so on' (*Hansard* [1973–1974], Vol. II, 1072, 1 November 1973); 'is our rage directed only towards the offender or is he a constant reminder of our own failure, that we are tainted with his guilt?' (*Hansard* [1973–1974], Vol. II, 1080); 'society has to take responsibility for these lost offenders' (*Hansard* [1973–1974], Vol. II, 1083). There was more to these statements, though, than an increasing sensitivity to the suffering of all classes of citizens – now extended even to murderers. It was predicated on the emergence of an increasingly strong central state authority, able to rebuild and reconstruct, able to absorb troubles and problems and then find solutions to them, able to absolve even murderers from responsibility for their actions: a state which no longer needed to exert its own authority through what was thought to be repressive law enforcement.

Nonetheless, the abolitionist cause was still a minority one, one that was increasingly articulated in parliamentary circles and reform bodies, but not one that was in keeping with more general public sentiments. Public support for the retention of the death penalty remained very substantial. In England, the public had been most opposed to the death penalty in an opinion poll of 1938 (40 per cent against, 49 in favour). In 1947, 65 per cent were in favour of retention and in 1964, 80 per cent.[10] Indeed, the sentiments of the general public had never been in favour of its abolition. This was in spite of a number of cases in the post-war period which raised further questions about the legitimacy of this sanction in the civilized world: the execution of those subsequently proved to be innocent, as in the case of Timothy John Evans in 1948; the execution of nineteen-year-old, mentally impaired Derek Bentley, an 'accessory to murder' in 1953; and that of the last woman to be executed in England, Ruth Ellis in 1955. Up to this time, small crowds had continued to gather outside prisons on the day of the execution, thus allowing the tradition of public involvement to linger faintly on (Rich, 1932; Grew, 1958). But now, angry demonstrations outside prison in the Bentley and Ellis cases in particular (Ball, 1956: 250; Cronin, 1967: 38–9) had the power to move the issue of capital punishment back into the public domain, making it unsettling and disturbing, again calling into question the moral authority of the state itself.

As *The Times* (9 May 1959: 7), now favouring abolition, wrote of the execution of Marwood:

What the courts decide is not necessarily always equitable – as civilized contemporaries see equity – and it is not even invariably right. So much may be advanced in extenuation of what has been said and done. Members of Parliament have thrown their weight into the scales. Clergymen have petitioned the Queen. Crowds outside the prison have demonstrated. At the one end of the scale these efforts to save the condemned man were legitimate, but at the other they set a dangerous precedent and revived an ugly custom. The fate of the murderer has always provoked emotional reactions. This is to the credit of the kindly humanity of the average man and woman. It is also a symptom of the sentimentality that can, if it is not kept in check, dilute justice at the dictate of mob rule.

In other words, the very retention of the death penalty had the potential to unleash penal sensitivities and emotion which the civilized world demanded be repressed and hidden away.

What we find, then, is a growing distaste for the death penalty – even if this still remained a minority distaste – and the growth of scientific knowledge which could disprove any case put forward by retentionists. Up to now the state had been increasingly prepared to restrict its use, to sanitize it as much as it could to the point where it had almost fallen into abeyance. In England, the mean number of executions per year between 1957 and 1964 was four. In the United States, there were only seven executions in 1965, one in 1966 and two in 1967. Of the last two men executed in England on August 13 1964, there was no report at all in *The Times*. Now the public were not even alerted to the execution by any reference to the death notice on the prison gates. *The Times* had simply carried a statement on the day before that their petition for a reprieve had been denied.

But what was it across these societies of the civilized world that now propelled governments into pushing for its abolition, when it had more or less fallen into disuse anyway? In New South Wales in 1955, in New Zealand in 1960, in England in 1965, in Victoria in 1967, in the United States in 1972 (where, rather differently and importantly, it was declared at that point *unconstitutional*, although this was in the aftermath of a series of state abolitions from 1957) and in Canada in 1975, the death penalty was effectively removed from the statute books and the penal repertoire of the civilized world. Why not let it simply rest in abeyance?[11] The reason for this was the way in which the state itself was increasingly prepared to assume a strong leadership role, over and above expressions of public opinion; relying on the research evidence produced by its officials and experts, acknowledging the importance of being seen to punish in accordance with the values of the civilized world, a status which retention of the death penalty ought to call into question, it now saw its duty as to lead public opinion, not follow it. It was prepared to use 'strong government' not to enlarge its own power but to rid itself of such uncivilized, totalitarian attributes as the death penalty.

Thus, in one of the 1960s' English debates on abolition, the following view was put forward:

> I doubt very much whether at the moment public opinion is in favour of the change, but I doubt also whether at any time during the last one hundred years a plebiscite would have carried any of the great penal reforms that have been made. The appeal in the time of Romilly was always the belief that public opinion would not stand it, but there are occasions when this House is right even if the public may not at that moment be of that opinion. (*Hansard* [536] 2083, 10 February 1965)

Similarly *The Times* (27 February 1965: 13), on the Abolition of Capital Punishment Bill: 'public sympathy may not be with the bill or its promoters and supporters, but it is right that it should be passed at last'. And in Canada:

> It has been said in this debate that parliament is a good deal ahead of public opinion, and I am sure that this is to a large extent true. I do not think we need be surprised at that ... the general public does not study the statistics, it does not see in fact how many murderers have not ... been visited with the ultimate penalty of death. We have had evidence cited today that judges and juries themselves feel uncomfortable about the present situation. The public may not be aware of this. But it is certainly not our business to wait for public opinion in such an important issue. (*Hansard* [1975 Vol. I] 527, 13 March 1975)

Public opinion, in fact, was something to be wary of, not to be trusted, allowing as it did sentiments of anger and uncontrolled emotion to blind it to more rational thinking: 'the public has based its opinions solely on emotion, not on facts'.

Its abolition across these societies, came to mark, nearly a century after the abolition of public executions had been one key turning point, a second decisive moment in the civilizing of punishment. By being prepared to abolish these last vestiges of punishment to the human body, the state was prepared to exert its own moral authority to govern in this area, and to place the way in which it punished its subjects above political interests and populist demands. As one speaker put the matter in the 1975 debate on abolition in Canada, 'the cry for law and order has been the cry of nearly every tyrant in history. "Law and order" was the cry of Hitler when he assassinated nearly one million (*sic*) Jews. Law and order has always been the cry of people who want to commit violence against others' (*Hansard* [1975 Vol. I] 803, April 17, 1975).

In societies that claimed to be civilized, it was now thought that the punishment of offenders should be one of those domains of everyday life that a curtain might be drawn across, and what then lay behind it should not be a matter of public debate. Behind that curtain, out of sight of the public, state bureaucrats, officials and experts would deal with the matter according to an appropriate mix of humanitarian sentiment and rational argument. This could only mean that there was no place for the death penalty in its spectrum. It was recognized by the US Supreme Court in Furman v Georgia (1972 408 US 238, 296–7) when declaring the death penalty 'a cruel and unusual punishment', that 'one role of the constitution is to help the nation become "more civilized." A society with the aspirations that ours so often asserts cannot consistently with its goals, coldly and deliberately take the life of any human being, no matter how reprehensible his past behaviour.'

Public opinion, with its common sense instead of reasoned, rational knowledge, had been detached from the law-making and punishment process. At least in relation to the death penalty the state and its officials in most countries of the civilized world would decide such matters and be prepared to move in advance of public opinion as it saw fit.

Notes

1 The transition from public to private execution took place elsewhere as follows: New South Wales in 1855, Victoria in 1856, New Zealand in 1858, and Canada in 1869. In the United States, the first private execution took place in Pennsylvania in 1834, to be followed by New York, New Jersey and Massachusettes in 1835; by 1845, public executions had been abolished in Michigan, New England and the mid-Atlantic region; they were then abolished in Rhode Island and Wisconsin in 1853 (Masur, 1989), although the last public execution in that country took place in Kentucky in 1936. Local cultural factors might still shape the way these developments were played out: they might take place in prison yards, still allowing the public to watch from a vantage point outside the prison (see *Toronto Daily Star* 26 May 1914). In Australia and Canada, colonial dynamics led to a relaxation of the privacy rule on at least one occasion when indigenous people where compelled to watch the executions of their own kin (McGuire, 1988). In New Zealand, the execution of the first white settler for killing a Maori in 1856 had been instrumental in the move to privatize executions thereafter (Pratt, 1992).

2 In England, there was no provision for the whipping of adults in the Criminal Law Act 1861. However, under the provisions of the Garrotters Act 1863, male adults could be whipped privately, although this was rarely done. *The Report of the Departmental Committee on Corporal Punishment* (1938: 57) noted that '[it] is out of accord with those modern ideas which stress the need for using methods of penal treatment'. It was abolished as a court sentence for adults in England in 1948.

3 See Thomas Hardy (1886: 201).

4 See, for example, Strutt (1830), Howitt (1840), Hole (1949), Cumming (1933), Cunningham (1980).

5 See *The Times*, 25 March 1854: 9.

6 Where an *Illustrated London News* picture depicts a family being shown them by a prison guard in the early 1870s (Gatrell, 1994).

7 A screened trapdoor was used in the United States as early as 1822 (Masur, 1989).

8 The number of executions in England between 1940 and 1946 seems to have been artificially inflated by war; the mean number per year between 1940 and 1946 was 19.

9 Dramatically so in New Zealand, New South Wales and Victoria, where after 1920, there were only around another 40 executions right across these societies to the point of final abolition of this penalty several decades later. In Canada, there had been 125 executions between 1930 and 1939; the number declined to 95 over the next decade. In the United States, there was a decline from an average of 167 per year in the mid 1930s to 72 per year by the mid 1950s.

10 Although in the United States, support for the death penalty was in decline over this period, there was never more than a marginal majority in support of its abolition. Those in favour of retention stood at 68 per cent in 1953. This had fallen to 53 per cent in 1960. In 1966, support for retention dropped to a low point of 42 per cent, those opposed to it now in the majority (47 per cent).

11 As governments in these societies were prepared to do with the largely defunct provisions for indeterminate sentences for repeat offenders at that time (Bottoms, 1977), another measure then thought more in keeping with totalitarian societies (Pratt, 1997).

3

The Disappearance of Prison

In the mid-nineteenth century, in place of the previous carnival of punishment, prison walls and gates were increasingly closing off the penal world from public scrutiny. One of the main functions of prison was to hide away those scenes and practices that had become so offensive and objectionable. What we then find, however, is that the prison itself came to be regarded as another spectacle of punishment, albeit one which was conducted on different economies and values from those of the carnival. Nonetheless, these differences did not shield it from the growing sense of distaste that its presence began to provoke. Eventually, the prison and its population would be another arena of punishment to be pushed behind the scenes of the civilized world.

Prison Architecture in the Early Nineteenth Century

> A large new building walled all round, with a long series of madhouse-like windows, showing above the tall bricken boundary. In front of this, upon the raised bank beside the roadway, stands a remarkable portcullis-like gateway jutting, like a huge square porch or palatial archway, from the main entrance of the building, and with a little square clock-tower just peeping up behind. This is Pentonville Prison. (Mayhew and Binny, 1862: 113)

The opening of Pentonville model prison in London in 1842 represented a major step in the 'civilizing' of punishment. Imprisonment in this manner would come to replace the distasteful, raucous, carnival of public punishment. Up to that time, there had been totally haphazard prison development. These institutions might be located in castles, courthouses and other civic buildings. As Brodie et al. (1999: 2) point out: 'They were also located in buildings which were essentially indistinguishable from adjacent houses and this practice continued until the late eighteenth century.' At this juncture there was no need for any differentiation between prisons and other public buildings (Evans, 1982), given the purpose of prison at that time: it was not used to isolate prisoners on account of their 'otherness' and to retrain them or discipline them so that they would be returned to society as 'normal' human beings. Instead, it was used, in the main, to retain them until it was time for the main business of punishment to take effect, such as transportation or execution. It was only when imprisonment became a penal sanction in its own right in the early nineteenth century that a set of barriers would be placed between prisoners and the rest of the community. Until that time, the absence of standardized rules and procedures meant that local practices whereby family and friends would be given free access to the prison to provide prisoners with the necessaries of life prevailed.

But now, as the main site of punishment, the prison would take on a recognizably modern form: the high walls, the gatehouse, the slatted windows, the imposing size. At the same time, as products of growing state power and responsibilities, these new buildings were regarded with pride. They attracted the interest of leading architects, for whom such designs generated considerable prestige (Johnston, 1960), and they were shown off to admiring foreign dignitaries, potentates and local worthies (see Ignatieff, 1978). As the model prison, Pentonville represented a distinctive break from the old prison forms and it was to be influential in the swift building of new prisons and the regeneration of old ones that then took place in Britain and elsewhere (Markus, 1993; Pratt, 1992).

The imposing view such prisons presented in England were by no means unique to that country. On a visit to the United States, William Crawford, the secretary of the London Prison Discipline Society and later Inspector of Prisons (1835, Appendix 1) described the Eastern Penitentiary at Philadelphia as being:

> situated on an elevated and healthy spot, about two miles from the centre of the city, the stone of which ... is built in granite of a greyish colour. The façade, or entrance gate, is in the gothic style of architecture, of a bold, impressive character, possessing the appearance of a great strength and solidity.

As regards Australia, in Darlinghurst, Sydney, 'is the great gaol, occupying a large area, and built of stone, with spacious wards radiating from the centre ... the prison stands on a high open spot in one of the fashionable quarters of the city' (Hill and Hill, 1875: 275). In Melbourne, the new gaol (built in 1840) was 'situated on top of the Russell Street Hill, and for decades the sombre grey stone gaol dominated the Melbourne skyline' (Broome, 1988: 2). In Canada, Dorchester Federal Penitentiary, opened in 1850, was described as 'being built one mile from the village: the buildings stand on a plateau which is elevated. From the train, passing along the Intercolonial Railway, they can be seen to advantage and present a very imposing appearance' (*Report of the Inspectors of Penitentiaries,* 1880: 21). However, what was so significant about Pentonville was that its design was one of three competing architectural influences then at work on prison construction; but it was also the one of these three which came to dominate prison building for much of the nineteenth century.

The others had been, first, neo-classicism. In England, Winchester prison, opened in 1788 was one of the earliest to be built in this style, drawing on architectural forms associated with Ancient Greece and Rome: clear cut lines, formalism, grandeur, 'precise ashlar stonework; plain, bold dentils; a powerfully simplified Ionic portico and entablature' (Crook, 1971: 943–4). In this example,

> the prison is enclosed on three sides by a low fence-wall, ten feet high. This is rendered very conspicuous by a noble and spacious gate, of the Tuscan order, constructed from a design of Vignola, at the Firnese gardens' gate or entrance into Campo Vaccini: and adorned with rustic columns and pilasters, supporting a handsome entablature. The spaces between the advanced structures are ornamented with niches, finished in a style of chaste simplicity, and the arcades are embossed with rustic quoins: over the niches are moulded square compartments, which give a simple and easy relief to the space between the crowning of the niche and the beautiful Dorick cornice; which is a grand and striking object, imitated from the theatre of Marcellus at Rome. (Neild, 1812: 381)

The exteriority of the prison itself, sometimes embellished with gargoyles or other forms of penal representation, meant that the public would now be able to 'read off' from it appropriate messages about its interior, as the new prison designs effectively screened from public scrutiny what was taking place behind their walls. We find fetters and chains above the gateway at Newgate (1784) and Dublin (1794). Robert Elsam's (1818) design for Dover Town Gaol above the adorning manacles by the gate had the inscription 'parum est coercere improbos poena nisi probos efficias disciplina'.[1] 'SOLITUDE' was engraved above the entry lodge of Littledean Bridewell in the Forest of Dean at the end of the eighteenth century. At Cold Bath Fields (opened in London in 1794) Mayhew and Binny later found,

> a gigantic pair of knockers, large as pantomime masks, lay low down on the dark green panels of the folding gates, and under them are the letter box and the iron-grated wicket, not larger than a gridiron; whilst, arranged in tunnels at the top of each side pillar, are enormous black fetters, big enough to frighten any sinful passer-by back into the pattern of rectitude. (1862: 279)

Figure 3.1 Gothic Architecture, Holloway

Second, and in contrast to these neo-classical influences, we see the imprint of gothic revivalism on prison design. This invoked medieval associations of penal confinement in dungeons and towers, with spires, flying buttresses, battlements, gables, perpendicular windows, three-cornered towers, turrets and extravagant gargoyles. In the United States, it was particularly evident in the work of John de Haviland, who designed the Eastern Penitentiary at Philadelphia and the Western Penitentiary at Pittsburg. In England, this influence was seen in the design of, for example, Holloway Prison in London (1852, Figure 3.1) and Armley Gaol, Leeds (1848, Figure 3.2). The Reverend John Field wrote of Reading, another gothic prison built in 1844, and where he was chaplain, that,

> every traveller by the Great Western railway is familiar with [its] exterior splendours ... the palace-prison as it is styled. After the regal residence at Windsor, it is the most imposing structure seen from the line of view between Paddington and Bath; it is beyond all question, the handsomest

Figure 3.2   Gothic Architecture, Armley Gaol, Leeds

building – [Windsor] castle alone excepted – in the county of Berkshire. (1848: 73)

Notwithstanding the differing effects in prison construction that these contrasting neo-classical and gothic styles had produced in the early nineteenth century, what unites both are, first, the imposing size of the prisons built in their fashions. The journalist and barrister Hepworth Dixon noted in relation to Millbank, opened in London in 1816, that,

> The outlines of the structure may be traced on any well-drawn plans of [the city]. In form it consists of six pentagonal buildings, surrounding an open courtyard; the whole surrounded by a lofty wall of octagon shape. This wall encloses an area of about sixteen acres, seven of which are covered with the buildings and airing yards; the outer nine laid out as gardens ... the corridors in which the cells are situated are upwards of three miles in length. (1850: 136)

Second, the impression of luxury and extravagance these buildings conveyed. In such ways, the idea of imprisonment could break free from its associations of squalor and disorder, initially exposed by Howard (1777) and subsequently condemned with vehement disgust in Dickens' prison novels of the 1830s and 1840s.[2] The neo-classical Manchester New Gaol was described as making 'a striking addition to the architectural beauties of the city' (Hepworth Dixon, 1850: 303). The Western penitentiary at Pittsburgh presented 'a handsome elevation being finished in the castellated style of gothic architecture' (Crawford, 1835: 15). As such, these two designs were able to demonstrate the different economy of scale that now

Figure 3.3 Neo-classical Architecture, Newgate

ordered imprisonment; while at the same time, in either style, the prison was still a site for the ostentatious, dramatic, communicative penality associated with early modern society (Foucault, 1978). If it was replacing the carnival of punishment with something more orderly and contained, something which now signified the transfer in ownership of punishment from the public to the state and its authorities, so that the public would be kept apart from it, they would still be able to read off particular messages about punishment from its carefully scripted designs. This might be in the form of the 'architecture parlante' of neo-classicism, or in the form of gothic 'architecture terrible' (Bender, 1987; Garland, 1990). Thus Hepworth Dixon, on Newgate (Figure 3.3), rebuilt after fire in the 1770s:

> Once seen, it is not a place very likely to be forgotten. Inside and outside it is equally striking: massive, dark and solemn, it arrests the eye and holds it. A stranger to the capital would fix upon it at a glance; for it is one of the half dozen buildings in this wilderness of bricks and mortar which have a character ... who can pass by it unmoved? ... is there one who heedlessly goes by, without bestowing on it a glance of curiosity, a shudder, a sign? It is doubtful. (1850: 191–2)

However, the very grandeur of both neo-classical and gothic prisons quickly came to be seen as offensive and distasteful. Thomas Carlyle (1850: 44) wrote ironically of a visit to 'one of the London prisons ...

surely one of the most perfect buildings within the compass of London ... in my life I never saw so clean a building; probably no Duke in England lives in a mansion of such perfect and thorough cleanliness'. By following such designs, it was as if prisons had been turned into buildings of magnificence and triumph, thereby rewarding and honouring crime. Instead, in the nineteenth century, the infliction of punishment was something to be regretted, to be carefully measured out and then dispensed frugally, so that all the penal excesses and extravagances from previous eras could be avoided. Just as the sight of punishment in the public domain had become offensive and distasteful to the sensitivities of a range of elite groups, such as reformers, essayists, novelists and philosophers, so too was the way in which the architecturally ostentatious new prisons seemed to turn punishment into an elaborate and expensive drama, providing those who broke the law with some kind of privileged existence, over and above the squalor and dilapidation of the surrounding communities. Such concerns had been registered, often from those same sectors which had also expressed revulsion at the old public punishments, from Howard (1777: 44) onwards who had complained that 'the new gaols, having pompous fronts, appear like palaces to the lower class of people and many persons are against them on this account'. The Society for the Improvement of Prison Discipline was critical of,

> architects [who] rank prisons among the most splendid buildings in the city or town where they have been erected, by a lavish and improvident expenditure of the public money in external decoration, and frequently at the sacrifice of internal convenience. Some prisons injudiciously constructed, present a large extent of elevation next to the public road or street: an opportunity was then afforded for the architect to display his talent, in the style and embellishment of the exterior. (1826: 36)

Instead, then, of 'palace prisons', the Society suggested that 'the absence of embellishment ... is in perfect unison with the nature of the establishment. The elevation should therefore be plain, bold and characteristic, but divested of expensive and unnecessary decoration'.

As the effects of industrialization in Britain and the acute levels of poverty and misery it had created in honest working-class communities became more apparent in government inquiries (see Chadwick, 1842), so too did 'palace prisons' and the like seem all the more incongruous and unjustifiable. The trade paper *The Builder* (1849: 519) wrote:

> The sums hitherto expended on prison buildings have in some cases been enormous. The cost is seldom less than £100 or £150 per prisoner (a sum sufficient for building two or three neat cottages, each able to contain a whole family) and in some instances it has been much more. A portion only (the newest) of the county prison at York, capable of accommodating only 160 prisoners, cost £200,000 which is more than £1,200 per prisoner; enough, if it had been desired, to build for each prisoner a separate mansion with stable and coach house.

The social reformer Roberts felt that: 'England surely cannot allow such a contrast to exist between the comparative domiciliary comforts enjoyed by those who have forfeited their freedom as the penalty of crime, and the wretched homes from which at present too many of our labouring population are tempted to escape to gin palaces or beer shops' (1850: 4).

Among the more influential elite groups, Dickens (1850: 714) articulates these concerns in the description of a visit to a new prison in *David Copperfield*: 'an immense and solid building, erected at a vast expense. I could not help thinking, as we approached the gate, what an uproar would have been made in the country, if any deluded man had proposed to spend one half of the money it had cost on the erection of an industrial school for the young, or a house of refuge for the deserving old'. Similarly, Hepworth Dixon (1850: 368), who singled out the grandeur and 'palatial character' of Wakefield New Gaol for particular criticism: 'ask some of the miserable creatures – miserable but honest – who live under the shadow of the new Wakefield Gaol, and who feel its grandeur insult their wretchedness – and they will tell you how it courts their attention, occupies their thoughts, and tempts them with its seductions'. In other words, not only did these prisons seem to unfairly elevate criminals above the status of the honest poor – thereby disregarding the social distance that now existed between them and the rest of society – but, by ostentatiously advertising their extravagance, they gave encouragement to lawbreakers. It was as if prison buildings in neo-classical or gothic designs were giving the message that the state and its officials would handsomely provide for the criminals who had taken up residence behind its walls, but would do nothing to assist those respectable citizens living on the exterior of them.

However, in contrast to the excesses of prisons reflecting these neo-classical and gothic designs, Pentonville seemed to have been constructed around principles of functional austerity (Figure 3.4), with an almost complete abandonment of exterior decoration in its architecture: although neo-classical themes were in evidence around the gatehouse, the point of entry to the prison, they were missing elsewhere. Given the new purpose of imprisonment and its detachment from the rest of society, it was perhaps appropriate that the gatehouse, through its architectural form, should highlight the importance of this point of departure from 'normal' life to the very different world that now lay behind the prison walls. But in other respects, the 'cheerless blank' (Teeters and Shearer, 1957) of the rest of its exterior gave a more appropriate message to onlookers about what was contained within it – the monotonous deprivation its regime imposed on its inhabitants, rather than any semblance of ostentatious extravagance implicit in the other contemporary designs. In contrast to the other two modern prison styles, Pentonville had given expression to a kind of 'architecture faisante' (Bender, 1987; Garland, 1990).

It was now recognized that the very starkness of the prison exterior itself would be sufficient enough to inspire trepidation rather than wonder, reticence rather than terror – sentiments more in keeping with the emerging values of nineteenth-century societies. Punishment at this time

Figure 3.4   Functional Austerity, Pentonville

was designed to strike no chord of affection with its citizens through majestic display nor awe-inspiring terror through its flamboyant representations: instead, the deliberate austerity of its architecture would convey the calculated sense of loss and deprivation that now met law-breaking. The general reaction to Pentonville, with its impressions of solemnity, frugality and restraint, was more favourable than it had been to its rival designs. Hepworth Dixon noted that, here:

> There is perfect order, perfect silence. The stillness of the grave reigns in every part. To a person accustomed to see only such gaols as Giltspur-street and Horsemonger Lane – with all their noise, filth and disorder – the change is striking in the extreme. The observer feels as if he had come upon a new and different world ... a model prison: an example of the efficiency and economy of the country at large. (1850: 157)

It was for these reasons that the Pentonville austerity in prison design gains precedence over its competitors – Pentonville did indeed become 'the model': not simply because of its internal disciplinary regimes (Ignatieff, 1978) but, in addition, because of its external appearance. From now on, elaborate castellation and decoration would be stripped down and concentrated only around the entrance: here was the defining moment of contemporary punishment, as one left the free world and entered the prison. Other than this, instead of gargoyles in the form of serpents, chains and so on, the prison clock tower (Figure 3.5) could become the new emblem of the modern prison: not only did it indicate the regularity and order of prison life itself, but in addition it would also

Figure 3.5   Nineteenth-century Prison Clock Tower, Bristol

signify the way in which punishment was now organizing itself around deprivation of time rather than the infliction of physical pain. Again, the prison buildings had to be sufficient to inspire remorse and trepidation about what they contained within, but at the same time would leave unspecified the exact nature of the deprivations occurring inside – the observer could only imagine these.

Prison location

Where, though, should these new prisons be built? Up to the early nineteenth century, there were no obvious hostilities to them being placed in the centre of towns and cities: the site would be determined by local tradition and convenience. The philanthropist James Neild (1812: 334), in a duplication of Howard's (1777) prison survey, commented that 'Leicester county gaol looks as it should do. It has a prison-like appearance. The noble stone face of the building extends 120 feet in front of the street, and near to it is the free school'. What clearly was of no concern to Neild at this time was the proximity of the gaol to the school, nor the fact that this building, like any other public building, bordered the main city thoroughfare – there was no dividing wall between the prison and the public. Even so, it was now possible to discern a clear pattern emerging in relation to the positioning of prisons: old prisons were likely to be found in the centre of their communities, new ones were more likely to be built on outlying, elevated sites. In contrast to Leicester, he noted (1812: 84) that 'Bury St Edmunds New Gaol (1805) is situated at the east-end of the South Gate, nearly a mile from the centre of town. The buildings are enclosed by a boundary wall, twenty feet high, built in an irregular octagon form'. Indeed, by the early nineteenth century, we find criticisms of prison buildings which were not located in outlying areas, as with the Visiting Justices' complaints about Winchester in 1817: 'the present gaol has been most injudiciously built nearly in the centre of the city, surrounded by buildings, which not only impede the free circulation of air, but are in many other respects of great inconvenience' (Society for the Improvement of Prison Discipline, 1826: 9).

Public health issues seem to have been the reason for the initial changes in thinking about prison sites, as Howard explained:

> Every prison should be built on a spot that is airy and, if possible, near a river or brook. They generally [should] have not ... subterraneous dungeons, which have been so fatal to thousands; and by their nearness to running water, another evil, almost as noxious, is prevented, that is the stench of sewers ... an eminence should be chosen; for as the walls round a prison must be so high as greatly to obstruct a free circulation of air, this inconvenience should be lessened by a rising ground. And the prison should not be surrounded by other buildings; nor built in the middle of a town or city. (1777: 21)

Similarly, the Society for the Improvement of Prison Discipline stated:

> The situation must be healthy, open and calculated to secure a free circulation of good air ... an elevated situation should be chosen, in order that a perfect system of ventilation may be effected, and that the prisoners may be exempted from the noxious effects of fogs, which are prevalent on low flat surfaces, or in the vicinity of rivers ... it is highly objectionable for a prison to be surrounded with buildings, or asked to have any, contiguous to its boundaries. It ought never to be placed in the midst of a city or town. (1826: 36)

In these respects, the humanitarian concerns of the authorities and reform-minded individuals and organizations embedded these principles of elevation, isolation and perimeter defining boundary wall (they were not unaware of the security implications of these new buildings) into subsequent prison construction (see *Report of the Inspector of Prisons of the Home District*, 1837). Holloway was thus 'built on a rising ground ... a ten acre site surrounded by a brick wall about eighteen feet high. At the back of the prison lie some beautiful green meadows ... one of the reasons for building it was to better preserve the health of prisoners' (Mayhew and Binny, 1862: 535). In Leeds, 'a large new prison [Armley] has been erected ... in a high and healthy situation, about a mile and a half from the town. It is constructed on the same general plan as the prison at Pentonville' (*Report of the Inspector of Prisons of the Northern District*, 1848: 427). Pentonville itself had been built 'in the country'.

The combined effect of these trends in architectural design and location was to transform the prison, both from its place as an unremarkable feature of everyday life, often indistinguishable from any other public building, and from its place as a kind of extravagant theatre of punishment, as was represented in some of the designs of the other early modern prisons, to a place where it would be set back from but elevated above modern society: looming over it, but at the same time closed off from it, with its windowless high walls and secure gate. Its size made it unmistakable, and the austerity of its design provided a chilling sombre threat, as we see in another description of Pentonville: 'at night [the] prison is nothing but a dark, shapeless structure, the hugeness of which is made more apparent by the bright yellow specks which shine from the easements. The Thames then rolls by like a flood of ink' (Mayhew and Binny, 1862: 119).

There had been no one plan, no one individual behind this transformation of prison buildings in the first half of the nineteenth century but instead a series of contingent alliances between influential organizations and individuals, often based on contrasting sensitivities: revulsion at squalor, disorder and chaos, and an equal revulsion of extravagance and flamboyance; humanitarian concerns for the health of prisoners, juxtaposed against a recognition that they had become one of modern society's most unwanted groups. Their confluence had produced an institution which at this juncture hid the administration of punishment from view, but one which in its turn would eventually become hidden from view itself; and yet, despite its own physical disappearance, its early representations were of sufficient force to remain in the public's imagination, with the power to haunt the *Weltanschauung* of the civilized world.

Hiding the Prison

For a good part of the nineteenth century, the new prisons continued to represent, for the authorities, an illustration of advanced social development: new prisons were a modality of punishment appropriate to a civilized society, certainly more so than public executions or floggings, certainly more so than old-style prisons which gratuitously threw together a festering collection of human refuse. The imposing structure and technology embodied in such buildings confirmed their rightful place in the civilized world. As regards Pentonville again,

> It is not the long, arcade-like corridors, nor the opera-lobby like series of doors, nor the lengthy balconies stretching along each gallery, nor the paddle-box-like bridges connecting the opposite sides of the arcade, that constitute [its] peculiar character. Its distinctive feature, on the contrary – the one that renders it utterly dissimilar from all other jails – is the extremely bright, and cheerful, and airy quality of the building; so that, with its long light corridors, it strikes the mind, on first entering it, as a bit of the Crystal Palace, stripped of all its contents. There is none of the gloom, nor dungeon like character of a jail appertaining to it. (Mayhew and Binny, 1862: 120)

And it was the possession of these new prisons that allowed Sir Edmund Du Cane to claim that:

> The creation of this prison system and the general improvement in all matters relating to the treatment of criminals or the prevention of crime have placed England in the foremost rank in this important social reformation. Our prison establishments, particularly those in which penal servitude is carried out, are visited by foreigners from all countries, studying the subject either on their own account or on behalf of their Government, with a view to improving their own practice. They are spoken of with the highest encomiums, and are the envy of most foreign prison reformers. (*Report of a Committee Appointed to Consider Certain Questions Relating to the Employment of Convicts in the United Kingdom*, 1882: 656)

Notwithstanding the pride of the prison bureaucracy in its own institutions, however, it is also possible, at this point in the late nineteenth century, to discern a growing sentiment that the 'prison look' of Pentonville and its successors was something that should be avoided in subsequent designs; as if that austerity and implicit deprivation had now become too threatening and unpleasant, at least for the more reform-minded members of the penal establishment. These sensitivities seem to have been first manifested in the design of Wormwood Scrubs Prison in London, opened in 1884 and the last significant English prison to be built in the nineteenth century.[3] As subsequent visitors confirmed, its exterior appearance had been beautified. Now, the architect's task was not to design turrets, gargoyles and battlements but, instead, landscaped gardens, fountains and flowerbeds:

> a visitor might, for a moment, imagine he had arrived at a school or university college. A well-kept drive encircled a flower garden, which in summer is bright with flowers. On either side of this garden are lawns,

in the centre of which are shady trees. At the background stands a fine chapel built in grey stone in the Norman style. To the right and left of the chapel run graceful arches like cloisters and reminiscent of a monastery. (Hobhouse and Brockway, 1923: 78)

Giving approval to the trend set at Wormwood Scrubs, the *Report of the Gladstone Committee* (1895: 23) noted: 'we see no reason why prison yards should not be made less ugly by the cultivation of flowers and shrubs'. The development of Camp Hill prison, Isle of Wight (1908) represented a further step away from the stark austerity of the Pentonville-influenced design: 'what may be called a "garden village" is being built, and as the site is on sloping ground in the forest, the grouping of the white and red and single and double and four cottage blocks amongst the trees will give a most pleasing effect when completed' (*Report of the Prison Commissioners,* 1908–9: 28). Nor were these attempts to beautify the prison confined to England. In New York state we find similar changes taking place at Sing Sing:

> at one of the main entrances to the prison yard an artistic marble gateway has been built, which will be equipped with a steel gate ... portions of the prison grounds have been elaborately laid out, kerbed and planted with trees and flowers. I am glad to say ... that the efforts of the last four years have made great changes in the inner and outer appearance of the prison. (*Report of the New York State Prison Department,* 1898: 37–8)

In New Zealand, it was reported that 'the general outside appearance of more recently constructed prisons is more elaborate and less grim than older ones' (*Report of the Controller-General of Prisons,* 1926: 3). Landscaping took place outside of Pentridge Gaol in Melbourne in the 1920s, so that its 'exterior lost some of its grim dominance by being softened in this way' (Broome, 1988: 16). In Canada,

> the most remarkable change at [Kingston Penitentiary] has been seen in the beautifying of [its] front – flowerbeds, sidewalks, roadway, pebbled concrete light sand, effective lighting system, ornamental stairway, one of the finest lawns, and flowerbed on terraces, pebble-dash concrete flower vase on concrete posts, bush cut down near the street, an orchard sown. (*Report of the Inspectors of Penitentiaries,* 1929: 6)

The penal authorities across the civilized world were attempting to draw a more attractive veil across what they now thought to be the unnecessarily spartan exterior of their own institutions. It was as if the functional austerity of the late nineteenth-century prison had become distasteful, as if the utter drabness of its cheerless walls in itself began to be seen as offensive, in just the same way that extravagance and ostentation in prison design had previously been. Just as the interiors of prisons were beginning to be redecorated with 'soft' colours and photographic montages of rivers, forests and the like (*Report of the Prison Commissioners, 1935*), so the exterior appearance could be similarly ameliorated. For the same reason, it was declared in New York that there were to be 'no more fortress prisons' (*Report of the State Commission of Corrections, 1931*). In England, in the early twentieth century, the borstal, built so that it had 'nothing of the prison about it' (Healy and Alper, 1941), became the new model institution, rather than Pentonville:

> In designing [new prisons] we shall take account of our experience in the development of Borstal institutions ... our object will be to provide institutions with opportunities for healthy outdoor work and exercise as far as possible. The [prisoners] will be housed in small groups in separate pavilions or houses which will allow of better classification and greater individualization than is now possible. (*Report of the Prison Commissioners*, 1936: 2)

Indeed, the term 'modern' was now applied to borstals precisely because they neither looked nor were positioned like prisons. The very qualities which had erstwhile provided the prison with an identification with the civilized world only indicated how outdated such institutions had become, in the sense that they no longer reflected the combination of humanitarian intentions and scientific objectivity which (formally at least) guided the authorities' administration of these institutions: 'for many years the Commissioners have drawn attention to the unsuitability for the development of reforms on modern lines ... the old prisons will always represent a monument to the ideas of repression and uniformity which dominated penal theory in nineteenth century society' (*Report of the Prison Commissioners*, 1937: 30).

Thus, by the early twentieth century, from being originally regarded as a source of pride, the early modern prisons the authorities had inherited were seen as obstacles to more progressive, therapeutic models of penal rehabilitation that their experts now wanted to pursue. For this reason they were increasingly prepared to experiment with simplistic designs that abandoned the previous nineteenth-century conceptions of prison building altogether: prison farms and camps in the outback, for example, in Australia and New Zealand (*Report of the Comptroller-General of Prisons*, 1926; *Report of the Controller-General of Prisons*, 1922). In England, in contrast to the earlier (and much criticized) grandeur of Wakefield New Gaol, at Wakefield Open Prison, established in 1934, 'there were no walls, not even a boundary fence – the men sleeping in wooden huts, and the boundaries designated, if at all, by whitewash marks on the trees' (Jones and Cornes, 1973: 5). Here, the defining features of the nineteenth-century prison had simply vanished, along with the interest of the architecture profession (Davison, 1931).

Removing the Prison

However, these successive attempts by the authorities to conceal or camouflage over the unseemly, distasteful spectacle that their prisons now represented were not sufficient to allay growing public distaste at any evidence of their presence. During the nineteenth and early twentieth centuries, urban development had eroded much of the distance that had originally existed between the new prisons and city outskirts. New estates were taking the general public right up to the edges of those prominences on which the prisons had been located; or alternatively, proposals for new prisons now threatened the increasingly precious 'greenbelt' areas of the urban environment. One of the first occasions in England when such issues were raised was in 1875, over the plans to build Wormwood Scrubs itself:

> Are we prepared for the infusion of a convict element in our population at Notting Hill? There is an establishment rising like Aladinn's [*sic*] Palace on the once pleasant site of Wormwood scrubs ... Why should Notting Hill submit to a penal establishment being quartered upon it? This is one of those matters which is nobody's business, and therefore the thing gets quietly done *sub rosa* until somebody suddenly wakes up and asks who would have thought of it? ... We want Wormwood Scrubs as a breathing space for our growing population; and object to its being made a country residence for the Claimant and his friends. (*The Kensington News*, 12 June 1875: 3)

In Victoria, Pentridge prison, built originally in 1851 to allow for rock breaking and quarrying by the prisoners, found itself in one of Melbourne's more respectable northern suburbs by the end of the nineteenth century: 'the worthy citizens of Coberg do not wish the prison to remain within the city boundaries' (Broome, 1988: 15). In New Zealand, it was reported that 'owing to local agitation, Mount Cook prison [in Wellington] was lying idle' (*Report of the Inspector of Prisons*, 1900: 3). In 1949 a plan was put forward to abolish Mount Eden prison in Auckland: 'erected some 70 years ago, it is now in a closely-built residential area. It is quite unsuitable and inadequate' (*Report of the Controller-General of Prisons*, 1950: 10). In Canada, nearly a century after the erection of Kingston penitentiary in 1834, it was suggested that:

> It should be removed from its present location to one which is an open district with necessary railway, water and building facilities. At present this penitentiary is very badly situated where five highways pass. Palace Street is one of the favourite automobile routes, and over it must pass all the inmates being employed on the farms. King Street

runs immediately in front of the main gate, on which there is a continual stream of pedestrians and vehicles. (*Report of the Inspectors of Penitentiaries*, 1921: 17)

For the general public, it was as if the very idea of the prison had become indelibly tainted with ugliness and morbidity, both in terms of what its design represented, and knowledge of the leper-like population hidden behind its walls. Indeed, it was as if the very remoteness and exclusion of the prison and its inmate population only made them both more undesirable. We thus find pressures to have the disfigurement that the prison represented for local citizens to be removed from view altogether, and the land be put to more tasteful use for the respectable members of the community. The *Report of the Prison Commissioners (1889: 4)* refers to 'a new prison ... near Nottingham, to take the place of one in the centre of town, which has been condemned on account of the unsatisfactory nature of its site'. There is a later reference to 'the erection of a new prison at Newcastle to replace the existing one, which *from its position* and construction is not up to modern requirements ... the site of Kirkdale Prison has been sold to the Corporation of Liverpool ... it is understood that the corporation propose to devote some of the site to "open spaces"' (*Report of the Prison Commissioners*, 1895: 11; my italics).

The prison, on the basis of what it now represented in the public's imagination, had become the least desirable of landmarks, as if its brooding presence on the nineteenth-century skyline was still physically visible. Aside from the dangers of the population housed within it, any plans to build one would immediately threaten local land values, so unwanted a neighbour had it become. Indeed, it was now recognized by the American architect Hopkins (1930: 12) that 'prison and prisoners will never be considered desirable neighbours and opposition to their placement anywhere must be expected'.[4] The authorities in post-war England found the same opposition as their plans for new prisons were vehemently rejected by any community in which they planned to situate them: 'the difficulty is that while it may be generally agreed that the Commissioners ought to acquire adequate accommodation for the prisoners, any specific attempt to do so almost invariably meets with a firm local conviction that they should do it somewhere else' (*Report of the Prison Commissioners*, 1947: 11). They were thus reduced to converting sites that had otherwise lost their original purpose or no longer had a role to play: disused army camps and airfields, on the one hand; and on the other, country homes in their surrounding estates (*Report of the Prison Commissioners*, 1949: 28) which belonged to a class structure and economic order in itself in the process of disappearing. Overall, by the mid-twentieth century, such remote sites, or socially redundant sites as in England, seemed to be the only ones available for prison building. As a result, these new locations further assisted in the camouflage and disguise of the prison, and its remoteness and isolation.

The Invisible Prison

The subsequent prison building programmes of the post-war period took this process a stage further, in the form of introducing designs that would make them completely anonymous, invisible to those members of the public who happened to come across them in the outlying areas of the civilized world where they were now to be built. Thus, the Home Office (1959: 92) reported as follows on the first major prison building programme in Britain in the twentieth century: 'the design, elevations and methods of construction and finishing are intended to get away as far as possible from the traditional appearance of a prison ... *this type of construction gives a pleasanter and quieter effect*, with better lighting, heating and ventilating' (my italics). Similarly, with the plans for the new Blundeston prison,

> two features of the new design will greatly change the forbidding aspect of the prison as the public sees it. There will be no high wall, but privacy will be maintained by an eight foot concrete wall, within which there will be a twelve foot chain link fence topped with barbed wire for security purposes. Visitors to the prison, whether on business or to see prisoners, will no longer have to pass through the formidable gate but will enter an ordinary office block which forms part of the perimeter. This will contain all the administrative offices and the visiting rooms for prisoners' friends. (Home Office, 1959: 117)

In effect, prison security, to avoid otherwise distasteful sights, was being maintained by means of a *trompe l'œil*. The offensive, exterior high wall, which might also give away the identity of the prison was scaled down: but behind it, of course, lay a further series of less obtrusive security fencing. Again, the dramatic effect of the prison entrance was now something that only prisoners need experience. Visitors would be spared such shameful, distasteful associations in the new forms of prison construction. As Sparks et al. (1996: 101; my italics) later noted in relation to Albany and Long Lartin (Figure 3.6) these 1960s' prisons had become hidden, anonymous, largely unrecognizable buildings: 'both were built in architectural styles which deliberately moved away from the traditional English Victorian "galleried" prison ... externally, like other modern high security prisons [they] *present the passer-by with a somewhat blank appearance*'.

This did not mean, however, that prisons were *completely* removed from view. The above specifications for architecture and location referred to the *new* prison building programme. Many of the nineteenth-century prisons remained in use, but now projected an appearance and a set of images that set them, and the localities in which they were situated, adrift from the civilized world. The grandeur and elegance that had initially placed them in its advance guard had largely turned to unsightly

Figure 3.6 1960s' Blank Appearance, Long Lartin

squalor and decay. By 1960, the formerly 'healthy situation' of the gothic Armley Gaol was described as follows:

> a walk from the railway station to Armley Road takes you through descending levels of civic blight. In the winter murk you pass ancient warehouses, untidy shops, and the unmaintained flats consigned to the very poor. Finally, you reach the sooty decrepitude of HMP prison at Leeds. This is the bottom. In all England, I saw no comparably resounding statement of man's persisting determination to render evil for evil. (*The Guardian,* 15 May 1960: 18)

Indeed, it was as if such prisons had themselves become imprisoned: trapped within their original locations which had been engulfed by urban development, but which were now denied any investment because of the proximity of the prison to them: these areas had come to represent a hidden pathological symbiosis of decay – the fate of the prison and its immediate locality linked together, as the rest of civilization carefully avoided any intrusion to this degenerating micro-world. Such prisons were still needed, despite periodic plans for their closure, but they could neither expand nor modernize through rebuilding because of lack of space, and there was opposition to any suggestion to move them elsewhere. In this way, they could only advertise urban blight and the kinds of sights the civilized world preferred to have hidden away and forgotten – and thereby make the prison still more of an undesirable, unwanted neighbour.

Because, by this time, for many citizens of the civilized world, the prison, for all intents and purposes did have a physical invisibility (hidden away in the rural hinterland or left to decay in inner city ghettoes), it could now only exist as a spectral memory of the gaunt, austere menacing institutions of the nineteenth century. From these obscure locations, prisons still had a role to play: as a hidden receptacle for those whose crimes placed them beyond the tolerance of civilized society. By the same token, any perceived departures from what had become the cultural expectations of prison design would provoke outrage; the legacy of the nineteenth-century prison, and its look of chilling austerity had been able to provide a lasting public memory about what prison should look like, if at the same time the cultural sensitivities of the civilized world also insisted that such buildings be camouflaged and hidden from view. For the penal authorities themselves, the nineteenth-century institutions were also unwanted, representing as they did the unnecessarily repressive remnants of the penal past and now out of place with the scientific, treatment-oriented ethos they had become committed to, more appropriate to psychiatric clinics than penal institutions.

Against such extensive distaste, it is hardly surprising that over the course of the nineteenth and twentieth centuries, prison became an increasingly exclusionary and prohibited site, even for those who broke the law, as more and more barriers were placed in front of it to keep them out. It was seen as too dramatic a penalty for an increasingly wide range of offenders – juveniles, initially, but then the mentally ill, the elderly and the destitute, first offenders, fine defaulters, alcoholics, young adults, even, by the 1970s some groups of persistent offenders. It still had its removal function to perform for some, of course, but it would now do this on the unobtrusive margins of modern civilized societies, which took exception to it having any more visible presence than this.

Hiding the prisoners

It was not simply the case, though, that the prison itself came to be obscured and hidden away during this period. In contrast to the largely unrestricted social intercourse that the pre-nineteenth-century prisons had allowed to take place between prison and the public, in the new penal institutions, the prisoners became steadily more entombed within them and thereby lost from public view and contact: the prisoners, like the prisons in which they were housed, began to be removed from sight. Initially, the novelty of the nineteenth-century prisons had turned them into sight-seeing attractions. In addition to the worthies who liked to visit Pentonville, Hepworth Dixon noted:

> the House of Correction at Preston has acquired a reputation among prisons. Foreigners of distinction visit it from all parts of the continent. Englishmen of all ranks think it worth an inspection. It is open to all comers. In the pages of its visitors book may be seen the superscription of the Russian or German prince and the Yorkshire artisan, the French marquis and the Yorkshire hand loom weaver, the Minister of State, the journalist, the magistrate and the peasant. (1850: 336)

These practices were to remain in some parts of the civilized world until at least the end of the nineteenth century. By then, the gratuitous prison visit – which might satisfy the curiosity of earnest elites interested in social reform, or provide opportunities for vulgarity and humour for those with less refined tastes – had come to be regarded with disapproval by the authorities. It disrupted the bureaucratic administration of the prison. Hepworth Dixon (1850: 3) observed that 'there is one reason why so little is popularly known respecting the London prisons to which attention ought to be drawn – the difficulty of obtaining access to them. In the case of the national prison, it is necessary to obtain a warrant from the Secretary of State ... in the case of city or county prisons ... the visitor must get an order from the magistrate of the city or county'. Even as the dignitaries were queuing to get into Pentonville, Chesterton (1856: 186) wrote of a magistrate who insisted that a charity visitor had no right to converse with the prisoners behind the walls, 'nor was it to be tolerated that Mr. Charles Dickens should walk into the prison whenever he pleased'. Increasingly, then, a firm dividing line was being placed between prisoners and the public: the latter should not be allowed to interfere with the administration of prison life – it was being turned into an occupational, quasi-professional activity, to be undertaken by those trained for it, and therefore something beyond the experience and capability of the general public.

But there was more to such prohibitions on public access than the desire not to disrupt bureaucratic routines: in addition, public visits began to be seen as distasteful. The *Report of the Inspector of Prisons of the Home District* (1836: 19) noted that 'we think the introduction of the visitors who now attend on Fridays the readings to the condemned men highly improper. On one occasion when we were present, there were twenty-three visitors while only twenty-eight prisoners could attend the lecture'. The *Report of the Inspectors of State Prisons* (1866: 17) complained that 'upon every week day, and particularly during the summer season, there are large numbers who visit the prisons ... An admission fee of twenty-five cents is demanded ... while not disposed to ignore the pecuniary advantage of this system we are still of the opinion that general visiting of the prisons is productive of much evil'. In New South Wales (*Report of the Comptroller-General of Prisons,* 1883: 2) there was concern that 'on some occasions females, after being conducted round, are accommodated with chairs, which are placed in a conspicuous position in the prison yard, so as to enable them to sit and scan the appearance of the various criminals ... And strange to relate, such local visitors are never required to subscribe their names in a visitor's book, in accordance with the adhered to regulations of other prisons'. In Canada the *Report of the Inspectors of Penitentiaries* (1897: 10) suggested 'excluding sightseers – they are embarrassing, inconvenient and it is dangerous to admit idle, curious strangers'. The opportunities to visit the prison, in a bid to keep out such entertainment seekers and thereby spare the feelings and embarrassment of the prisoners, would become more restricted and orderly. Visitors would have to gain permission in advance and then sign a book recording their arrival and departure (a rule that had been introduced in England in 1843). It was later reported in New South Wales that 'under the new rule, visitors are admitted on the production of an order from this office on Saturday afternoons, and this, only to those parts of the gaol occupied by members of their own sex. As a further restriction they are debarred access to any place where prisoners can be seen' (*Report of the Comptroller-General of Prisons,* 1904: 2).

Just as the barrier to public access to the prison was being set up, so we find moves to prevent the prisoners working beyond the prison walls. In British Columbia it was noted that 'the objectionable practice of marching prisoners through the streets and working them in irons on public highways has been wholly discontinued at Victoria, and it is to be hoped that in the near future it will be entirely abolished in all parts of [this province], as the effect on white prisoners in particular is most degrading' (*Report of the Superintendent of Police Respecting the Prisons of British Columbia,* 1891: 2). In 1900 the New York prison inspectors proclaimed that 'the presence of convicts in their distinctive garb upon public highways is an insuperable objection to their employment on road making. The public should never be familiarized with criminals or crime. Such familiarity universal experience demonstrates to be demoralizing' (*Report of the New York (State) Prison Department,* 1900: 13). It had become equally distasteful in urban New Zealand: 'the influence of prisoners in cities is not good and when we see children in front of the Terrace Gaol at Wellington playing prisoners, it showed a familiarity with the system which could not be for good' (*Hansard,* 13 August 1907, 40, 191).

There was, then, the issue of the easy identification of prisoners on transportation to new prisons or courts: during the nineteenth century, little or no effort had been made to 'anonymize' such removals – the prisoners would be paraded in chains and uniform in the streets, at railway stations and so on as they made these journeys. They expressed their own concerns about this degrading spectacle. Oscar Wilde wrote that,

> on November 13 1895 I was brought down [to Reading prison] from London. From two o'clock till two thirty on that day I had to stand on the centre platform of Clapham Junction in convict dress and handcuffed, for the world to look at ... of all possible objects I was the most grotesque. When people saw me they laughed. Each train as it came up swelled the audience. Nothing could exceed their amusement. (Hart-Davis, 1962: 490–1)

However, it was not just celebrity prisoners like Wilde who could attract the attention and vulgarities of the crowd. The more mundane, non-descript, unknown prisoners, such as Jock of Dartmoor were just as capable of doing so, when openly 'displayed' on such journeys:

> then came the most ghastly, the most degrading experience of all: I cannot describe – no words could convey – my feelings as I walked down the public platform of Paddington in the full gaze of the people and chained to [other prisoners]. A section of the public made a rush to see us, but I noticed that there were some who had the decency to turn their heads away. I felt that the last shred of decency was being torn from me and soon I should be a beast indeed. (1933: 22–3)

The prison authorities and some of those more sensitive members of the public who did turn their heads also expressed their repugnance at such sights:

> Anyone who has had the experience of railway travelling in Great Britain knows the strange spectacle at a terminus when a convoy is setting out for Portland, Dartmoor or other convict establishments. The wretched prisoners, clad in yellow garments with striking design (the black arrow conspicuous on every part of their person), as if dressed for an *auto-da-fe*, hustled in chains through an excited and gaping crowd to an ordinary third class railway carriage, compelled to exhibit themselves in degradation. (Spearman, 1895: 718)

Just as it became increasingly difficult for the public to gain access to the prisons, so various other possibilities of catching glimpses of prisoners came to be shut down, in the light of complaints about these distasteful public spectacles: 'transfers between prison and prison are now carried out in civilian clothes, to avoid exposure to the public in prison dress' (*Report of the Prison Commissioners*, 1922: 14); 'in recent years advantage has been taken of the improvement in motor transport to convey a large proportion of prisoners by road and so avoid the publicity involved when they travel by rail' (*Report of the Prison Commissioners*, 1935: 10). In addition, the prison authorities began to reserve railway carriages for their transports and to keep the blinds closed for the entire journey.

In 1920, a screen was placed in front of the Dartmoor prisoners at work quarrying to keep them from the view of sightseers (Grew, 1958). After the war, the necessary invisibility of the prisoners was incorporated within the prison rules in England: 'they shall be exposed to public view as little as possible, and proper safeguards shall be adopted to protect them from insult and curiosity' (Fox, 1952: 164–5). In the civilized world, the sights of prisons and prisoners had become distasteful and repugnant: something out of place with its values and standards, something it was necessary to hide from view.

In Canada, the *Report of the Commissioner of Penitentiaries* (1961: 4) noted that 'last month fourteen inmates [of one institution] who were graduating from a public speaking course at the prison travelled in civilian clothing to Victoria, where they held their graduation ceremony at a private club. This function was attended by the mayor and other civic officials. It was impossible to separate the inmates from the guests'. Scenes such as this had become the ideal for penal authorities in the civilized world. Not only had penal institutions through their remoteness, disguise and seclusion become largely invisible to the general public, but it was also the intent of the authorities that, on leaving prison, its prisoners should carry no stain, no mark, no reminder of what they had come from (at least no reminder that would be visible to the public). Having designated that it was essential to remove them from the world beyond the prison, then on their release they should be allowed to surreptitiously re-enter that world, in such a way that it would be impossible to separate them out from the rest of society. The lack of adverse reaction, the lack even of any recognition of their immediate past, showed that these Canadian prisoners at least had been able to pass that test.

Notes

1 'It is not enough to restrain the bad by punishment unless they are made good by training'.

2 For the appropriate Dickens novels, see *Pickwick Papers* (1836/7); *David Copperfield* (1849/50); *Barnaby Rudge* (1841a); *Nicholas Nickleby* (1837/8); and *Oliver Twist* (1838).

3 It is usually seen as significant because its telegraph pole layout seems to have been the first departure from the radial style of Pentonville and its successors (Matthews, 1999).

4 In societies such as New Zealand and Australia, for example, we find shifts in prison building away from urban environments and towards more provincial towns. In New Zealand, after plans to build a pre-release prison hostel in its major city, Auckland, had been 'dashed by local resistance' (*Report of the Controller-General Prisons*, 1960: 12), approval was then given for one in the small town of Invercargill, at the opposite end of the country: 'it is gratifying that the people [here] having "adopted" our borstal should now accept our first pre-release hostel. Their attitude is in marked contrast to the hostility encountered elsewhere' (*Report of the Controller-General of Prisons*, 1961: 10). In such cases, it is possible to discern quite distinctive sensitivities at work, which separate out the provinces in these new societies from their urban counterparts, where opposition to their presence became just as intransigent as that to be found in the longer-established societies of modernity. Such towns, with little tradition, no earlier existence without an institution in their midst, no other kind of identification that could transform them from being at the frontier of the modern, developed world, seemed more readily able to tolerate the presence of penal institutions. Indeed, with no in-built sense of reserve or distaste for them, their prisons began to be seen more as community assets than embarrassing, unsightly stains. For example, in Victoria, it was claimed that 'Geelong prison is very much part of the local community ... in country areas the local prison looms fairly large and its efforts to help the community make an immediate impact ... in a large city efforts by prisoners to help go largely unnoticed' (*Report of the Inspector-General of Penal Establishments and Gaol*, 1902: 4). In effect, these new provincial towns could be organized around the prison – there were unlikely to be any other significant or competing landmarks which would show off the prison in shameful contrast and, indeed, as today, they came to be an important source of local employment. But by the same token, these exceptions seem to prove the more general rule that in the modern urban environment, the prison could only be the least desirable of landmarks and faced much more significant pressure to be removed from view.

4

The Amelioration
of Prison Life

However, it was not sufficient that punishment in the civilized world simply be invisible: otherwise it would have associations with penal trends in some totalitarian societies, taking the form of a hidden terror, some nameless, silent space for the disappeared. In contrast, another of its hallmarks came to be the way in which its penal sanctions were progressively ameliorated. Changing official attitudes towards prison conditions, in particular, two essential features of prison life – food, on the one hand, clothing and personal hygiene on the other – have been chosen to illustrate this. However, this process was not of necessity a unilinear one. It was capable, under particular conditions, of being overridden by contradictory sentiments which demanded more severity. Nonetheless, interruptions of this nature proved to be temporary, before giving way again to the flow of penal sensitivities more in line with the general thrust of the civilizing process.

Prison Food

In England in the first half of the nineteenth century, the provision of an adequate diet had been one of the distinguishing features of the new model prisons. Until then the dietary arrangements had been left to the discretion of the local bodies in charge of each particular prison, with prisoners often having to make their own arrangements with the help of friends and family, or by paying – 'garnishing' – the prison officers. On their visit to Pentonville, Mayhew and Binny observed the superior quality of its diet, which confirmed the high standards that the prison authorities had claimed for themselves:

> It struck us as strange evidence of the 'civilization' of our time, that a person must in these days of 'lie-tea' and chicory-mocha, and alumed bread, and bran-thickened soup and watered butter – really go to prison to live upon unadulterated food ... the most genuine cocoa we ever supped was at a Model prison, for not only was it made of the unsophisticated berries, but was of the very purest water too – water not of the slushy Thames, but which had been raised from an artesian well several hundred feet below the surface, expressly for the use of these same convicts. (1862: 130)

During this period, the authorities had felt able to boast about the quality of the diet they provided. Griffiths quotes the Governor of Newgate prison asserting in the late 1830s that:

> No gaol in England now fed its inmates so well as Newgate. So plentiful was this dietary that although the old permission remained in force of allowing the friends of prisoners to bring them supplies from outside, the practice was falling into abeyance and the prisoners seldom required private assistance to eke out their meals. (1884: 210)

By the same token, it was unconscionable that prison diet be used as an 'instrument of punishment'. As Sir James Graham, Home Secretary, explained, it should be determined by 'the minimum amount which can safely be afforded to prisoners without the risk of inflicting a punishment, not contemplated by law, and which is unjust and cruel to inflict; namely the loss of health and strength through the inadequacy of the food supplied' (Home Office, 1843: 24–5). To this end, it was suggested that breakfast and supper were to consist of bread (6–8 oz) for all but those serving three days or less with one pint of gruel. Dinner was likely to be made up of bread and various combinations of meat (3 oz), potatoes (8 oz) and soup (1 pint).

In the first half of the nineteenth century, the authorities need have no reticence or reservations about proclaiming its quality since they were trying to institutionalize, as a bureaucratic task, the tradition of humanitarian reform that enlightenment reformers such as John Howard had pursued as individuals. However, during the 1860s, prison diet in England came to be set by different criteria: from being determined by the need to maintain health, it comes to be used instead as a tactic of penal discipline, which now overrides the former principle.

Less Eligibility

Following successive Commissions of Inquiry,[1] the most generous diet in the central state's convict prisons in 1864 was as shown in Table 4.1.

Table 4.1 Diet Proposed for Male Convicts at Public Works,
Experiencing Hard Labour (1864)

Meal	Day	Ration
Breakfast	Everyday	3/4 pint of cocoa, bread
Dinner	Sunday	4 oz of cheese, and bread.
	Monday and Saturday	5 oz meat with its own liquor, flavoured with 1/2 oz onions and thickened with bread and potatoes left from previous days, 1lb of potatoes and bread.
	Tuesday and Friday	1 pint of soup containing 8 oz of beef, 1 oz of pearl barley, 2 oz of fresh vegetables, 1 oz onion, 1 lb potatoes, bread.
	Wednesday	5 oz of mutton with its own liquor, flavoured and thickened as above.
	Thursday	1 lb suet pudding containing 1½ oz of suet, 8 oz flour, 6½ oz water. 1 lb potatoes and bread.
Supper	Everyday	1 pint of gruel, containing 2 oz oatmeal and 1/2 oz of molasses, and bread.

Source: *Report of the Committee Appointed to Inquire into the Dietaries of Convict Prisons*, 1864

In contrast to the earlier boasts about the quality and generosity of prison food, we find denunciation of any suspicion of this. Cocoa, for example, had become an outrageous luxury, as a visiting justice now proclaimed: 'I find it wicked; there is no justification for it' (*Report from the Select Committee of the House of Lords on Prison Discipline*, 1863: 320). Instead of the assumptions that it would liberally maintain the health and well-being of the prisoners as its first objective, a much more restrictive diet was linked to the perceived need for prisons to be made deterrent:

> The effect must be very prejudicial, in this way, that persons do not object to going to prison, there is not so much to deter them from prison, and therefore to deter them from crime, as there ought to be; I think that by *a system in which the food is only just sufficient to meet the wants of the human frame*, and where it it is of a very simple kind, and where the system is rather one of punishment, you will deter a person from crime much more than you do, under present circum-stances. (*Report from the Select Committee of the House of Lords on Prison Discipline*, 1863: 120; my italics)

The ameliorative responsibilities of the authorities had been arrested by conjoining them with a secondary set of issues, which demanded that the state's least worthy citizens would not unduly gain from their involvement with crime, being more advantaged in such circumstances than the respectable poor. In effect, the attempts to ameliorate, improve, and standardize prison diet (as part of a more general reform process designed to alleviate the debilitating consequences of imprisonment itself, Howard, 1777, Taylor, 1824) would be subordinated to the more general imperative of English social policy at this time: those who became dependent on the state in one capacity or another would endure less favourable living conditions than the poorest free citizens – the less eligibility principle.

This had been introduced in the 1834 Poor Law to regulate state responsibilities to paupers and other indigents and was extended in the 1860s to prisons. Fears had been building up for several decades that the prisons were becoming too luxurious. Indeed, there seems little doubt that, in the 1840s, prisoners at this point *were* better fed than significant sections of the respectable poor: agricultural workers in the South of England, for example, lived mainly on 'bread, with occasional cheese, or bacon, potatoes, a little milk and meat only a rare luxury' (Burnett, 1966: 84). It is also clear that the living conditions of workhouse residents were more severe than those of prisoners. There were disclosures that the destitute poor would break the law to go to prison in preference to being received in to the workhouse:

> Several of the prisons continue to be attractive to certain classes of persons, instead of repulsive; owing apparently in some instances to the better dietary of the prison as compared with that of the workhouse; in others, to the good medical treatment generally provided in prisons; and in others to a practice of giving prisoners clothing on their liberation. (*Report of the Inspectors of Prisons of the Home District*, 1851: vii)

Scandalous revelations, as at Andover Workhouse (*Report of the Select Committee on Andover Union*, 1846), where it was reported that inmates were so hungry they had resorted to eating the meat off putrid bones, led to an extension of sympathy for those in the workhouse and a growing resentment of the seeming generosity (by comparison) of prison conditions: a hierarchy of worthiness and desert was generated even within outsider groups.

Dickens, again, helped to galvinize public sentiments against the supposed privileges of prisoners and thereby redesignate them at the bottom of that hierarchy, with a reduced tolerance of their everyday living conditions. In *David Copperfield*, he satirized their dietary arrangements:

> It being then just dinner-time, we went first, into the great kitchen, where every prisoner's dinner was in course of being set out separately (to be handed to him in his cell), with the regularity and precision of clockwork. I said aside ... that I wondered whether it occurred to anybody that there was a striking contrast between these plentiful repasts of choice quality and the dinners, not to say of paupers, but of soldiers, sailors, labourers, the great bulk of the honest, working community; of whom not one man in five hundred ever dined half so well. (1850: 714)

The luxuries and privileges of the prisoners contrasted with the deprivations of the workhouse, as he had characterized them in *Oliver Twist*:

The room in which the boys were fed was a large stone hall, with a copper at one end, out of which the master, dressed in an apron for the purpose, and assisted by one or two women, ladled the gruel at meal times. Of this festive composition each boy had one porriger, and no more – except on occasions of great public rejoicing, when he had two ounces and a quarter of bread besides ... the bowls never wanted washing. The boys polished them with their spoons until they shone again; and when they had performed this operation (which never took very long, the spoons being nearly as large as the bowls), they would sit staring at the copper with such eager eyes as if they could have devoured the very bricks of which it was composed, employing themselves, meanwhile, in sucking their fingers most assiduously, with the view of catching any stray splashes of gruel that might have been cast thereon. (1838: 24)

Growing public recognition in this way of the differences in the regimes of these separate institutions (Field, 1848; see also Delacy, 1986) generated sympathy for the more deserving workhouse residents and resentment of the prisoners, making their contrasting living conditions increasingly unjustifiable. The Deputy Governor of Chatham Prison complained:

I find that the scale of diet in convict prisons is vastly beyond that in any gaol or workhouse, and in the most ridiculous disproportion. A pauper in [the workhouse] gets only 4 oz of meat per week, while the convict on public works gets 39 oz of solid meat without bone per week, 27 oz of bread and one lb of vegetables daily to enable him to do little more than the average seven hours of work daily throughout the year. (*Report of the Committee Appointed to Inquire into the Operation of the Acts Relating to Transportation and Penal Servitude,* 1863: 446–7)

In these respects, the responsibilities of the state to its differentiated categories of dependents would vary in relation to where they fitted on the sliding scale of worthiness/unworthiness. Dr Edward Smith (1858: 299), for example, who was later to assume the position of nutritional adviser to the government, advocated increases in the workhouse diet. As regards prisons, however, his suggestion was that 'whilst the aim should not be to improve the condition of the prisoners generally, it should be in reference to those who are exceptionally below a fair standard; and upon the whole, I think that the basic principle involved in the dietary and occupation of prisoners should be, not to injure the system, *but to allow prisoners to leave the prison in as good a condition as they entered it*' (my italics). He was advising that state responsibility for prisoner health should be rewritten: there was no longer any onus on it to improve the prisoners, only to ensure that there was no deterioration in their condition.

The subsequent readjustment to the diet in the 1860s ('[it] differs considerably from the old diet, and contains only 284 oz of solid food per week as against 306 oz per week [before]', (*Report of the Commissioners Appointed to Inquire into the Operation of the Acts relating to Transportation and Penal Servitude*, 1863: 13), was fuelled by the concerns to ensure that prisoners were recognized as the least worthy of all dependent groups; and was set at a level determined by the scientific knowledge that was given in evidence to the 1863 Committee. Smith (*Report from the Select Committee of the House of Lords on Prison Discipline*, 1863: 77), for example, suggested that 'cocoa and meat were unnecessary luxuries and that the functions these provisions performed could be provided by other less extravagant means: cocoa as a stimulant could be replaced by fresh air; meat as a nutrient should be replaced by other farinaceous substances and vegetable foods, so that the main elements of prison diet would consist of bread, rice, oatmeal, potatoes, milk and liquor.' William Guy, Medical Superintendent of Millbank Prison, while disagreeing with Smith on points of detail (arguing, for example, for brown bread in preference to white bread and for a progressive stage rather than a unitary diet) was more restrictive. He believed it impractical to keep prisoners in 'the highest possible state of health and vigour' and saw benefits to be derived from ensuring that, the lower scale of diet, especially, was 'so scanty and uninviting, as to be itself a punishment' (*Report from the Select Committee of the House of Lords on Prison Discipline*, 1863: 498). More specifically:

> I have no hesitation, then, in expressing an opinion in favour of the sufficiency of a dietary from which the meat element is wholly excluded. I have no doubt that health may be preserved, and with it the capacity for labour, on a diet consisting of milk and vegetable food; and I should have no hesitation in prescribing for all criminals under short terms of imprisonment a diet consisting wholly of bread and potatoes. (*Report from the Select Committee of the House of Lords on Prison Discipline*, 1863: 208–9)

In the aftermath of these scientific assessments, the standard recommended by the Home Secretary was that 'the prison dietaries should be sufficient, and not more than sufficient, in amount and quality to maintain the health and strength of the prisoners, and that the diet ought not to be in more favourable contrast to the ordinary food of the free labourers, or the inmates of the workhouses, than sanitary conditions render necessary' (*Report of the Committee on Dietaries of County and Borough Prisons*, 1864: 561). The negative duty to maintain, rather than the positive duty to improve, was now written into the administration of prison regimes.

In contrast, reports from similar societies during the remainder of the nineteenth century show, at most, a much more qualified inscription of the less eligibility principle than had been the case in England. In New Zealand and New South Wales, their penal histories had been clearly tied to that of England due to colonization and their remoteness from other influences, and we find periodic references to a rather less vigorous version of it. In the former, the *Report of the Royal Commission on Prisons* (1868: 15) had referred to prisoners being given 'an unnecessarily abundant' diet of one pound of meat, one pound of potatoes, and one pound of bread per day (at a time when English prisoners were being fed one pound of meat per week). The first New Zealand Inspector of Prisons, Captain Arthur Hume, who had trained under Du Cane in England, complained that 'prison diets are too liberal ... prisoners leave heavier in weight than on reception' (*Report of the Inspector of Prisons*, 1881: 2). However, little if any adjustment seems to have been made. He later notes 'the liberal scale of rations ... compared to England' (*Report of the Inspector of Prisons*, 1890: 2). In New South Wales, although the diet was intended to be as 'low as is consistent with health with due provision for exercise', it prescribed a quantity of food superior than that to be found in the English prisons: 'the rations scale fixed by a Board of medical men is: short sentenced prisoners up to 12 months, sliding scale: 3/4 lb wheat bread, 3/4 lb maize meal, 1/2 lb fresh meat per week (served in 2 meals), 3/4 lb veg, 1/2 oz salt, 1 lb per week rice: increased in labour gaols to 1.5 lb wheat bread, 1 lb fresh meat, 1/2 lb veg, 1/2 oz salt, and sugar, 1/4 oz rice' (*Report of the Comptroller-General of Prisons*, 1885: 2).

In the United States as a whole, Wines and Dwight (1867: 243) reported that prison rations were generally 'abundant and good', referring to the menu at Sing Sing as consisting of 'Breakfast: beef hash, bread, coffee; Supper: mush or molasses; Dinner: corned beef and beans/peas, or stew; beef and soup; pork and potatoes and bread.' The *Report of the New York State Prison Inspectors* (1874: 260) simply refers to 'an abundant supply of wholesome and varied food' in the prisons. That there is no reticence or qualification to such a statement indicates the absence of any significant injection of the less eligibility principle to the relationship between the state and its dependents in New York. As further evidence of this absence, it seems to have been commonplace that each prisoner was allowed to eat as much as they liked. In Canada, the *Report of the Inspectors of Penitentiaries* (1881: 3) noted that 'the diet is healthy, substantial and sufficient; it is well and properly cooked'; and 'the food supplied is good quality. Objection is sometimes made that criminals are too well fed, clothed and lodged ... they stress that the convicts should be on a low diet and that plum pudding on Christmas Day is once too often. However, *it is the role of the government to provide properly for their health and comfort*' (*Report of the Inspectors of Penitentiaries*, 1887: 3; my italics).

What was it about England, then, that allowed less eligibility to be inscribed on the prison diet so firmly here, much less so in some societies, not at all in others? Certainly, one reason for the frugality of the diet was that food provision in England for the lower classes in general was much less than in these other countries:[2] on this basis, we can also expect the prison dietary to be significantly less than elsewhere. This does not explain, however, the particular care and scrutiny that was taken to scale down the prison dietaries in England. What was responsible for this? First, centralized bureaucratic control in that country was already more extensive and more powerful than in these other societies and was in a better position to harness science to justify its aims and practices (putting a stop to the free-flowing humanitarianism associated with much of the early nineteenth-century history of penal reform), which does not seem to have been the case elsewhere: it thus had the bureaucratic means to insist on such a careful calibration.

Second, unlike the New World societies, the prisoners had no utilitarian value: while there was a shortage of labour and population in the former, there was an overabundance in the latter; while prisoners could be put to work on road making and other public works in the former (albeit with increasing reticence), such sights in England only seemed to confirm that the prisoners were the least deserving of all the dependent groups that now proliferated in that rapidly industrialized and urbanized country:

> The convicts are pampered ruffians ... they are healthy looking, clean shaven and have a lazy style of working ... it is high feeding and low work, almost encouraging ticket of leave men to return. When 12.00 midday comes, the convicts who have done the most quarrying that day, may be seen sitting down to their meal of bread and cheese, sometimes with a bit of dried fish or a tin pot of sweetened coffee. The convicts leave work at 11.30 to wash up, comb their hair, take a toilet break before they are rewarded with their ample dinner. (*The Times*, 21 November 1862: 8)

As such, a different set of responsibilities on the part of the central state authority was established towards its prisoners than in these other societies, and a different set of tolerances about the level of their deprivations. In England, the duty of the state was to keep prisoners apart from the more worthy sections of the population and ensure that their living conditions were not more generous. In Canada, as indicated above, the duty of the state was seen as much more extensive and inclusive.

Third, we need to look at the way in which the dramatic urbanization of English life in the first half of the nineteenth century upset existing interdependencies, and needed new ones to be forged, before the civilizing process was able to continue in that country. What is evident in many of the social commentaries of the time is the huge social and spatial gulf that had been thrown up by industrialization (Dennis, 1984; Poynter, 1969). This accounted for the weakening of pre-industrial social bonds and any sense of community; it accounted for the attendant growth of central government and bureaucratic organizations at the expense of local understandings and paternalistic obligations; and it accounted for the geographical separation of the industrial classes in the new cities. Faucher thus wrote of Manchester:

The town, strictly speaking, is only inhabited by shopkeepers and operatives; the merchants and manufacturers have detached villas, situated in the midst of gardens and parks in the country. This mode of existence within the somewhat contracted horizon of the family circle, excludes social intercourse, and leads to a local absenteeism. And thus at the very moment when the engines are stopped, and the counting houses are closed, everything which was the thought – the authority – the impulsive force – the moral order of this immense industrial combination, flies from the town, and disappears in an instant. The rich man spreads his couch amidst the beauties of the surrounding country, and abandons the town to the operatives, publicans, mendicants, thieves, and prostitutes, merely taking the precaution to leave behind him a police force, whose duty it is to preserve some little of material order in this pell-mell of society. (1844: 26)

Crime control was already becoming specialized and professionalized, reducing the obligations on other citizens to become involved in such duties.

In effect, then, the social distance that had come about as a result of advanced industrialization and urbanization not only allowed for the possibility of the less eligibility injection to social and penal policy, but also sheltered much of the dominant class from having to see and be affected by its uncomfortable consequences. If some stirrings of conscience had been provoked by scandals about workhouse conditions and had ultimately led to some improvement, the new prisons were known only for their luxuries; and the prisoners only for their unworthiness. Under such circumstances, a very repressive penal culture begins to take effect in England, directed at removing any vestiges of the privileged life of prisoners.

But again, even under these new arrangements where severity is now to outweigh humanity, it is not allowed to eclipse the latter (Sparks, 1996). If the prisoners were not to be advantaged at all, then at the same time, their health should be maintained, not allowed to deteriorate. In societies that professed to be 'civilized', it was no longer sufficient for its prisons to discharge starving human wrecks (*Report of the Prison Commissioners*, 1887–8). The succession of inquiries to determine how low the dietary's scale could be made in the early 1860s was then followed by a succession of others to ascertain whether or not this had been set too low to maintain this level of duty (*Reports of the Commissioners on the Treatment of the Treason-Felony Convicts*, 1867, 1871). In fact, the diet was changed in 1878, with the addition of beans and bacon as an alternative to meat and potatoes. The stated principle was that the authorities should 'avoid any approach to indulgence or to excess, but to arrange that the diet shall be sufficient and not more than sufficient to maintain health and strength' (*Report of the Committee Appointed to Consider and Report upon Dietaries of Local Prisons*, 1878: 55).

What had changed since the 1864 Committee set the seal on the matter was the dropping of the stipulation that the prisoners' diet should not exceed that of more deserving groups, indicating already, perhaps, a softening of the rigid adherence to less eligibility. As with the inquiries of the 1860s, the 1878 Commissioners relied strongly on medical evidence and scientific knowledge to determine the appropriate level of prison diet, in the light of which they advocated that more protein should be included: 'we follow the example of the Committee of 1864 in giving hot food once daily; but we give it in the shape of a nutritious stirabout, composed of oatmeal and Indian meal'.[3] And, for the first time, it seems, attention was paid to food preparation now thought to be

> Of no less importance than the regulation of the quantity, and in order that due attention may be paid to this subject, we ... have obtained the services of a medical adviser, who, besides other important duties ... will supervise the introduction of the new dietary, and we propose, with his assistance, to establish systematic instruction in the art of preparing food, so that by degrees we hope to spread throughout the prisons sound scientific and practical knowledge of the subject. (*Report of the Committee to Consider and Report upon Dietaries of Local Prisons*, 1878: 1, 10)

However, if nutritional science could be called upon to justify improvements in some respects, it could also be used to justify the continuance of restrictive diets in others. The Committee disclaimed any relationship between prison diet and weight loss; if this did occur, then it was only likely to be beneficial to health: 'it is a matter of universal experience that partial abstinence from food is not only safe under ordinary circumstances, but frequently beneficial, and we think that a spare diet is all that is necessary for a prisoner undergoing a sentence of a few days or weeks'.

It is towards the end of the nineteenth century that we begin to see a shift back to more obvious signs of ameliorative influences on the English prison diet. By this point, the new interdependencies of industrial society had begun to take root: knowledge of the suffering of the poor and other dependent groups was becoming more widely available through a range of investigative journalism and inquiries thereby helping to raise the threshold of sensitivity and embarrassment (Booth, 1890; London, 1903). It was possible to further reduce the restraints of less eligibility as embryonic welfarism began to take effect, increasing central state responsibilities, particularly as advances in scientific knowledge highlighted the deficiencies of the diet across most of the population of England, such as the absence of vitamins A and B (Drummond and Wilbraham, 1939: 420). These concerns about inadequate diets now included the prisons, indicating some reduction in the social distance between these institutions and the rest of society, some lessening of the intensity of the prisoners' outsider status. There could thus be an improvement in the quality of food they provided. The *Report of the*

Prison Commissioners (1899: 21) stated that 'having regard to the grave dangers which would accrue should the lowest scale be unduly attractive, [the diet] should consist of the plainest food, but good and wholesome and adequate in amount and kind to maintain health'.

Instead of earlier injunctions against exceeding 'sufficiency', instead of assuming a completely neutral stance, neither improving nor harming the condition of the prisoners on arrival, the prison now had a positive duty: to maintain the health and strength of the prisoner, 'as well as to fit him for earning his living by manual labour on discharge (*Report of the Prison Commissioners*, 1900–1: 19). With this aim, around the end of the nineteenth century the standard prison diet in England changed from consisting largely of stirabout to one based on porridge for breakfast and variations of bread and potatoes and bread and suet pudding for dinner. The qualitative and quantitative dietary changes that this duty necessitated are indicators of the changing relationship between the modern state and its criminals.

Again, scientific opinion was used to justify these changes. Weight loss was now recognized as detrimental to health: 'I am still of the opinion expressed by the Dietary Committee, that when applied to large bodies of men, all placed in similar circumstances, in other respects as regards food, a general loss of weight affords a fairly reliable indication of the inadequacy of a dietary for due nutrition' (*Report of the Prison Commissioners*, 1900–1). At the same time, the scientific accreditation of the new diet provided a bulwark against criticisms that it had become too generous – more so in fact than was the case in workhouses:

> The new dietary is based on the opinion of experts, is framed on scientific principles, so as to present a sufficiency, and not more than a sufficiency, of food for an average man doing an average day's work. The scale of tasks is based on the experience extending over many years of what can reasonably be expected from a man working his hardest during a given number of hours per diem. We believe that both the dietary and the tasks strike a fair average, so as not to err on the side of severity or leniency.

Two decades later, further changes had taken place in prison diet: Hobhouse and Brockway (1923: 127) were able to refer to 'vegetables which are sometimes allowed as substitutes for a part of the potatoes in the ordinary diet: – cabbage, carrots, leeks, onions, parsnips and turnips. These vegetables are always greatly appreciated by the prisoners'. The *Report of the Prison Commissioners* (1926: 12) refers to a 'more balanced and varied diet, which included the provision of regular vegetables'. During the 1930s, the prison menu took the following form, as shown in Table 4.2. The English prison dietary had now moved broadly into line with the ameliorative principles at work in corresponding societies; what differences there were in diet between these respective countries would now be more reflective of the availability of

Table 4.2   A Typical Day's Menu in Prison in the 1930s

Breakfast	Dinner	Supper

Porridge ½ pint
   Bread: 6 oz, margarine,
   1 pint tea
	Meat Pie (4 and ½ oz meat,
	   4 oz veg, onions, flour, suet,
	   12 oz potatoes (unpeeled)
		Bread 8 oz, margarine
		   ½ oz, cheese 1 oz,
		   cocoa 1 pint.

Source: *Report of the Prison Commissioners*, 1960: 67.

local produce and general standards of diet in them, rather than philo-
sophical issues about what was tolerable for prisoners. Thus, in contrast
to the plain prison food in England, fish was served once a week in New
South Wales from 1914 and in New Zealand from 1918, where it was
later (*Report of the Controller-General of Prisons*, 1937: 3) claimed that:
'ten years ago the food was noteworthy for its bulk and plainness, now
it is more innovative: puddings, pastries, gravy, cocoa, more milk and
butter'. Similarly, in Victoria, 'over the last twenty years there has been
an immeasurable improvement in the food ration: meat, bread, oatmeal,
potatoes and vegetables and also dried fruits; milk cheese and jam'.
(*Report of the Inspector-General of Penal Establishments and Gaols*,
1943: 3) In Ontario, the menu was changed daily from 1923: 'the quality of food is excellent – increases in vegetables and decreases in the
number of steamed dishes and the pasteurization of all milk' (*Report of
the Inspector of Prisons and Reformatories*, 1933: 40).

   In another innovation, we find references to improvements in the
ambience of serving arrangements. In England, prison 'cans' were to be
abandoned and replaced with aluminium trays and utensils; in addition,
some prisoners were now allowed to 'dine in association' (*Report of the
Prison Commissioners*, 1926: 20), in the hope that this would increase
their self-respect. In the Canadian federal prisons, 'tinware in which
men's food was formerly served has been replaced by white enamelware.
Perhaps the best indication that the men appreciated the change is
evidenced by the fact that they take care of their dishes ... the new dishes
have a more cleanly and appetising appearance' (*Report of the
Inspectors of Penitentiaries*, 1915: 5). In Sing Sing, 'those employed in
the kitchen and mess hall are dressed in white check suits. Tables with
enamel tops and chairs with backs are being installed' (*Report of the
State Commission on Prisons*, 1917: 5). In New Zealand: 'standard
bowls, plates and pannikins are on issue – it had been either enamelware
or tin' (*Report of the Controller-General of Prisons*, 1927: 3). Changes
in diet and food preparation at this time are indicative of changing
tolerances towards what were acceptable prison conditions and further
reductions in the social distance between the prisoners and the rest of
society – at least on the part of the prison authorities. Any need to talk
about the frugality of what they provided was being increasingly
reduced. In Victoria, there had been criticisms from prisoners of poor
food. The authorities replied that

It may interest the public to see what the rations really are. These ... vary somewhat from week to week and are supplemented by salad vegetables such as lettuce, onions, tomatoes, beetroot etc ... the quality [of the food] is the best procurable. Prisoners invariably gain in weight during imprisonment and there has never been an ascertainable case of disease due to deficiency in diet. (*Report of the Inspector-General of Penal Establishments and Gaols*, 1944: 4–5)

The Normalization of Prison Food

According to Rule 98 of the 1949 Prison Rules, the diet in English prisons was to be 'of a nutritional value adequate for health and of a wholesome quality, *well prepared and served* and reasonably varied' (my italics). A higher standard has now been placed on the authorities as regards dietary provision. It was no longer sufficient for them to merely maintain health and to ensure appropriate preparation of food. In addition, as with improvements to diet beyond the prison that begin to be set in place (Mennell, 1985), there must also be variation to it:

There was a general upward trend in the standard of cooking ... gradually the meals are becoming more in proportion to the civilian eating habits. Sweet puddings of *normal portions* are now given on most days of the week and some relish for the supper meal in the form of cake, bun or savoury dish is served every day: in short, the food is more evenly spread over the day and this is much appreciated by the inmates. (*Report of the Prison Commissioners*, 1949: 66; my italics)

Alongside this apparent commitment to adjust the quantity of prison rations to the same standards of the world outside the prison, the prisoners were to be provided with a full range of eating utensils. Furthermore, eating arrangements were to be improved by the replacement of 'old wooden dining tables with tables having inlaid linoleum tops and many of the forms for seating were replaced by wooden chairs' (*Report of the Prison Commissioners*, 1949: 65). These changes were followed by the introduction of 'a cafeteria tray ... during next year all prisons whose meal service arrangements allow of its use will be equipped with it. The results so far gained suggest that the prisoners and staff have welcomed the use which can be made of the tray, which enables the food to be served in more variety and with improved presentation' (*Report of the Prison Commissioners*, 1950: 76).

In line with the increased responsibilities of the post-war welfare state, various additions were made to improve the prison menu, formally bringing the prisoners' eating habits into line with the standards of the rest of society: previous social divisions that were intended to separate them out

Table 4.3   A 1960s' Prison Menu

Breakfast	Dinner	Supper
Porridge, bacon, savoury, marmalade, bread, margarine, tea	Vegetable soup, meat pie, cabbage, mash, steamed fruit pudding, custard, bread roll Evening Cocoa, bread roll (perhaps with savoury filling)	Cold ham and tomato and/or yeast bun, bread, margarine, tea.

Source: Report of the Prison Commissioners, 1960: 68

were being reduced. The 'traditional breakfast of porridge' was now supplemented by 'sausage and gravy' or 'bacon and fried bread', with 'a reduction in the amount of oatmeal and bread being balanced by an additional item of food suitable for providing an extra dish. This welcome break in the breakfast monotony has been almost universally appreciated and it also resulted in an improvement in the overall nutritional value of the dietary' (*Report of the Prison Commissioners*, 1956: 126).

Variety, choice, quality and quantity in food and the ambience of its serving arrangements were a feature in the annual reports as wartime and post-war shortages, restrictions and regulations were eased. What we now find from this time are steady, incremental improvements in line with the more general improvement of diet beyond the prison that the final abolition of food rationing in England in 1954 made possible: 'dietary changes will include a substantial increase in allowance for fresh meat, a reduction in the amount of sausage meat and an increase in potato and fresh fruit allowances' (*Report of the Prison Commissioners*, 1958: 98); 'potatoes are peeled and cooked in a variety of ways' (*Report of the Prison Commissioners*, 1960: 67); 'the milk ration was increased by half a pint weekly for all adult inmates and sufficient cornflakes for two breakfasts a week were introduced' (*Report on the Work of the Prison Department*, 1963: 59); 'eggs now form a part of the regular weekly dietary ... the increased cash allowance has also made it possible to increase the amount of fresh fruit available and to provide tinned fruit and other extras' (*Report on the Work of the Prison Department*, 1964: 51). In the 1960s, the standard prison menu was as shown in Table 4.3.

These developments in England were again in line with those taking place elsewhere. In New South Wales, milk was provided for the first time, as was jam and golden syrup. There were to be two meat meals daily and porridge was eliminated from the evening meal. The formal aim was that 'food is simple but ample in quantity and good quality' (*Report on the Operations of the Department of Prisons*, 1949/50: 12). In Canada, 'prisoners' rations have been greatly improved and the complaints of stomach trouble are not so frequent. Kitchen facilities have improved – there are more attractive servings and an officer to inspect meals each day and report on them. Food inspection charts are morale boosting to inmates since they know food is checked daily' (*Report of the*

Inspectors of Penitentiaries, 1945: 8). In some Canadian penal institutions, the serving arrangements now confirmed the reduction in the social divisions and hierarchies between prisoners and guards: 'certain members of staff partake of meals with inmates in cell blocks at common tables, giving direct, continuous supervision. As a result, the use of table-cloths and knives and forks ... are now being enjoyed at all cell-block dining tables' (*Report of the Commissioner of Penitentiaries*, 1960: 8).

Then, as these societies in the civilized world began to become more cosmopolitan, so the greater diversity in diet associated with this was reflected in prison food. In New York State, 'inmates welcome the opportunity to choose the type and quality of food desired as opposed to the old methods whereby it was impossible to make a choice' (*Report of the Department of Correctional Services*, 1967: 18). In England, 'diets have been more interesting and more varied. Some establishments are able to offer as many as four choices at the main meal. Arrangements for both the preparation and the service of food are being modernized; the cafeteria system has been introduced at some establishments, and new rotary bread ovens are installed in all new establishments' (*Report on the Work of the Prison Department*, 1967: 29). This was followed by references to the provision of 'more fresh fruit and vegetables. Poultry has been put on the menu for the first time, and arrangements have been made for salads to be supplied from prison department farms and market gardens' (*Report on the Work of the Prison Department*, 1973: 19–20).

By now, it was as if the 'hard fare' and so on of the mid-nineteenth-century English prisons lay in the prehistory of punishment in the civilized world, a temporary interruption to the process of ameliorating this aspect of prison life that had become one of its distinguishing features.

Prison Clothing and Personal Hygiene

Until the mid-nineteenth century, the provision of prison uniform and the arrangements for personal hygiene had been provided on an irregular, ad hoc basis. On his tour round English prisons John Howard (1777: 31) found a uniform in existence in only three of them. Thereafter, it became a regular feature of prison life, reflecting both the humanitarian concerns of the authorities, and broader security interests (which inured uniform, unlike food, from excessive intrusions of the less eligibility principle). The early uniforms were deliberately ostentatious in design, involving stripes and multi-coloured garments, ensuring the prisoners would be recognized if they escaped (Society for the Improvement of Prison Discipline, 1826: 26). The wearing of them, in conjunction with other aspects of prison discipline and hygiene such as head-shaving, the wearing of masks (in England to prevent recognition by other prisoners), the display of one's prison number on the breast, and movement in lockstep formation in the United States also had humiliating consequences for the prisoners.[4] Although at the end of the eighteenth century there had been some support for uniforms that produced exactly this effect (Ignatieff, 1978: 93), during the course of the nineteenth such stigmatization was increasingly thought of as undesirable. For some observers, the sight of prisoners clothed in such attire could lead to pity for them and disgust at what they had been turned into. Mayhew and Binny (1862: 141), on their visit to Pentonville, reported that 'each of the prisoners is not only clad alike – and brown as so many bees pouring from the countless cells of a hive – but everyone wears a peculiar brown cloth cap, and the peak of this hangs so low down as to cover the face like a mask, the eyes alone of the individual appearing through the two holes cut in the frame'. Similarly offended, the *Report of the Inspectors of [New York] State Prisons* (1862: 17) urged the authorities to 'take away the degrading stripe in prison clothing and banish the everlasting lockstep'.

In England, the prisoners' appearance was given consideration in the *Report of the Commission of Inquiry on Prison Rules and Prison Dress* (1889). It was now recognized that '[prison clothing] has too long been associated with all that is vile and shameful to be assumed by the lesser offenders without a sense of degradation and a shock to self-respect which should never be unnecessarily inflicted'. When providing his own written evidence to the Committee, Du Cane himself acknowledged that 'the idea of humiliating and degrading prisoners, and especially of making a spectacle of them ... is quite opposed to modern principles and practice, and belongs rather to the period when stocks and the pillory were in use' (*Report of the Committee of Inquiry on Prison Rules and Prison Dress*, 1889: 44). However, the prison uniform itself had become a 'necessary incident to imprisonment.' Furthermore, it was argued that any relaxation of the rules regarding the wearing of them 'would produce in the mind both of the prisoner and of the public the impression that certain classes of offenders are exceptionally favoured' (*Report ... on Prison Dress*, 1889, 46). Even so, the uniform could also serve humane concerns:

> the present practice whereby prisoners of different classes are distinguished by different colours and patterns of dress, and every prisoner has on various articles of his clothing distinguished badges ... not only make it unnecessary for the warder to know or address him by his name, but avoid the necessity for making each prisoners' name known to the other prisoners with the disadvantages which might result to the prisoner therefrom.

Bureaucratic necessities and an intolerant and unforgiving public meant that it had to be worn.

Nonetheless, we do find a number of initiatives designed to ameliorate its effects. The wearing of masks in English prisons was abolished in

1878, for example, and prisoners waiting to be tried on another charge would be allowed to appear in court in their own clothes. At least the prisoners' own clothing could now be cleaned:

> We have taken steps to provide that the clothing in which prisoners are received shall be disinfected by exposure to heat in a hot air chamber and have given directions ... that effective measures shall be taken to have such articles as are capable of it thoroughly cleansed and purified before being put into store, that the underclothing of all prisoners sentenced to ten days and upwards shall be washed. (*Report of the Prison Commissioners*, 1883: 11)

The standards of cleanliness were to be normalized by the Prison Rule 33, 1898, which stipulated that 'the prisoner shall be required to keep himself clean and decent about his person'. To this effect, weekly baths were introduced and the rules regarding the severity of hair clipping were relaxed in 1911.

In New York State, the lockstep was abolished in 1900:

> [The convicts] now march in double or single file ... with a fair degree of precision ... drill gives them a more erect and manly bearing. The aim is to soften the necessary rigor of convict life and to apply more fully the forces, which distinctly seek to better and reform the prisoner. The lockstep was a distinctive prison march ... it was a badge of prison humiliation ... some methods of the old system which tended unnecessarily to humiliate prisoners and lessen self-respect have been discarded. (*Report of the New York (State) Prison Department*, 1900: 17)

The distinctive prison stripes were abolished in 1904. From thereon the uniform was to consist of 'suits and caps of gray cloth. The coat, which is cut with a standing collar and fitted to the form, has steel buttons. The cap is of semi-military style ... stripes had come to be looked upon as a badge of shame and were a constant humiliation and irritant to many prisoners' (*Report of the New York (State) Prison Department*, 1904: 22). Hair clipping was abolished in 1907, with 'shirts and underwear numbered on an individual basis, with indiscriminate garments from the laundry prohibited' (*Report of the New York (State) Prison Department*, 1907: 14). Similarly, in New South Wales, hair cropping was abolished in 1907. In Ontario, 'prison stripes' were abolished in 1909. In the federal prisons, there was an 'abandonment of checked and striped clothing' and its replacement by 'plain blue for winter and plain brown for the summer' (*Report of the Inspectors of Penitentiaries*, 1922: 12). In New Zealand, 'the days of the Broad Arrow are long since past ... the aim is to supply an outfit with a touch of individuality, especially for leisure time' (*Report of the Controller-General of Prisons*, 1938: 3).

In England, a further series of reforms was introduced in the 1920s. Until then, the sight of prisoners could still be a distasteful experience, for elite observers at least. Sir Alexander Paterson (Ruck, 1951: 11), subsequent Head of the English Prison Commission, described what he saw on a visit to Dartmoor in the early twentieth century: 'their drab uniforms were plastered with broad arrows, their heads were closely shaven ... not even a safety razor was allowed, so that in addition to the stubble on their heads, their faces were covered with a dirty moss, representing the growth of hair that a pair of clippers would not remove'. In a bid to improve the prisoners' appearance, the 'convict crop' was abolished and 'broad arrows' were removed from uniforms: 'a new style of clothing is being devised which though of the simplest kind will give a better chance to self-respect' (*Report of the Prison Commissioners*, 1922: 14). Furthermore, 'we have given clear instructions (a) that every prisoner must receive a clean suit or dress on admission and (b) that all under-clothing worn next to the skin must be washed weekly. To this end, outer garments, as well as under, which are discarded by prisoners on discharge are to be washed'. As a result, it was claimed that 'the hang-dog look so characteristic of many prisoners in former days tends to disappear' (*Report of the Prison Commissioners*, 1924–5: 19). Through these reforms, it would be possible for the prisoners, in these accounts of the authorities, to throw off the debasement and lack of pride in themselves that their previous appearance had advertised and instead take on a more 'normal' look.

There were further attempts to improve prison clothing in the 1930s and a 'kit system' was introduced, as if this form of ownership would encourage the prisoners to take more responsibility for their clothing and pride in their appearance (see *Report of the Prison Commissioners*, 1937: 26). There were also attempts to improve hygienic arrangements and to end the shamefulness and squalor now associated with slopping out[5]. In response to criticisms of such practices, it was noted that 'the Commissioners have not yet quite completed the task of bringing the existing recesses up to modern standards. [However,] those who remember what they were like before will appreciate that this is no small contribution to the provision of better hygiene' (*Report of the Prison Commissioners*, 1935: 81).

The quest for improvement in personal appearance and hygiene continued during the war – this was not allowed to interrupt this commitment:

> The Commissioners have, within wartime limitations, done their best to get a better standard of neatness and cleanliness in the appearance of the prisoners. They recognize, however, that with the present style of prison clothes no great success is to be expected in getting men to take any pride in good appearance and they have set up a Committee to consider this question and make suggestions for improved clothing, which can be put into effect as soon as supplies permit. In the meantime they have paid special attention to questions of repair and conditions of shoes and clothing and have issued short aprons to protect the trousers in those shops where the work is dirty. (*Report of the Prison Commissioners*, 1942: 35)

The same report notes that shaving had now become compulsory every day. Then, in a further attempt to personalize the prisoner, the wearing of cell badges, stamped with a prison number, was abolished in 1944. For the first time in nearly a century, prisoners had been formally granted the right to a name: they could begin to think of themselves as having an identity as a human being. It was now claimed that the prisons enforce:

> a high standard of cleanliness both in premises and in the person of prisoners, many of whom are received in a filthy condition and are not naturally clean in their habits ... a bath must be taken on reception and thereafter weekly and underclothing is changed weekly. Regular shaving and haircutting are required. (*Report of the Prison Commissioners*, 1945: 25)

After the war, improvements in clothing and personal appearance continued to be made, notwithstanding rationing: 'some progress has been possible with the implementation of the Clothing Committee's recommendations ... new pattern shoes and socks have been supplied to all establishments. The distribution of new pattern underclothing, over-alls, jackets and trousers will, it is to be hoped, be completed in 1948' (*Report of the Prison Commissioners*, 1947: 36). In 1949 it was reported that 'to improve the finish of a new type of prisoners outer clothing steam presses have been installed in all tailors shops' (*Report of the Prison Commissioners*, 1949: 41). As regards personal hygiene, the 1949 Prison Rules had stipulated that 'arrangements shall be made for every prisoner to wash at all proper times, to have a hot bath at least once a week, and for men ... to shave or be shaved daily and to have their hair cut as required' (Rule 95); and 'every prisoner shall be provided on admission with such toilet articles as are necessary for health and cleanliness and arrangements shall be made for their replacement when necessary' (Rule 96).

By the early 1960s prisoners were wearing 'dark blue battle dress' instead of a 'grey woollen suit' (Morris and Morris, 1963). This in turn was replaced as the authorities professed to show some recognition of the broader changes in attitudes to variety in dress and self-presentation:

> A start was made in 1968 on a programme that aimed at improving practically every article of prison wear and at bringing scales of issue up to modern standards of living and hygiene. Outer wear has already been radically altered with a smarter jacket to replace the outmoded battle dress style blouse. More and better shirts, socks and sets of underwear were issued. (*Report on the Work of the Prison Department*, 1968: 29)

Different shades and colour were introduced, not for the earlier purposes of classification and humiliation, but to allow choice and personal preference: 'it should soon be possible to allow most men and boys in custody choices of what they will wear. It should be possible, for example, to have a range of shirts in different colours. [Furthermore] pyjamas are now being issued in prisons as in borstals ... Among the Victorian traditions was one that required prisoners to sleep in their clothes' (*Report on the Work of the Prison Department*, 1969: 27). The authorities were indicating how far behind they had left such shameful, distasteful remnants of the penal past: as with any normal citizen in the civilized world, day clothes would be removed at night, and special sleeping garments would be provided.

Outside England, we find that in New South Wales (*Report of the Department of Prisons*, 1965/6) 'improvements since 1960 include clothing and footwear'; in 1972, free dental services were introduced and a new uniform approved in 1975. In Victoria, 'saluting has been abolished, prisoners are not required to swing their arms shoulder high when marching, [there is] regular bathing, the provision of two clean shirts per week and the prisoners no longer have to wear hats' (*Report of the Director of Penal Services*, 1972: 36). In the Canadian Federal Prisons, 'inmate grooming conforms to contemporary standards now. A new design and colour for work clothing has been introduced to reduce the drabness [of the uniform]; leisure time clothing is made available in a range of colours' (*Report of the Solicitor-General of Canada*, 1971–2: 48).

At this point, the prison authorities were formally committed to ameliorating the essential living conditions of prison to the point where they could be seen as entirely normalized. Earlier images of the wretched hopelessness of the prisoners, informed by their stigmatic uniforms, and the other practices of subjection and dietary restrictions, which thereby cast the prisoner apart from the rest of society, had long since disappeared from official penal discourse. They had been removed from it, as the authorities themselves frequently pointed out, because of their commitment to the amelioration of prison and their disassociation from those remnants of it that seemed to belong more to the uncivilized past, not the civilized world of the present. Around 1970, what should formally differentiate prisoners from the rest of the population in these societies was the fact that they were in prison, not the circumstances of prison life itself.

Notes

---

1 See the *Report from the Select Committee of the House of Lords on Prison Discipline*, 1863, *Report of the Commissioners Appointed to Inquire into the Operation of the Acts Relating to Transportation and Penal Servitude*, 1863,

Report of the Committee Appointed to Inquire into the Dietaries of Convict Prisons, 1864.

2 See, in relation to diet in England in the late nineteenth century, Chinn (1995); in contrast, see Graham (1992) on New Zealand; on Canada, Russell (1973); on Australia, Davison et al. (1998); on the United States, Levenstein (1988).

3 Stirabout (also known as 'skilly') was a regular feature of working-class diet in England in the late nineteenth century. In prison, it consisted of one and a half pint servings, consisting of three ounces of Indian meal, three of oatmeal and the rest water.

4 'A curious combination of march and shuffle, the march aiming to impose discipline, the shuffle to make certain that the men did not become too prideful' (Rothman, 1971: 120).

5 'Slopping out' was prison slang for the practice of English prisons of the morning emptying of chamber pots, in the absence of internal sanitation in the cells. See also p. 109.

5

The Sanitization
of Penal Language

Another of the hallmarks of punishment in the civilized world relates to the way in which its formal language of punishment came to be sanitized: stripped of the emotive, pejorative force that its infliction might invoke in favour of one that spoke of punishment in more neutral, objective, scientific terms. This reflects the growing influence of expert knowledge on the development of official penal discourse. This language of punishment became the property, by and large, of elites (reform groups, members of the penal bureaucracies and so on) rather than the general public. For the most part, popular discourse changed from celebrating and romanticizing the criminal in the eighteenth century to fearing and shunning him during the nineteenth and twentieth. In contrast, the language that came to be spoken by the penal authorities over the same period reflects the growing sensitivity of these elites to the circumstances of criminals and prisoners, and their professed commitment to reducing the social distance between them and the rest of the population.

The Fear of Convicts

In England in the mid-nineteenth century, nonetheless, there was still a much closer resonance between these two languages of punishment. Charles Dickens' (1860) *Great Expectations* provides one of the most famous literary descriptions of 'the criminal', using language that was then being spoken across all social groups and which indicated a very different set of sensitivities and ways of thinking about such individuals than that which eventually came to be spoken in sanitized official discourse. The book opens with a scene set on the south coast of England, in the early 1800s. An escaped convict from a prison hulk, awaiting transportation to Australia, surprises the hero Pip. The convict is described as having 'a terrible voice', and as a fearful man, all in coarse grey, with a great iron on his leg. A man with no hat, and with broken shoes, and with an old rag tied round his head. A man who had been soaked in water, and smothered in mud, and lamed by stones, and cut by flints, and stung by nettles, and torn by briars; who limped and shivered, and glared and growled; and whose teeth chattered in his head as he seized me by the chin. (1860: 1)

This escaped convict – Abel Magwitch – demands that Pip bring him food and drink, and should he fail to do so threatens him with another convict even more terrible than he:

There's a young man hid with me, in comparison with which young man I am a Angel ... That young man has a secret way pecooliar [sic] to himself, of getting at a boy, and at his heart, and at his liver. It is in vain for a boy to attempt to hide himself from that young man ... I am a-keeping of that young man from harming of you at the present moment, with great difficulty. I find it very hard to hold that young man off your inside. (1860: 1)

As Pip flees home, his last sight of Magwitch is of him 'limping on towards ... a gibbet, with some chains hanging on to it, which had once held a pirate, as if he were the pirate come to life, and come down, and going back to hook himself up again. It gave me a terrible turn when I thought so' (1860: 2).

What is clear from this description of Magwitch (and his non-existent associate) is the absence of any romanticization of the criminal, a theme that had been prevalent in much eighteenth-century popular literature.[1] Such a theme did not end at this juncture – it continued into the early twentieth century and well beyond this.[2] But what we now find in the work of Dickens and others is the existence of a much more prominent, more powerful counter-discourse: those who were previously outlaws – living outside of society – have here been turned into eponymous 'convicts'. And thereby, everything we are told about Magwitch turns him into an outcast, not an outlaw: someone whom society wished to be rid of, to put him out of sight, beyond its imagination; as opposed to the outlaw, whose decision to live beyond its reach was their own, but who would still make periodic returns to it to take on and challenge the authorities. There is nothing in Magwitch to celebrate or admire; nor is there the slightest pity for the starving, shivering chained creature he had become. Instead, marked off from the rest of society by his own appearance as dangerous and to be avoided at all costs, he can command only terror and horror, as Pip acknowledges: 'I have often thought that few people know what secrecy there is in the young, under terror, so that it be terror. I was in mortal terror of the young man who wanted my heart and liver; I was in mortal terror of my interlocutor with the ironed leg' (Dickens, 1860: 2).

In the period in which the novel was set (as opposed to when it was written), the penal system was designed to act in such a way that Pip and the rest of society would be spared such terrors: convicts such as Magwitch would normally face some form of expulsion from society, whether by means of transportation or the death penalty. Magwitch, of course, had been sentenced to the former and only by cheating his fate with his escape, did he come to threaten Pip. However, at the time of the book's publication – which no doubt helps to explain its popularity – there was no longer any such protection. The death penalty (in effect) was available only for murder cases, and the gibbets had long since been taken down (while the execution site itself was shortly to be moved behind prison walls); furthermore, transportation from England had been finally abolished in 1856. The spectacle of punishment, affirming that expulsion of one kind or another would take effect, was in itself in the process of being removed from the nineteenth-century penal agenda. Now creatures such as Magwitch would be housed right in the heart of the civilized world, in the new prisons, where they would be eventually released, free to commit their crimes again, as the growing interest in criminal statistics seemed able to confirm.[3] By the time Dickens' novel was published, as we saw in relation to the development of attitudes towards prison diet and other necessaries of prison life around this time, whatever the humanitarian channels of penal reform that had been pursued in the early nineteenth century, these were evaporating before a growing intolerance of the convicts. There were demands from right across the social body that they should be recognized as the most undeserving of all social classes.

As such, Mary Carpenter, herself active in penal reform, in a passage very redolent of Pip's experience, summarizes the dilemma that the shift from a penality of expulsion to one of incarceration had brought about:

> The very name of 'convicts' excites in the mind an idea of moral corruption which would make one shrink from such beings with a natural repulsion, which would lead one to wish only that like lepers of old they should dwell apart in caves and desert places, warning off the incautious passenger with the cry 'unclean, unclean.' We might desire to rid ourselves of them by sending them off to some remote region, where nature herself should guard them with her impregnable walls of ice, scantily yielding them bare subsistence from a barren, grudging soil – or to some spot where they should be cut off from the civilized world by the mighty ocean – and where their fiend like passions should be vested upon each other, not on peaceable and harmless members of society. (1864: 1)

Carpenter, then, is speaking to the same fears that her audience had of the convict that were expressed by Pip. His experience, though, took place at the beginning of the nineteenth century, when the then existing penal arrangements would normally have removed such creatures and the threat they posed in one way or another. However, for her, the problem was that 'many would fain thus separate themselves from convicts;

would gladly thus rid themselves of the awful responsibility which is in the words – "our convicts." *But they cannot*. These convicts are men, are women, reared to manhood and to womanhood among us' (1864: 2: my italics). In a world without transportation and where executions would only be used sparingly, Pip's aberrational encounter would become a much more regular possibility: the penal transformation that had taken place meant that the convict menace had become an endemic feature of nineteenth-century society. While the prison might temporarily remove Magwitch and his associates from it, ultimately it would only release them back into it – society would never be rid of them. As Plint (1851: 153) put the matter, '[the criminal classes] are in the community, but neither *of* it, nor *from* it ... the large majority was so by descent, and stands completely isolated from the other classes, in blood, in sympathies, in its domestic and social organization – as if hostile to them in the whole ways and means of temporal existence'. The social organization of the civilized world itself, with its new interdependencies, boundaries and values provided a more humanitarian economy of punishment while simultaneously engendering a sense of revulsion rather than romanticism towards those who were punished. The importance given to prison at this time meant that its inmates had become, in Carpenter's words, 'our convicts'.

This dawning, perturbing recognition was then confirmed by their physical appearance. Just as the sight of Magwitch had immediately set him off as a creature apart from the rest of society, so Carpenter (1864: 2) wrote: 'the first sight of the inmates of a Convict prison, to one unaccustomed to the criminal portion of our community, awakens emotions of mingled sorrow, pity and intense moral repugnance, never to be forgotten'. At this time, the commonsensical revulsion that their appearance provoked was in line with scientific thinking on the significance of physical propensities and human development. Such morbid ugliness was understood as a natural attribute of those who possessed it, in keeping with their low levels of intellectual capability. Cox referred to criminals as being 'persons of very low mental and bodily organization, with small heads and stupid aspect ... nine tenths of them really and truly were both mentally and physically diseased' (1870: 458). Similarly, Tallack: 'they are not very drunken as a class, but incorrigibly lazy. Work is the one thing they most abhor; they are often too indolent to wash themselves; they prefer to be filthy; their very skin in many instances almost ceases to perform its functions. Nearly all the discharge from some of their bodies is by the bowels; and if compulsorily washed such people become sick' (1889: 216).

Descriptions of their conduct befitted their depiction as savages – uncontrollable and untameable. The Reverend Kingsmill, Chaplain of Pentonville, observed that 'criminals are persons who more than others have shaken off all restraint, and indulged in licentious freedom, from their youth. They derive countenance and support in a profligate and lawless career, from confederacy with others of a like character, and with companions in criminality, they forget in confused excitement all fear and self-reproach' (1854: 33). Du Cane himself described them as having characteristics

> entirely those of the inferior races of mankind – wandering habits, utter laziness, absence of thought or provision, want of moral sense, cunning and dirt may be found in which their physical characteristics approach those of the lower animals so that they seem to be going back to the type of what Professor Darwin calls our 'arboreal ancestors.' (1875: 302–3)

Indeed, much of the criminological discourse of this period bears a strong imprint of Darwin's (1859) *On the Origin of Species by Means of Natural Selection* – with criminals seen as little more than unfeeling brutes, degenerate, anthropomorphic misfits, but now, of course, with the penal changes that had been put into effect during the first half of the nineteenth century, allowed to remain within the civilized world rather than expelled from it.

On this account, the penal language of the authorities, prison officials, and other significant members of elite groups allowed no sympathy for the convicts: they were simply brutish creatures to be feared and hated. It expressed the need to crush and control their animalistic natures: 'the will of the individual should be brought into such a condition as to wish to reform, and to exert itself to that end, in co-operation with the persons who are set over with him. The state of antagonism to society must be destroyed; the hostility to divine and human law must be subdued' (*Report of the Inspectors of Prisons of the Home District*, 1837: 16). Once it was assumed that the prisoners were insensitive to human feelings, then the only sentiment likely to have any effect on them would be repression. The authorities spoke, at this time, without any reservation, of using whatever legitimate means they could to crush whatever spirit the prisoners might bring with them on admission. In these respects, the very internal darkness of the prison could become one such tactic of control, as we see in the following comments on the design of its exercising yards (*Report of the Inspectors of Prisons of the Home District*, 1839: xiii):

> [They] radiate from a central point, round which there is a dark passage, having an inspection into each yard – the advantage of a dark passage is that it affords the opportunity of a close and unobserved inspection, which experience has proved to be a more effective check upon irregularity than any other mode. The darkness of the passage renders it impossible that the prisoner can be aware when the eye of the officer is upon him.

That they could speak in this way indicated their total lack of respect for the convicts as human beings. The convicts had been reduced to objects; if they had any sensitivities of their own, then these were only 'brutish instincts' – thereby further justifying such a callous intrusion on their privacy.

In the 1850s and 1860s especially, the authorities felt no reticence in boasting about their own unremitting severity towards them:

> restrictions in the use of corporal punishment which have been intro-duced seem to be injudicious; the infliction of four dozen lashes, and with these a severer cat than formerly used, ought to be allowed in place of two dozen lashes with a lighter cat, which is the maximum of corporal punishment now permitted ... the practice of giving each con-vict half a day's schooling a week, in the hours that would otherwise be devoted to labour, is objectionable. It is in effect giving the men a weekly half holiday, and thus diminishes the amount of labour which is necessarily, for other reasons, less than would be desirable. (*Report of the Commission Appointed to Inquire into the Operation of the Acts. Transportation and Penal Servitude*, 1863: 43)

Similarly, the *Report of the Commissioners on the Treatment of the Treason-Felony Convicts in the English Convict Prisons* (1867: 23) acknowledged unequivocally that penal servitude was 'a terrible punish-ment; it is intended to be so, and so it is'. The *Report of the Directors of Convict Prisons* affirmed that:

> No offender who has gone through a course of punishment in a convict prison now speaks of it with contempt, or as a chance which may be accepted without much regret ... they are kept to hard, never ending work, with no social enjoyments, and none of the luxuries which even the poorest enjoy from time to time, the condition of the convict is certainly one of punishment. (1872: vii)

There should be no expression of sympathy, no pity, no respect nor any affinity for the convicts – as if such brutes, with their animalistic cunning would immediately spot any such sentiment, and, seeing it only as a weakness in the penal armour that had been constructed to protect society from them, take advantage of it, burst through its defences and threaten destruction to all they then encountered. If at this time, prisons were spoken of, then it was as the terrible punishment the authorities now intended them to be.

Prisoners as Human Beings

Such a language of hatred, contempt and condemnation has not, of course, remained unique to this period in the nineteenth century. What we find taking place from this point, however, is a change in the language of the penal authorities, scientific experts and other elite groups. Increasingly, expressions of loathing and of contempt, of a proclaimed readiness to inflict suffering on prisoners to the very limits of what was tolerable in the civilized world, become more associated with the sentiments of the general public and sections of the press, and even some of the lower tiers of the penal establishment, such as prison officers and some governors;[4] but it would now be spoken less and less by most other establishment groups, especially by those who were regarded as experts in penal matters, or who were more involved in policy development rather than face-to-face contact with the convicts: a gulf opens up between the emotive language of popular discourse and the rationalistic, objective language of the penal establishment. Across the civilized world, the latter distance themselves from the merciless language of revulsion and denunciation and instead begin to speak in ways which recognize the prisoners' possibilities of self-improvement and reform:

> It may be true that some criminals are irreclaimable, just as some diseases are incurable, and in such cases it is not unreasonable to acquiesce in the theory that criminality is a disease, and the result of physical imperfection ... but criminal anthropology is in an embryo stage ... so much can be done by recognition of the plain fact that the great majority of prisoners are ordinary men and women, amenable, more or less, to all those influences which affect persons outside. (*Report of the Gladstone Committee*, 1895: 16)

The language of the experts thus begins to move away from anthropological determinism towards that of a more remedial humanitarianism. This shift in conceptualizing the prisoners is also reflective of changes in state formation at this time: it was increasingly seen as the duty of the early welfare state to make provision for the well-being of all its subjects, even those such as the prisoners who had demonstrated their own unworthiness. Now the state, through its officials, was beginning to express some notion of acceptance, of respect, some duty towards even those most unworthy citizens, some recognition that even these creatures were actually human beings. As such, and in a way that indicated a reduction in the social distance between the prisoners and the rest of the population (as far as the authorities were concerned), we find far fewer boasts of penal repression in official penal discourse (indeed, there would come a time when to do so would only be seen as indicative of the brutishness and savagery of those making such comments). By the late nineteenth century, the very word 'convict' was falling into disuse, to be replaced by what was then the less emotive, less disdainful term, 'prisoner', as the Gladstone Report suggests above. Furthermore, this group is increasingly spoken of as human beings with all their feelings and sensitivities, able to appreciate and respond to acts of kindness and forbearance, hurtfully recoiling before displays of repression and severity:

> We think that the privilege of talking might be given after a certain period as a reward for good conduct on certain days for a limited time

and under reasonable supervision ... the present practice of imposing silence except for the purposes of labour and during the visits of officials and authorized persons, for a period, it may be of fifteen to twenty years, seems to us unnatural ... with regard to education, we think that better results would be obtained by establishing a practice of teaching in classes, and by extending tuition to the prisoners. (*Report of the Gladstone Committee*, 1895: 25)

Penal language begins to reflect a changing attitude to order within the prison: darkness is no longer thought of as functional to maintaining control but, instead, it is recognized as a contributor to poor health and demoralization. Now, in the prison depths, darkness should give way to light:

> We have been giving much attention to the question of providing better light in the prisoners' cells, both natural and artificial and we propose gradually to discontinue the use of the opaque glass which has generally been used hitherto, by which the admission of light is greatly diminished, hindering the employment of prisoners by unduly taxing their eye-sight, especially in the short and gloomy days of the year. We propose gradually to introduce improved gas burners and when possible ... to take advantage of any public source of electric supply. (*Report of the Prison Commissioners*, 1902: 16)

Even in death, there is now a greater dignity and sensitivity being shown to the prisoners by the authorities. Thus, as regards the burial of those who died in prison, Thomson (1907: 205) reported that 'up to 1902 graves were not marked unless relations chose to put up a headstone, and in only one case was this done. Since 1902, however, small granite headstones have been erected by the Prison Commissioners, bearing the initials of convicts buried there and the date.' Once disowned by their relatives and buried with no earthly reminder of their existence, the authorities themselves were now prepared to mark their demise with some indication of respect. Thus, in contrast to Mr Justice Stephen's (1883) exhortation that criminals should be 'hated', which fitted within the language of punishment that was being spoken by the authorities in the mid to late nineteenth century, by the early twentieth we find the Reverend Quinton (1910: 12) noting that '[the prisoner] is nowadays a much milder, and more civilized person than his predecessor of thirty years ago, who too often was an ignorant, truculent and intractable monster, for whom a very stern code of discipline was required'. In view of these perceived changes in the prisoners, pity and empathy now seemed more appropriate sentiments than hatred.

The break that takes place in the formal language of punishment from utter loathing for the prisoners, on the one hand, to one of respect, on the other, is well demonstrated in Australian examples from this time. In New South Wales, while it was reported that 'the object of this treatment is to send [the prisoner] out of prison with the feeling that the place is to be dreaded' (*Report of the Comptroller-General of Prisons*, 1893: 4), a short time later, the language of punishment reflects a different set of sensibilities at work: 'punishment as simple revenge for an offence is of no use to anybody ... sentences should be of such a nature as to be deterrent and reformative rather than merely punitive ... every effort should be made to keep first offenders out of prison' (*Report of the Comptroller-General of Prisons*, 1896: 45). And in Victoria: the claim that 'prisoners as a rule show great ignorance of moral duty and a corruption of principle' (*Report of the Inspector-General of Penal Establishments and Gaols*, 1887: 10) is succeeded by the recognition that 'as criminals are human beings and not inanimate machines, their disposal is a matter of education, and as the treadmill and other brutalizing modes of punishment have given way to rational scientific methods, it has been my aim to brighten the necessarily sombre atmosphere of gaol with an infusion of kindliness' (*Report of the Inspector-General of Penal Establishments and Gaols*, 1910: 8). Instead of being seen as beyond society due to their biological deficiencies and degeneracies, it was gradually being recognized that there was a duty on the modern state to bring about their rehabilitation, as with its other sick or deficient citizens. In contrast to Du Cane's own language of 'laziness', of 'cunning' and 'dirt', his successor, Sir Evelyn Ruggles-Brise (1921: 87) pointed out that 'upon a certain age, every criminal may be regarded as potentially a good citizen ... it is the duty of the State at least to try to effect a cure'. To this end, it was recognized that the relationship between prisoners and the state extended beyond the prison walls: it would no longer leave them to their own devices, clutching only their 'tickets of leave',[5] whereby, after terrorizing local communities, they would then make their inevitable return to prison: 'the duty of aiding prisoners on discharge has been recognized from the beginning of the century as a public duty to be borne by public funds ... the Voluntary Aid Society being ancillary for this purpose, that is to assist in the disbursement of public money and incidentally at least in the first instance to increase it by private benefaction' (*Report of the Prison Commissioners*, 1918–19: 14). Now the wretchedness and helplessness of the prisoners, the legacy of a prison system which in the past had been deliberately designed to crush the human spirit, were spoken of with concern and dismay, rather than in the form of boastful proclamations: this new language spoke of addressing the sufferings of a fellow-citizen, rather than remorselessly crushing a vainglorious enemy. On the Dartmoor visit referred to earlier, Sir Alexander Paterson noted (Ruck, 1951: 26) how, 'as [the prisoners] saw us coming, each man ran to the nearest wall and put his face against it, remaining in this servile position, till we had passed behind him ... the men looked hard in body and in spirit, healthy enough in physique and colour, but cowed and listless in demeanour and response'. It was no longer the formal expectation that prisons would produce such disturbing sights.

Those members of the establishment who saw them – the only ones to whom such sights were available other than prison staff – could now only express sadness and pity. To offset such consequences, Ruggles-Brise (1921: 194) argued for more scientific, efficacious and humane treatment and of the need for 'criminal laboratories', as in 'the United States where science and humanity march hand in hand exploring prisons as places of punishment'. Now, the formal language of punishment disowned any suggestion of penal repression, and spoke of attempting to bring about productive change in the prisoners – prisons were no longer places to destroy their spirit, but instead were intended to turn them into better people. For example, in New Zealand: 'there is no such thing as hard labour – this is a dehumanizing and degrading practice – prisoners are placed at useful work to stimulate interest and self-respect' (*Report of the Controller-General of Prisons*, 1934: 3); and, 'there is no statutory provision for corporal punishment ... our experience is that the necessity for rigorous methods diminishes in inverse ratio to the development of humanitarian standards' (*Report of the Controller-General of Prisons*, 1938: 2). And in Canada: 'efforts to stimulate reform are now regarded as of vital moment in the present day treatment of offenders ... it is important to dispel dependency, abandonment and isolation' (*Report of the Inspector of Prisons and Reformatories*, 1938: 8). Indeed, the language of psychological expertise that, during the 1930s, began to feature with increasing prominence in penological discourse, stressed the 'normality' of prisoners. As the research findings of these experts illustrated, there seemed little difference between most of them and the rest of the population:

> There is no doubt that the tendency to break the law and acquiesce in certain forms of crime is widespread, and the occurrence of antisocial behaviour cannot be taken to imply 'abnormality,' unless the word is used in a very special sense. The 'normal' group will include at least eighty percent of offenders. (East and Hubert, 1939: 6)

What was spoken of in this language of punishment was not the prisoners' differences from the rest of society but, instead, of their similarities to it. As the former Chairman of the Prison Commission, Sir Alexander Maxwell (1942: vi) put it: 'that persons found guilty of criminal offences are, for the most part, ordinary folk, seldom showing abnormal characteristics, is one of the first things noted by everyone who is brought into contact with a considerable number of offenders'. Expert knowledge now confirmed these similarities. The new Head of the English Prison Commission, Sir Lionel Fox (1952: 111), argued that 'between a hundred prisoners and a hundred persons chosen at random from the street outside, the resemblances are more noticeable than the differences'. The more the formal language of punishment came to blur the division between the criminal and the rest of society in this way, the more it became possible to speak of the criminal as a subject to be restored to full citizenship rather than an enemy to be excluded.

Inadequacy and State Responsibility

During the post-war period, the formal language of punishment changes again. It is no longer even sufficient to speak of prisoners as normal, unremarkable human beings, undeserving of any severity in punishment, but responsible enough to be punished for their crimes all the same. Instead, it begins to show an awareness that such individuals are likely to have been damaged: not through anything that they should take responsibility for, but because of what other individuals, or more general social arrangements had done to them. Their criminality was not their fault: they deserved increasing state assistance to alleviate the difficulties and burdens that had been unfairly placed on them. In this post-war penal discourse, it was as if it was the prisoners who were frightened of the world beyond the prison, rather than that world being frightened of them. The previous imagery of wild beasts is replaced by concepts of inadequacy and depictions of unfulfilled lives: 'the man who commits [crime] is almost certainly one who cannot lead a fully satisfying life, adequately expressing his personality. He is a man in need of treatment: of psychiatric or medical attention or guidance into new fields of work and opportunity where he can be in harmony with conventions of behaviour we all accept' (Howard, 1960: 128). What we thus see happening in this new way of talking about prisoners is that all the old references to their character traits of degeneracy are removed; nor are they seen as relatively 'normal' subjects, as had been the emphasis in the interwar period; instead, the emphasis is on the inadequate, helpless creatures they had become:

> [They] were lonely men who had become inept in handling personal contacts and from their experiences had developed paranoid attitudes towards other people. In their view the world was a threatening and frightening place. They were unable to establish satisfactory contacts often because they were unable to tolerate the emotional demands which such contacts made on them, their reaction being to break away on the slightest pretext or without one. (Taylor, 1960: 35)

Now, from being portrayed as a creature that should be hated and despised at the beginning of this period, at its end, the criminal had been turned into an object of pity rather than fear. And if, at the start of this period, the dreadful Magwitch who had tried to cheat his fate, represented the degree of fear and terror that the unleashed convict personified, at the end of it it is possible to see a very different representation of the prisoner – as in the case of the 1962 movie, *Birdman of Alcatraz*. This was about the American murderer Robert Stroud who was to serve 54 years in prison for his crime, but who had become a world renowned figure through the publication of his scholarly treatises on bird life, and their health and care. One review of the film stated:

> I hope it will help [to secure his release] but it does not place enough blame, it seems to me, upon the old-fashioned and vengeful attitude by federal prison authorities who have kept this man behind bars when horrible child murderers, prisoners, rapists and vicious criminals, even traitors to the country, and many of them not rehabilitated like Stroud have been paroled. (Babyak, 1994: 261)

The penal language that was now capable of being spoken by liberal elite groups could appreciate the bathos of a life such as Stroud's, could express pity at its waste, and repugnance not at Stroud for what he had done but at those penal authorities who did not incorporate such sensibilities into their penal policy and release him.

Indeed, it was almost as if those who broke the law were only the innocent victims of a malfunctioning society: 'they have certainly injured their fellows, but perhaps society has unwittingly injured them' (Glover, 1956: 267). There was thus a duty on expansive welfare states to both correct their individual deficiencies and at the same time ameliorate the social conditions that might have contributed to them: such a commitment had by now become a test of the extent to which a given society could claim to be civilized (Jones, 1965). By now, references to punishment are minimized, as far as possible. Thus, in New Zealand: 'the causes of crime lie in the personality of the delinquent himself and in the conditions of society in which he lives ... *the aim of penal administration is not to punish* ... the primary objective is to effect the rehabilitation of punishment through a carefully devised individualized programme of treatment and training' (*Report of the Controller-General of Prisons*, 1947: 8, my italics). In England, it was claimed 'that we have come to recognize that people received into prison are not simply creatures to be kept locked up, but persons to be studied and handled in manageable groups according to their character and weaknesses' (*Report of the Prison Commissioners*, 1955: 17). Similarly, 'the deterrent effect of imprisonment must finally lie in the loss of personal liberty and all that this involves under any kind of regime, and that effect is not reinforced if the period of loss of liberty is used in a *mere repressive and punitive way*' (Home Office, 1959: 13: my italics). Instead, 'we have found that the study of art, music and drama has for those in prison a particular appeal, and that these arts may bring for the first time in to the lives of depressed and distorted men and women, perceptions of beauty, goodness and truth' (*Report of the Prison Commissioners*, 1951: 52). And rather than deliberately kept ignorant of it, deliberately starved of any contact with it as part of their punishment,

> It is important that prisoners should be able to keep in touch with what is going on in the world outside. A selection of daily newspapers at the rate of one to ten is provided in rooms where prisoners associate ... at all times, treatment of prisoners shall be such as to encourage their self-respect and sense of personal responsibility. (*Report of the Prison Commissioners*, 1956: 31)

Nor should the prison be a place of darkness anymore: 'the brightening of establishments by redecoration, in new colour shades has continued and the installation in all blocks of the modern type of sanitary recess has made progress' (*Report of the Prison Commissioners*, 1958: 109).

By the same token, penal language reflected the growing importance given to the place of psychological experts within the penal system to uncover and repair the inadequacies of the prison population: 'training is to be the aim of imprisonment ... there is a need for the separate establishment for the study and treatment of psychological abnormalities' (Home Office, 1945: 8). The subsequent *Report of the Prison Commissioners* (1946: 28) had a new section: 'Psychology, Investigation and Psychiatry: the Psychiatric Unit of Wormwood Scrubs has continued to work and expand ... there is a need for a second psychiatric unit at Wakefield.' Similarly in Canada:

> New appointments have been made for full time medical officers, psychologists and social workers ... modern institutional treatment stresses the prime importance of re-education and training if the individual is to be restored to society as a self-supporting, self-directing person. It cannot be too strongly emphasised that whatever element of punishment is involved is satisfied by depriving the individual for the period prescribed by the court of his freedom and liberty of action. (*Report of the Commissioner of Penitentiaries*, 1953: 8)

In England, the important *Penal Practice in a Changing Society* illustrated the extent to which the prison configuration had accommodated the new forms of expertise:

> A modern prison service requires an adequate and specialized service of doctors with psychiatric experience, psychologists and such other qualified persons as go to make a psychotherapeutic team. During the period since the war it has been possible to make much progress in these directions ... the value of psychiatry is not limited to the treatment of those abnormal states of mind which require the kind of psychotherapy that will be given in the new [psychiatric prison hospital]. A psychiatrically experienced doctor can do much to help disturbed prisoners not only adjust themselves to prison life but also to change their general attitudes so that they make a better adjustment in society after release. (Home Office, 1959:18)

A decade later, the authorities were able to report:

> The last few years have seen a substantial development in psychological services ... about fifteen to twenty percent of all offenders receive some form of psychiatric treatment during their sentence ... psychiatric work in prison is not confined to the treatment of those who are manifestly ill. There are many offenders who need some degree of psychological support and supervision at various stages in their sentence. (*Report on the Work of the Prison Department*, 1969: 34)

However, this new language of punishment was not just intended to be the exclusive property of a body of white-collar professionals. It was also expected that it would be spoken by the prison officers as well, who would then use their influence on the prisoners accordingly: 'in the control of prisons, officers shall seek to influence prisoners through their own example and leadership, and to enlist their willing co-operation: at all times the treatment of prisoners shall be such as to encourage their self-respect and sense of personal responsibility' (*Report of the Prison Commissioners*, 1956: 31). Now, as evidence of this psycho-therapeutic approach to prison administration, we find references to the establishment of group work in England (1956), and in New South Wales (1960), New York (1960), and Victoria (1961): 'group counselling [enables] closer relationships with inmates and allows guards to have an even greater impact in terms of changing inmate behaviour' (*Report of the Director of Penal Services* 1961–2).

All the syntax of repression and deprivation that had once existed had been stripped away from this sanitized language of punishment, as it spoke with increasing frequency of therapeutic institutions rather than prisons, medico-psychological penal professionals rather than guards:

> towards the end of the year it was possible to develop the observation and assessment side of the work of the remand centre ... any man who needs individual treatment is seen by a medical officer or psychologist. Each prisoner is then seen, some five days later, by an assessment board who have before them reports by staff of the observation wing, and information about the prisoner's family background and personality, on any treatment which it is suggested he requires, and any special problems that may have shown themselves. The board have available also the tests undertaken by the prisoners, a record of his medical history and a report by the deputy governor or principal officer. (*Report on the Work of the Prison Department*, 1967: 71)

The terrifying 'convicts' of the Victorian period had long since disappeared from penal discourse; even the term 'prisoner' could in its own turn be replaced, in some jurisdictions, by the still more neutral, less stigmatic 'trainee'. By the same token, it was reported in Canada that 'the title prison guard has been changed to security officer' (*Report of the Director of Corrections*, 1963: 3). Even the bureaucratic organizations responsible for the administration of punishment might now have to change their name to bring their identity more into line with contemporary sensibilities. In New South Wales, the 'Department of Prisons' disappeared and was subsumed under the more mellifluous sounding 'Department of Corrective Services': 'the change now conforms with the service's contemporary function of supervised liberty, detention and conditional liberty, and places emphasis on its theme of corrective, re-educational treatment programs for offenders rather than the historically adopted concept of a simple punitive detention' (*Report of the Director of Corrective Services*, 1969–70: 7).

It was again claimed that 'prisoners are not easily distinguished from non-prisoners' (*Report of the Director of Corrective Services*, 1969: 38). They certainly no longer had the distinguishing characteristics that had once made Abel Magwitch and his kind so terrifying, so different from the rest of the population. By now penal language – at least that to be found in official discourse – had been sanitized to such an extent that the huge gulf that was once thought to exist between prisoners and the rest of society had almost closed: what differences there now were, were thought to lie beneath the surface of the prisoner not in his physical appearance, which expert intervention could draw out and then provide appropriate forms of treatment and rehabilitation. On completion of this kind of therapeutic intervention, there would then be no distinction between prisoners and non-prisoners. The prison experience should no longer leave any distinguishing marks. The official penal language of the 1960s reflected the shift, over the course of a century, from emotive, moralistic denunciation to that of scientific, rationalistic objectivity. Just as prisons had disappeared, just as prisoners were not easily distinguished, it was thought, from non-prisoners, so in the formal language of punishment, punishment itself had been considerably diluted. It was now difficult to find traces of it in a language dominated by references to treatment and rehabilitation, therapeutic institutions and correctional services.

Notes

---

1 See, for example, Fielding (1743), Defoe (1722, 1726), Smollett (1757), Gay (1712, 1716, 1728), Johnson (1734).

2 See, for example, Ainsworth (1838), Rockwood (1834), Hornung (1899).

3 Carpenter (1864: 158) thus refers to Metropolitan Police Commissioner Sir Richard Mayne's concerns about escalating crime statistics which 'confirmed a large increase in crime in London, particularly violence, burglary and highway robbery'.

4 Former prison governor Rich (1932: 263) wrote: 'I do not believe the slightest good can ever be achieved with such specimens of humanity as compose the population of [Wandsworth] prison except by handling them on the lines of the strictest military discipline.'

5 'Tickets of leave' were introduced with the establishment of penal servitude in place of transportation in 1853; these referred to early release on licence, approved on a form 'signed by the Secretary of State ... which set out [the convict's] name, offence and sentence and informed him that he was on licence subject to it being revoked in the case of misconduct' (Radzinowicz and Hood, 1986: 248).

6

The Memories of Prisoners

The formal penal language that was being spoken in the 1960s, stripped of pejorative, emotive content, by and large, and replaced by that of scientific, objective rationality, had been sanitized: in line with the values of punishment in the civilized world, it reflected both the technocratic efficiency of the authorities and their humanitarian intent. By the same token, it was as if the concept of punishment itself had become too delicate, too unpleasant a matter to be spoken of – at least in the elite circles of penal reformers, experts, administrators, and the like. But this kind of language, claiming to represent what was taking place behind the prison walls, represented only one version of the reality of prison life. Running alongside it throughout the whole period from the mid-nineteenth century to the 1960s, a very different version of the reality of prison life was being provided. This took the form of a counter-discourse from the prisoners themselves. Here, in their memoirs and biographies, the reality of prison life that had been put forward by the authorities had been contested on almost every level.

At the same time, however, these prisoner accounts do more than simply provide a different version of 'the truth' about prisons, in the form of a history of contradiction to set against the claims being made by the authorities. They also help to show the way in which prison came to be so well suited to the values of the civilized world: they show the way in which it became possible to remove society's unwanted and then keep them, by and large, quiescent, thereby not allowing any distasteful ugliness associated with punishment to trespass upon its social contours. These biographies help to illustrate how prison achieved this task: not simply because of what the authorities were allowed to do to repress the prisoners, largely unchallenged behind the scenes, but, in addition, because of the prisoners' own subjectification to and acquiescence in this process of control. To take such an approach is not to deny the acts of individual and collective resistance that took place in the prisons over this period. Rebellions, violence, escapes did take place. But it is not these isolated events that interest me here so much as the more prevalent themes in prisoner literature of the everyday ingrained, mundane, deprivations of prison life: for most prisoners, this was their normality, and subjection to which became second nature to them.

What would seem to lend the prisoner memoirs particular authenticity (aside from the fact that they are intermittently confirmed in the memoirs of some former governors and guards) is not that they provide a blanket condemnation of everything to do with prison, and a reversal of everything the authorities claim; on the contrary, it is often the case that particular individuals, particular features of prison life, particular prisons may be singled out for praise and acknowledgement. In these respects, their subtleties, qualifications, and ambiguities strengthen the claims they make, while at the same time the general, critical thrust of what they say provides a counterweight to 'the truth' being told by the prison authorities. This is evident when we examine the prisoners' own responses to the essentials of prison life and the claims that had been made about these features by the authorities.

Prison Food

After the 1860s' changes to prison diet, the Irish political prisoner Jeremiah O'Donovan Rossa claimed that the eternal hunger he experienced while in Pentonville led him into a state of desperation:

> for years this feeling of hunger never left me, and I could have eaten rats and mice if they had come my way, but there wasn't a spare crumb in any of those cells to induce a rat or mouse to visit it. I used to creep on my hands and knees from corner to corner of my cell sometimes to see if I could find the smallest crumb that might have fallen when I was eating my previous meal. When I had salt in my cell I would eat that to help me to drink water to fill my stomach. (1882: 94)

Against the later claims of the authorities that in such prisons there was 'a lesser sickness than in the most luxuriously appointed and comfortable houses' (*Report of the Prison Commissioners*, 1887–8: 5), Rossa, in contrast, was able to describe the way in which the diet in that prison was as life-threatening as famine: 'I had lost eight pounds since I had come to London, but others had fared worse. Cornelius, Kane, Michael O'Regan and a few more [Irish prisoners] had lost as much as thirty pounds' (1882: 108).

Notwithstanding the authorities' contemporary claim that science proved the harmlessness of weight loss, in his prison recollection, One who has suffered (1882: 48) asserted that 'when, by and by, he can eat the unpalatable mess provided, he acquires chronic indigestion, dimness of eyesight, *tinnitus aurum*, roarings in the head, gastric spasms, shortness of breath, sickly giddiness and absence of staying power generally'. That is to say, *under the normal conditions of imprisonment*, as they were, the diet could lead to symptoms of chronic debilitation. But in Rossa's case, the fact that he was for all intents and purposes a political prisoner, meant that there were still more privations which the authorities could inflict by manipulating the formal prescriptions governing the provision of food. Regular doses of the punishment diet (bread and water), for example: 'twenty-eight consecutive punishment days was the worst I yet had, and time hung heavily with nothing to read and very little to eat' (1882: 138). Rossa, given his status, had been effectively placed outside all the other prisoner-outsiders; and being beyond those established/outsider parameters of governance within the prisons, which at least set formal rules and standards, it was as if he was lost in some secret recess of it, that was cut off from any such safeguards. In recognition that he had now been cast apart even from other prisoners, he underwent a differential process of subjection – being forced to eat his food in the manner of an animal, for example:

> The doors were locked and I was left in darkness with my pint of stirabout. With my hands in cuffs I put the dish to my mouth, but it was thick, not running, stirabout, and it wouldn't come near my hungry lips ... no way evidently to get it down but to lay the dish on the floor and support myself on my knees and elbows. You may call this eating on all fours if you like, but it was the way I had to take my dinner that day. (1882: 181)

In the more mainstream experiences of prison life, there might still be differences in quality of the diet, if fewer differences in quantity, given the standardization that had been enforced in English prisons in the late nineteenth century. Thus, One who has endured it (1877: 36) found that the diet at Newgate was the worst of the four prisons he experienced; in contrast, the food at Millbank 'is plain but good and well cooked, and considering the little exercise the men have, not insufficient, although the serving tins are dirty'. For Michael Davitt, another Irish prisoner,

> The food in Dartmoor I found to be the very worst in quality and the filthiest in cooking of any of the other places I had been in. The quality of daily rations was the same as in Millbank, and with the difference of four ounces of bread more each day and one of meat less in the week ... from about November till May [the food] is simply execrable, the potatoes being often unfit to eat, and rotten cow carrots occasionally substituted for other food. To find black beetles in soup, 'skilly', bread, and tea was quite a common occurrence; and some idea can be formed of how hunger will reconcile a man to look without disgust upon the most filthy objects in nature, when I state ... that I have often

discovered beetles in my food, and have eaten it after throwing them aside. (1886: 17)

Again, on this basis, the regular prison diet (and not the 'special treatment' given out to Rossa) was in itself sufficient to jeopardize the prisoners' hold on their health. Davitt goes on to write of men being reported and punished for eating 'candles, boot oil and other repulsive articles ... I have seen men eat old poultices' (1886: 18).

After the reforms introduced by the 1878 Committee which included the provision of a 'nutritious stirabout', Bidwell (1895: 184) still writes of being in a perpetual state of hunger, as a result of which 'no vile refuse we would not devour if the chance presented itself'. Balfour (1901: 189) described lunch at Parkhurst: 'an eight ounce loaf of coarse brown bread, one pound of very inferior potatoes, a ration of two ounces of boiled bacon and of twelve ounces (or it might have been sixteen ounces of haricot beans)'. In addition to the permanent hunger he experienced, he also complained of the timing of the meals (something which the authorities never seem to speak of at all) – breakfast 5.45 a.m., lunch 11.30 a.m., supper 4.30 p.m. – to suit prison officer shifts: hunger would now have to conform to time as it was organized by the prison bureaucracy, rather than by nature. Jock of Dartmoor, nonetheless, comments more favourably on prison diet at the end of the nineteenth century. In contrast to Davitt's experience of Dartmoor, this convict found that '[here] food is mainly good, wholesome and plentiful' (1933: 25). He goes on to add, though, that 'very few convicts will admit this, however, because of its monotony' (1933: 37). As Nevill commented on the standardization and routine of dietary arrangements, as with all other aspects of prison life at this time, 'only those can appreciate it fully who have known nothing but sameness, tastelessness and too often repulsiveness in everything they have had to eat for years' (1903: 52).

Writing of the same period, Lee (1885, 1985: 61) felt that the consequences of the 1878 dietary changes were that 'before the reforms, less food was provided to keep you in a practically starving condition'. What happened after the reforms was that, while the quantity of food improved, its quality still made it, on occasions, inedible, no matter how hungry the prisoners were. He thus complained of being fed 'disgusting pieces of fat pork, bad potatoes and poor bread'. In his last sixteen months prior to release his diet had consisted of 'dry bread and a pint of tea for breakfast and supper and for the midday meal a combination of bread, potatoes, beans and bacon' (1885, 1985: 62). Thus, notwithstanding some adjustment to the quantity of food being served around the end of the nineteenth century, and notwithstanding some variations at least in the quality that had by then been introduced, the coupling of diet and discipline inevitably led to a state of chronic hunger within the prisons and various forms of debilitation as a result of this. So long as the diet was arranged around that particular axis, the kind of adjustments that were being made by the authorities were inconsequential over time (even if they were able to reduce the immediacy of hunger pangs, so that after the 1878 changes, there are no more reports of starving prisoners being driven to eat candles and poultices in these prisoner sources).

As we know, further adjustments to the diet were made in the early twentieth century. It was linked again to maintaining health rather than enforcing disciplinary control. The authorities now had to ensure that they not only maintained the prisoners while in their charge, but, in addition, on their release, they should be fit enough to earn a living beyond the prison. The variations and improvements that were introduced in the first few decades of the twentieth century were intended to address these responsibilities. Now the menu in an English prison could advertize 'treacle pudding' 'beef-steak pudding', 'savoury bacon', 'sea pie', 'beef stew', 'pork soup', and so on. Nonetheless, Wood still complained that 'one of the greatest privations men endured under the system then in force was hunger, owing to the insufficiency of the diet supplied. One was eternally hungry' (1932: 64). Similarly, McCartney (1936: 122) reported 'being in a state of semi-starvation'. As to the above additions to the menu, he complained:

> the vile concoction masquerading under these honest names might make a hungry pig vomit with disgust. 'Sea pie' is a mess in a filthy tin, defying analysis. The top is a livid scum, patterned with a pallid tracery of rolling grey grease, and just below this fearsome surface rests a lump of grey matter like an incised tumour, the dirty dices of pale-pink, half-cooked carrots, heightening the diseased anatomical resemblance. (1936: 123)

Furthermore, notwithstanding the increasing attention that was being given to the ambience of the serving arrangements at this time, which included the abandonment of serving food in cans (*Report of the Prison Commissioners*, 1926), Sparks (1961: 83) confirms their continuity at Dartmoor into the 1930s, where the 'food was fed to you out of cans like old paint tins'.

These memoirs of a different kind of reality to prison life from that claimed in the official discourse of the authorities are given added legitimacy by the way in which they are confirmed by two former prison officers. Warden agreed that 'meat is always badly cooked. Potatoes stand in water for a couple of hours before they are served, and reach the convicts half cold and sodden. Vegetables are impregnated with grit and dirt. The tea is stewed and utterly spoilt, and the cocoa has a layer of fat always on the top' (1929: 219). Similarly, Cronin reflecting on his work in the inter-war period:

> The normal diet was far from exciting. Breakfast was a pint of tea and milk – except for the hard labour man during his first twenty-eight days – with a half pint of porridge (without milk or sugar!) and an ounce of margarine. Typical dinners to which the men adjourned from the workshops were: corned beef, potatoes and bread; every item was carefully weighed to conform with the regulations on quantity. (1967: 21)

In other words, whatever improvements had been made to the diet itself, in the early twentieth century, it could still be rendered unpalatable by the absence of modern serving and cooking facilities and the bureaucratic administration of the prison, which dictated precisely when and how meals should be served and so on, providing a timetable which bore no relation to the world beyond it.

It need not always be like this, of course. Christmas day festivities and Christmas lunch had by now become fabled hallmarks of the prison authorities' humanity.[1] Leigh seems to have experienced one of the happier Christmases among this group of writers:

> In the library was a pile of large paper bags, one for each man to receive his Christmas letters and cards. Some of the bags were filled to overflowing; some remained empty. But a friendless man must not be shamed at Christmas before his fellows: he, too, received his bag, and in it something from the chaplain ... dinner consisted of a double ration of meat and potatoes and a hero's portion of Christmas pudding. (1941: 198)

Similarly, Behan 1959:

> I got out the dinner on the plate. It lay hot and lovely, the roast potatoes, the Yorkshire pudding, the chopped greens and the meat, and a big piece of bread to pack with, and it wasn't long before I had it finished, and the plate clean for the [plum] duff and custard. And then the door opened again, and the screw gave me the *News of the World*. (1959: 110)

Others, though, were less fortunate. For Phelan (1940: 8), there were no festivities, and in his London prison, Christmas lunch was reduced to a 'tin can of watery soup and three potatoes'.

The attempts to normalize the prison diet in the post-war period (the standard was now to be food 'of a wholesome quality, well prepared and well served and reasonably varied' (Rule 98, 1948) were confirmed by ex-prison governor Clayton:

> their meals have been improved, not just the dietary but in the matter of variety. The traditional monotony of the breakfast (bread, margarine and porridge) and supper meals has been broken by the introduction of cooked dishes, jam, cake, cheese etc. Prisoners can also augment the meals by buying sauces, treacle, sugar and margarine at the canteen. The old dinner tin has gone, too. In its place is a plastic compartmentalised dish on the lines of those used in American cafeterias. (1958: 36)

But Runyon (1954: 72), writing of the same era, complained of 'terrible food and the monotony of the diet: for dinner and supper a convict orchestra did its best to make the tasteless food more palatable – and at the same time it served to drown the complaints of those who had to eat it'. Wildeblood (1955: 118) observed that 'the midday meal consisted of soup, two slices of gristly meat, a wedge of washed out cabbage and three potatoes'. Croft-Cooke refers as follows to the claim in the *Report of the Prison*

Commissioners (1952: 60) that 'the quality of the food and the way in which it is prepared have been maintained at a consistently high standard':

> I can only wonder at the cold cynicism of such statements ... most of the prisoners became chronically constipated due to the nature of the food [which consisted of] pieces of stale fish in a greasy batter, potatoes which even if they had been properly cleaned ... would still have tasted mouldy ... heavy tasteless deep coloured liquid intended as soup, an occasional stew which varied only from the soup in that minute fragments of twice cooked or tinned meat were sometimes found in it. (1955: 118)

Norman's (1958: 26) regular menu consisted of 'soup, mincemeat, potatoes and cabbage'. However, the reality was that, 'I have never seen such cabbage as you get in the nick.' And a variation of the diet – suet pudding – was 'like trying to eat a piece of rubber'. He, too, suffered a disappointment over Christmas lunch where the main course was meant to be pork: as he saw it, there was 'a lump of congealed fat on a plate together with cold roast spuds and some greens' (1958: 86). Baker, while claiming that Christmas lunch in prison was the best food he had ever tasted, still felt that, in general:

> Meals were so unpalatable that it was impossible to eat them. Although food improved very greatly between 1954 and 1959, even by then quantities were only just adequate and the general standard of cooking was not even reasonably satisfactory. In 1954 it was quite execrable; apart from the inevitable cabbage, there was no fruit or fresh vegetables at any time of the year, the quantities were insufficient and the cooking so appalling and much of the food so dirty that only wild animals could digest it. (1961: 35)

As for the cafeteria-style changes, Dendrickson and Thomas reported on the eating arrangements at Dartmoor:

> [There are] latrines ... situated a few yards from where the prisoners eat their meals and pass time in the evenings. The stench that wafts from it and into the hall is enough to put the hungriest prisoner off his dinner ... the tin in which one's dinner is served usually has portions of someone else's breakfast adhering to it. (1954: 124)

Similarly, Crookston (1967: 114), while confirming the new availability of salad, still complained that 'meals were served in an extremely depressing room, where there was a slop-basin full of greasy crusts and old bacon rinds, with terrible chipped enamel plates'. On the basis of these accounts, it would seem that, by the 1960s, the dietary arrangements as they were then, were producing a different kind of deprivation and deterioration from that experienced by late nineteenth-century prisoners. Prison food need no longer be life-threatening in its frugality and poor quality, but it could still lead to a sense of chronic debilitation caused by its unrelenting monotony, poor quality and lack of cleanliness and care in preparation and serving, whatever assurances to the opposite the authorities were then providing.

Clothing

The prison reformer and secretary of the Howard Association, William Tallack, noted the presence of the convicts at hard labour outside Chatham convict prison in the 1860s:

> I was struck with the care which had been taken to keep the prisoners in a comfortable condition. I observed that those men not merely had sufficient clothing but had warm jerseys and good thick boots. I was also informed they were allowed additional pairs of stockings for change, they had gaiters, and even mittens to keep their hands warm ... what contrast to the condition of the labouring poor. (*Report of the Committee Appointed to Enquire into the Workings of the Penal Servitude Acts*, 1879: 208)

Such comments inevitably contributed to the popular wisdom that prison conditions had become luxurious, certainly in excess of the living conditions of many much more worthy members of the general public. The prisoners themselves, however, had different opinions. Rossa complained that warm clothing was not permitted during winter: 'the prison doctor had decided we were to have no flannels after reception. It was mid-winter ... and snow was covering the ground. To give any idea by words of the cold I felt is something I cannot do' (1882: 114). Rossa's working garb was completed with the issue of regulation prison boots,

> fully fourteen pounds in weight. I put them on and the weight of them seemed to fasten me to the ground. It was not that alone, but the sight of the impression they left on the ground as you looked at the footprints of those who walked before you, that struck terror to your heart. There was the felon's brand of the broad arrow impressed on the soil by every footstep ... the nails in the soles of your boots and shoes were hammered in an arrow shape, so that whatever ground you trod left traces that 'government property' had travelled on it.

However, it was not just the inadequacy of the clothing to provide protection from the elements that was of concern to the prisoners; in addition, it was the knowledge of how, by wearing prison uniform, their own appearance could be made degrading and humiliating. One who has endured it (1877: 41) wrote that after putting on his prison clothes, 'I heartily thanked God there was no looking glass near.' In his own mind he no doubt saw himself as he saw other prisoners:

> fantastically and picturesquely costumed. I could not avoid recalling certain chorus singers I had seen at the opera. Each man was dressed in

a short loose-jacket and vest, and baggy knickerbockers of drab tweed with black stripes one and a half inches broad. The lower part of their legs were encased in blue worsted stocking with bright red rings round them; low shoes and a bright grey and worsted cap, which each man wore in accordance to his own taste, completed the costume. One thing spoiled it. All over the whole clothing were hideous black impressions of the broad arrow [↑], the 'crow's foot', denoting the clothes belonged to Her Majesty. (1877: 68–9)

Similarly, Balfour's observations on prison dress:

There appeared a person dressed in the most extravagant garb I had ever seen outside a pantomime. It was my first close view of a convict ... the clothes were of a peculiar kind of brown (which I have never seen outside of a prison), profusely embellished with broad arrows. His hair was cropped so short that he was almost as closely shawn as a Chinaman. A short jacket, ill-fitting knickerbockers, black stockings striped with red leather shoes. (1901: 36)

Jock of Dartmoor (1933: 25) then reported changes in the early twentieth century: 'Dartmoor prison garb was handed to us – khaki tunic, knee-breeches, stockings, cloth leggings and regulation boots. The uniform bore no markings, the hideous "broad arrow" is a thing of the past.' Wood (1932: 290) confirmed that the convict uniform now consisted of 'two sets of underwear, jacket, waistcoat, knee breeches, a cap bearing one's registered letter and number in the convict hierarchy, one pair of boots, one pair of shoes and stockings'. However, if a uniform of this nature no longer had the look of a pantomime or circus outfit, it was still likely to be made up of clothing that could only degrade through the squalor of its poor quality and poor fit. Even amongst some members of the prison establishment there was recognition of this. The former prison chaplain Rickards, now showing considerably more sensitivity to the self-respect of prisoners than Tallack had earlier done, recognized that:

[there is] nothing more disfiguring and disgusting than the dress and tenure of the man in prison is it possible to imagine, and some of them feel it acutely, especially when a friend or relative is allowed to visit them, and they see how shocked their visitor is when faced with the grotesque Guy Fawkes opposite and realises that it is the man he has known outside in decent garments. (1920: 130)

Such humiliations and embarrassments could also be compounded by the way in which the prisoners' clothing signalled a total lack of care and lack of personal respect in their appearance. Holt's first sight of his fellow prisoners, after reception at Liverpool, was as follows: 'there were tall men, short men, fat men, thin men, young men, old men, fair men, dark men, clean shaven men, and men with beards, but all dressed clumsily in coarse grey clothes and most of them showing holes in the heels of their socks at each step' (1934: 34). By wearing such uniforms, the prisoners had been turned from their nineteenth century appearance as jesters or court fools into some utterly grey, beaten and crushed army of men. Certainly, these feelings seem to have been exacerbated, not removed by the changes to prison uniforms that were put into effect in the post-war period. When growing attention was being given to personal care and presentation in the world beyond the prison, the lack of it within stood out all the more. Heckinstall-Smith (1954: 63) refers to 'unhygienic and badly fitting clothes'; Wildeblood (1955: 138) felt that the prison clothes were 'designed to rob [one] of the last vestiges of self respect'. Baker (1961: 8-9) was issued with 'trousers about two sizes too small and a coat similarly too large'.

There were differences in the experiences of individual prisoners, of course. Croft-Cooke (1955: 48) describes being issued 'with a reasonably well fitting shirt with faint stripes, a blue tie, grey socks and comfortable fitting black shoes'. His concern, however, was with the cleanliness of the clothing:

> it was on bath-day ... that we received an issue of clean clothes with which to pass another week, clearly an inadequate allowance. A shirt had to serve one week as a shirt and another as pyjamas while socks should certainly have been changed more often. How is a man to feel that self respect to which he is adjured? (1955: 103)

Again, former prison governor Clayton concurs with the prisoners' sentiments, noting:

> the present uniform is supposed to resemble an ordinary lounge suit. But, as it has to be washed every time its wearer is released, it falls far short of the ideal. The remainder of the outfit consists of a striped shirt and collar, a black and unmanageable tie, vest and drawers, woollen socks, and a handkerchief startlingly like a housewife's duster. What induced the Prison Commissioners to substitute it for the neat khaki uniform which was worn when I first joined the service will never be known ... nothing could be more degrading than the present quite shapeless clothing. (1958: 40)

Whatever humanitarian intent there had been to ameliorate the conditions of prison life by changes in uniform over this period, wearing it could still be a matter of extreme debasement and shame for the prisoner.

These prisoners' accounts do not of necessity nullify the ameliorative claims being made by the authorities; what they do show, though, is how the slow-moving, inert, cold bureaucracy of prison itself could nullify any such intentions and by so doing make tolerable standards of squalor that now had no legitimate place in the world that lay beyond the prison. Even so, for some prisoners, there was still a further stage of degradation that the wearing of prison clothing might subject them to. Houghton reported that after reception into prison:

> the humiliation process was put into force. The prison uniform of grey trousers and jacket ... was taken away from me. On the floor lay a number of uniforms which would have brought a laugh if worn in the ring

by a circus clown. I had the degrading experience of having to pick out from the floor a previously used and not cleaned harlequin uniform which would more or less fit – less rather than more. This consisted of grey trousers with a broad, yellow stripe running from waist to ankle on each leg back and front, and a jacket with a large yellow patch on the front. The prime object is to humiliate: nothing can make a human being look and feel more idiotic than to be forced to dress in such outrageous garb. (1972: 142)

Houghton, in fact, was a convicted spy and maximum-security prisoner. He thus had a status which placed him (as with Rossa in the nineteenth century) beyond that given to most ordinary prisoners, and in respect of which the formal rules and standards of the civilized prison did not seem to apply. As the obvious symbolism of the patch on his breast jacket signified, he too was an outsider even among outsiders and was therefore denied whatever sensitivities might be shown to them, whatever standards of decency and codes of protection that regulated mainstream prison life.

Personal Hygiene

The prison authorities had always assured the public of the hygienic quality of their institutional arrangements. Indeed, official visitors had been quick to write of the startling cleanliness and hygiene of the prisons – Mayhew and Binny on Pentonville, for example:

> The first thing that strikes the mind on entering the prison passage is the wondrous and perfectly Dutch-like cleanliness pervading the place. The floor, which is of asphalt, has been polished by continual sweeping, so bright that we can hardly believe it has not been black-leaded, and so utterly free from dust are all the mouldings of the trim stucco walls, that we would defy the sharpest housewife to get as much off upon her fingers as she could brush even from a butterfly's wing … the cells distributed throughout this magnificent building are about the size of a large and roomy omnibus, but some feel higher … and they seem really comfortable apartments. (1862: 119)

For much of the nineteenth century, the outward, ostensible cleanliness of the prison continued. Balfour (1901: 38–9) wrote that 'the cells at Wormwood Scrubs are clean, large and well lit, and the temperature is always maintained at a proper heat for the human body. The floors actually shine with cleanliness.' However, the hygienic arrangements for the prisoners themselves were reported as being of a different order. Lovett (1876: 226) describes his reception to Pentonville in the 1840s, for example: after being examined, his hair cropped, his clothes stamped with a highly visible marker in indelible ink, and of being exhibited to public visitors, he was then compelled to strip again, along with 'not less than eight prisoners ... some of whom were in a filthy state ... and to bathe in the same cistern of water as the men did, and dry themselves as well as they could on the same towel'. Half a century later, there seems to have been little improvement. Brocklehurst claimed that:

> for a whole month I had to wash in a pannikin little larger than a glorified soup dish, and the only other opportunity or means of cleanliness which was afforded me was when, in conjunction with the other men in my block, I was taken to have the fortnightly bath which had two inches of water, a piece of soap as big as a domino and neither sponge nor brush. (1898: 60)

Similarly, Convict 77 experienced no increased sensitivity on the part of the authorities in relation to these matters: 'the sanitary arrangements at Wormwood Scrubs, like those at most prisons, leave much to be desired. A line of horse troughs, divided by a very light partition (not at all calculated to insure strict privacy to those occupying the divisions) constitutes the closets' (1903: 213).

Other aspects of personal cleanliness were treated with little regard for the dignity of the prisoners. One who has endured it (1877: 137) was told that 'if you are particular about your teeth my man, use the corner of your trowel'. On other occasions, however, the rigorous enforcement of some standards of cleanliness and hygiene might only add to the prisoners' immiseration. Thus Balfour's experience of his prison haircut on reception:

> my barber advanced, appliances in hand ... the shaving was performed with a curious instrument which I had never seen before. I expected to be shaved, for I knew that beards were not permitted in convict prisons ... for the hair cropping I was not prepared, nor did I know to what extent it had taken place till I put my hand to my head when the process was half finished, and felt that my head was already almost as smooth as a billiard ball. What kind of spectacle I presented I know not. There was, happily, no looking glass in the prison. (1901: 36)

Half a century later, the subsequent relaxation of the prison rules meant that Croft-Cooke (1955: 195) was able to write that 'the shaven headed convict is so much a figure of the past that a man must obtain the governor's permission to have his hair clipped short'. However, he goes on to write that 'as the government pamphlet somewhat euphemistically states, "a man's hair is trimmed regularly, but not in any regulation style"'. The relaxation of the rules at one point might only open up a channel for new debasements at another. Unlike the provision of food, where there was undoubtedly some significant quantitative and qualitative improvement over time (even if it could still remain unpalatable, the diet in post-war prisons at least was no longer life-threatening), there seems no doubt at all that into the twentieth century, standards of cleanliness and hygiene actually deteriorated. As the nineteenth-century prisons aged, it was impossible to maintain their initial standards, particularly as both government investment and public interest declined:

it was as if the more remote the prison became, the more it could deviate from the standards of the world outside it, whatever the authorities might claim to the contrary. Wood (1932: 370) describes the sanitation at Dartmoor as 'appalling ... toilets were no more than sheds in the exercise yard, emptied by a cart outside the prison'.

Even so, it is clear that standards of hygiene were better in some prisons than others. Thus McCartney on the arrangements at Parkhurst:

> a stool, a jug, a chamber pot, and a washbasin complete the cell. When one is in special stage – that is, when one has served four years – one can have a chair and a wash stand. The wash-basin is tiny, but the new enamel basins now coming into use are better ... The cells in Parkhurst are the most comfortable in English prisons. (1936: 56)

Notwithstanding any such improvements in material provisions, however, the stench produced from decades of use had embedded itself into the fabric of the prison:

> My cell, like every cell on [Dartm]oor, stank of staleness and sweat and people of long ago. A place nine feet by seven, inhabited by generations of men compelled by circumstance to have dirty habits, must stink, however much the smell be layered with tar and whitewash. Hanging on the wall was a quote from the code. It said ... that one should not excrete in cell vessels. In fact, the paper used the second person of address and almost appealed to people to go to the lavatory at night ... the moment one came into a hall, a whiff of sweat, lavatory, hair, tar, jackdaw, mice and dampness struck at one like a dirty sack being forced over the head ... I never managed to draw a full breath the whole time I was on the Moor at night. (Phelan, 1940: 138–9)

Perhaps the most significant attempt to actually improve cellular hygiene – the removal of water closets from cells (their design meant that they gave off foul-smelling odours) and their replacement with corridor latrines (*Report of the Prison Commissioners*, 1890) – was to have the most profoundly humiliating consequences for the prisoners. It meant that 'slopping out' every morning became an institutionalized feature of English prison life:

> I staggered out of my peter [cell] still dopey from sleep, with my piss pot in my hand and walked to the other side of the landing. There was about 50 men there already with their pots queuing up to empty them. The stink was enough to turn my guts over. Eventually it was my turn, the sink into which the slops were emptied was blocked and there were lumps of shit and pieces of paper floating in it. I reached and closed my eyes, so that I wouldn't see this charming sight. I blindly threw the contents of my pot into the sink on top of the rest, and rushed away without looking, back to my peter. I did that same thing every morning and afternoon for two years. (Norman, 1958: 10)

Without dramatic reconstruction of the prison system, which the authorities at that stage where in no position to undertake given the unpopularity of prison building and public expenditure austerities, hygienic conditions could only worsen:

> C wing [in Brixton] housed more prisoners, since they were crammed three to a cell. This leads to the most filthy pollution. Imagine an airless cell scarcely large enough for one man filled with the bunks, the bodies, the clothes and the chamber pots of three. If it were an ordinary bedroom or a ship's cabin it would be monstrously unhygienic, but when it is an almost windowless cell in which the men are locked without respite from half past five in the afternoon to seven o'clock next morning it becomes foul and pestilential beyond all words. (Croft-Cooke, 1955: 204)

Furthermore, the building programme which began in 1960 in England was premised on the belief that:

> as the cells in the new prisons will be used only as sleeping accommodation, it is no longer necessary that they should be arranged in long wings ... this arrangement, which is the standard plan of the Victorian prison, creates a very gloomy impression and makes it difficult to provide efficient heating, lighting and ventilation. Noise and smells penetrate to every quarter of the prison ... what is required is effective supervision of the movement of prisoners to and from their cells and during periods when they are engaged in various activities within the prison. (Paterson, 1961: 310)

Another example, then, where an attempt to ameliorate conditions within the prison could lead to further inhumanity and demoralization as overcrowding became extended and activities restricted: built for one prisoner, on the assumption that they would be empty for most of the day, these new prison cells might in time be used to house three, for up to twenty-three hours a day. Far from representing the equivalent of a sanatorium, as had been some of the claims made about prisons by the authorities in the nineteenth century, there was now a tangible stench of decrepitation about them, the combined effects of its various arrangements for personal hygiene over the course of a century or so: by now, as Crookston (1967: 111) made the point, there was another form of deprivation associated with prison: 'fresh air ... that is what you crave most. The rancid smell of the place seems to permeate your skin.'

The Internalization of Subjection

What we have considered so far is a series of examples of the way in which the prisoners' accounts compete with those of the prison authorities in precisely those aspects of prison life which came to be regarded as a test of the civilized standards to be expected of prisons in England and similar societies. But these prisoner accounts provide us with something more than just a different version of the truth. They also provide us with a history of how the prisoners came to internalize their own subjection to prison rule: the assumption of the role of cowed, subservient prisoner became 'second nature' to them – it became their habitus. Their marked physical deterioration as a result of the conditions they experienced inevitably played a role in this. Bidwell, writing of a time when these effects of prison life were at their most acute, saw the initial bravado on reception that some prisoners displayed give way to a remorseless decline:

> the first part of their body to be visibly affected by the effects on them of hunger and torment of the mind is the neck. The flesh shrinks, disappears, and leaves what look like two artificial props to support the head. As time goes on the erect posture grows bent; instead of standing up straight the knees bulge outward as though unable to support the body's weight, and the convict drags himself along in a kind of despondent shuffle. Another year or two and his shoulders are bent forward. He carries his arms habitually before him now; he has grown moody, seldom speaks to anyone, or answers if spoken to … everyone understands that the end is coming. The projecting head, the sunken eye, the fixed expressionless features are the outward exponents of the hopeless sullen brooding within. And so he keeps on in that way, wasting more and more, body and soul, every day, until he drops, and is carried off to the infirmary to die. (1895: 187)

This is an extreme example, but an example of what could then happen, given the conditions of prison as they existed. No doubt as well that the prisoners' own awareness of their physical deterioration added to their sense of shameful subjection, as we see in the comments of Rossa (1882: 120) to his warders: 'you should have seen what a handsome man I was when I was in the world'. His own knowledge of what he has now become, his understanding of prison as some kind of different universe altogether that does not simply deprive one of freedom, but takes one out of life itself, seems all too obvious to him. Indeed, on a subsequent visit by relatives he claimed that 'they hardly knew him' – his physical appearance had deteriorated so much (1882: 122). Similarly, Balfour (1901: 36) on putting on prison clothes: 'what kind of spectacle I presented I know not. There was, happily, no looking glass in the prison … I never saw myself in a looking glass for nine years.' It was as if he did not want to see his own reflection – he knew well enough what he must look like. It is also important to recognize that this physical deterioration did not necessarily end with the ameliorative reforms which begin in the early twentieth century. Phelan wrote:

> nearly everyone was heavy and sluggish in the morning. Bad air and little sleep with worry-hours not counted in the code, turned the men

out swollen eyed and frowning. The healthy sun-bronze of the [Dartm]oor prisoners is often mentioned in apologetics. It is mostly dirt ... For me ... the strain was considerable. From the beginning I had refused to let myself go, had driven myself hard, physically and mentally, so that I should not slide off into the quietude of fantasy life which helped the seven year men to sleep. (1940: 143)

Dendrickson and Thomas (1954: 180) describe physical deterioration in the post-war period: 'food was designed to keep weight up to a certain standard without giving any energy ... muscles turn to flab, short-windedness, flacid bodies of even those who are working on the quarry and farm parties. Ailments of under-nutrition are rife'. Croft-Cooke (1955; 155) felt the effects of a few weeks of prison diet and lack of sufficient air and exercise when he had to move cell: 'by the time I had hurried up the three flights of iron stairs to my cell ... packed my few personal belongings and those items of prison gear which move with a prisoner, and brought them down to the ground floor, I found myself shaking with exhaustion'.

A sense of utter subjection and helplessness could be induced by the prison's own security procedures. Balfour, quoting with irony the rules of the time that 'the searching of a prisoner shall be conducted with due regard to decency and self respect', describes 'dry bath searching' and the automotive behaviour of the prisoners when commanded to perform even such a degrading spectacle as this turned out to be:

> as the party of men to be searched was being marched back from labour to its parade ground for dismissal to the baths, it would be met by a principal warder, who would utter the single word 'baths' ... the direction of the party would at once be changed, and instead of proceeding to the parade ground, the party would march to one of the exceedingly well-appointed ranges of bath-house ... [there,] the party was halted and formed up into the regulation double rank, and ordered to 'stand at ease' ... at the word 'first ten men', the numbers indicated broke off from their ranks and entered the bath house. As they entered they found an assistant warder stationed at the door of every bathroom or compartment, and each man would be directed to enter a separate bathroom. The command given will best indicate the disgusting business that then went on, it being, of course, understood that the assistant warder stood close by and carefully watched the prisoners. (1901: 45)

It involved the prisoner removing his clothes on command and to 'stoop down, and touch your feet with your fingers. Keep like that till I tell you to move'. At the end of the matter, Balfour writes: 'garment after garment having been minutely examined by the warder, they were handed back to the prisoner, who, after, shivering with cold and invariably trembling with shame at the ordeal he has passed through, resumed his clothing as best he might'.

What amelioration there was to this practice during Balfour's confinement consisted of prisoners at least being allowed to retain their shirts while standing appropriately in the bath. However, after half a century when the authorities claimed to have been developing prison regimes and conditions that promoted prisoner self-respect, Croft-Cooke (1955: 95) reported that this very practice continued. It had become just one of the numerous ways in which 'self-respect is destroyed: a prisoner, for instance, may never move from one part of the prison to another unaccompanied. He may not cross the yard to the recess; he may not go to work or obey a summons to see the governor unless a screw or leader is with him. There can be no reason of security in this, its object when it was first introduced must have been to humiliate prisoners, and it has been retained because no-one has bothered to think about it.'

All kinds of everyday prison rituals confirmed the prisoners' sense of isolation and powerlessness: 'it seems to be part of the etiquette in the handling of prisoners that they should be kept waiting as long as possible ... there is always an immense amount of key-jangling at the entrance to HM convict establishments; a good deal of it I believe to be purely theatrical' (Balfour, 1901: 31); or the practice of keeping prisoners ignorant of the formal rules of the prison, let alone the informal codes on how to get by (Runyon, 1954: 70) or Croft Cooke (1955: 56). Alternatively, bureaucratic ineptitude could enforce their subjection, by deepening their shame, reinforcing the stain of being a prisoner. As we know, during the 1920s and 1930s, the prison rules were changed to try and protect the privacy of the prisoners. But, again, these intended safeguards could easily be breached by lack of care or sensitivity by the authorities, as if formulistic compliance with the rules themselves was the only requirement on those putting them into practice. Hence Wood, although now allowed to wear his civilian clothes on being transferred, still found the experience deeply humiliating: 'I travelled with two warders, clad in prison clothes, stared at and pointed at by hundreds of people who thronged the platforms and the steamer that carried me from Portsmouth to Newport. Not an experience to nourish one's self respect' (1932: 277). Some decades later, Baker was similarly shamed: 'our burly and uniformed escort grouped menacingly around us, and made it quite clear to the world that we were apprehended felons. The railway carriage had a notice: "reserved for HM Prisons party and escort"' (1961: 16).

For some, subjection was brought about by the entombment their cell represented:

> I do remember vividly the awful sense of isolation and helplessness that made me feel as if I were shut way in a whited sepulchre, and almost as tomb like. There were fourteen small panes of opaque glass in the heavily barred window high up, out of reach, with a wooden ventilator attached. Leaning against the wall was a three-planked bed board with dirty blankets and a red and yellow bedcover hanging over it, crowned with a hard coir pillow. A slimy water can and a thickly furred utensil

were propped up against the wall ... under the window there were two iron quadricircular shelves ... a table similarly fixed on one side of the door and a wooden stool ... I felt that I wanted to scream out at the black, menacing darkness that enshrouded me like a pall – darkness so utter that not a single ray of light could be seen or even the outline of the barred window, it was like being buried alive in a vault. (Wood, 1932: 27)

Others did scream out, though, eerily, helplessly, penetrating this darkness, and at the same time forcibly bringing home to those who had to listen a reminder of their own helplessness and sense of isolation. Davitt (1886: 31) refers to the howling of the '"barmy blokes" or madness, the shouting and crying of the poor fellows in dark cells on bread and water, and the singing of those who chose to satisfy their hunger with a snatch of some favourite song'. Balfour (1901: 44) heard similar sounds: 'at Wormwood Scrubs it was a gruesome and not uncommon experience to hear the shrieking of some half-demented or conscience-stricken creature in a nightmare'.

Such agonized despair could be heard well into the twentieth century, even if it could not break through the sanitized language the authorities now used to describe prison life:

I have heard strong men crying all night, only pausing to shout 'Mother, Mother', as loudly as [they] could. I have heard a man smashing up his cell furniture and heard of sheets being ripped and windows broken, out of sheer loneliness and despair. I saw the faces of prisoners when they were first released in the morning and was able to guess from them some of the agonies of the night. (Croft-Cooke, 1955: 85)

Instead of some sense of unity and comradeship amongst the prisoners, what we see in such accounts is only a kind of shameful, furtive isolation, which not only made imprisonment a more painful experience, but also reinforced the sense of helplessness and subjection. Again, this is not to deny that the amelioration of prison conditions and so on – as the authorities claimed – did take place. But what such changes failed to do – and perhaps they could never do this anyway – was to remove or lessen the demoralization that going to prison could cause. The substitution of numbers for names, for example, in the mid-nineteenth century – ostensibly to give prisoners anonymity – came to represent how, on reception, their identity would be stripped from them: 'twenty-six was the number of my cell and was to be my name in prison. I was newly christened, and the name of Rossa was to be heard no more' (Rossa, 1882: 96). Later on, the liberalization of the rules regarding association and communication meant that the prison's former silence became a precious commodity, to be treasured (McCartney, 1936; Phelan, 1940), against the bedlam-like experience that it had now become: 'the wireless loudspeakers, roaring out distorted dance music, made conversation impossible. Lights were dim and unshaded. The smell of sour food and sweaty feet hung over everything like a fog, and everywhere one looked one saw men sitting there, hunched in their capes, their eyes blank, waiting, waiting' (Wildeblood, 1955: 136).

In effect, the prisoners did not really need training or instruction in practices that made them acquiescent to the prison authorities. It was as if acquiescence came 'naturally' to them; as soon as they assumed the role of 'prisoner', they also assumed the habitus that came with this. Thus Davitt's observations while performing hard labour:

> at about ten o'clock the man next to me threw down his spade with an oath and swore he would do no more work. Putting on his jacket, he walked up to the warder and quite as a matter of course turned his back to him and put out both hands behind him. The warder took out hand-cuffs and without any comment handcuffed his hands in that position ... the handcuffed prisoner came trudging along behind, and to my surprise I noticed that several of the other parties also had an *enfant perdu*, hands behind his back, marching in the rear. As soon as we were back at the prison each of these poor sheep in the rear fell out without even being ordered to do so. (1886: 27)

It was as if the prisoners knew exactly what to do under such circumstances. In these respects, the prison itself, and the transmission of its cultural values and role expectations simply allowed the prisoners to internalize their own sense of worthlessness and subjection. Conformity to discipline and order not only produced utterly degraded prisoners; it also produced subservient prisoners. Balfour (1901: 46) refers to 'the prison shuffle': 'after exercise we shuffled back to our cells, and I use the word "shuffle" advisedly, because this is a kind of walk – a gait – peculiar to prisoners. I do not know why it becomes a habit but it certainly is one.' But as we see here with Balfour, it was also conduct that they came to perform 'automatically' – it was second nature to them: he cannot explain how he picks up such habits, only observing that he does pick them up. Every part of prison life seemed able to contribute towards this sense of subjection: the exercise routine, for example, of walking round in circles:

> four yards from each other, and the four warders at the cardinal points watch us with eyes keen as eagles. Tramp, tramp, tramp, the dull monotonous sound is heard for some thirty five minutes and at its conclusion you are taken from the fleeting sunshine to the coldness and gloom of solitary confinement. (Brocklehurst, 1898: 20)

More than half a century later, Baker (1961: 80) wrote of the 'humiliating nature of exercise – most of the prisoners that passed went by with heads and eyes half covered, as though my disgrace was contagious'. He and every other prisoner he could see had become one of the 'grey clad men – who marched stolidly around [making] up a weird mime of the retreat from Moscow' (Hignett, 1956: 245). Even after the various reforms of the twentieth century, it was as if the echoes and spectres of the past – the tramping feet, the shuffling march, the shaven heads and arrowed uniforms – provided their own ghostly pedagogy of subjection for each new prisoner to learn.

The sense of helplessness was likely to be confirmed if the prisoners sought assistance from those in the world beyond the prison most likely to provide it. Illness, like diet, clothing and hygiene was also subject to institutional rules, requirements and procedures Brocklehurst reported as follows after being taken to the doctor when he felt ill: 'he received me in a kind of dispensary under the central dome. There were several prisoners desirous of seeing the doctor at the same time as I, and in order to prevent us from "communicating" with each other, we were placed about two yards apart, with our faces turned to the wall' (1898: 130). In the inter-war period, criticisms of the doctors became more forthright as the prisoners saw them indelibly on the side of the authorities, harnessing the treatment of illness to the bureaucratic routines of the prison rather than the needs of the prisoner patient. Wood (1932: 130) suffered from the following symptoms: 'great sores had broken out all over my scalp, and large fissured ulcers in the anus made stool an intolerable agony ... my appeals to the doctor, a part time official with a practice outside, were received with scepticism and daily doses of salts, which made me vomit and weakened me more and more'. After the war, Dendrickson and Thomas confirmed that:

> Illness has to obey prison times. Prisoners are supposed to report sick first thing in the morning. They are then shut up, in their cells until such time as the doctor comes to see them. A man who feels suddenly ill in the middle of the afternoon is considered an unmitigated nuisance and will be advised in no uncertain terms to hold over his complaint until the following morning. If he insists on seeing the doctor immediately he may be sure of a somewhat frigid reception. (1954: 122)

By now, the prisoner's medical examination on entry had become matter of fact and routine, notwithstanding the high concentration of medical problems that they experienced: 'the prison doctor read out a series of questions and looked up only if I did not answer immediately ... most of them were of a personal nature and I think he could have used a little discretion in not bawling them out as if I were a computer' (Vassall, 1975: 157). It was as if the habitus of the medical staff had also been transformed as a result of their prison work:

> the doctor treated me as if I was a malingerer ... as soon as they entered the prison they seemed to regard their tasks as the promulgation of discipline rather than of medicine ... the attitude of doctors on morning sick parade was little short of scandalous ... far too many seriously ill prisoners were treated as malingerers or were given reasonable treatment only after long delay. (Baker, 1961: 130)

As such, it became second nature for the medical staff to disregard or dispute as a fabrication any symptoms that the prisoners might report to them:

> I was asked by a prison doctor if I had any ailments, and I said 'Yes,
> I've got osteo-arthritis in both hips'. Without examining me he said this
> was quite untrue. I had no such thing. In fact it got worse under prison
> conditions ... [b]ut the prison doctors job is not to cure; it is simply to
> keep the inmates in a 'reasonable state of health' as they put it; in other
> words, to make sure they do not actually drop dead before they're
> tossed out into the outside world. (Houghton, 1972: 125)

This claim is correct. The job of the doctors was not to cure. They
simply had to maintain the health of the prisoners to the appropriate
bureaucratic requirements – that was the prison version of the
Hippocratic Oath. It was this that routinized the approach to the treatment of prisoner illness within the mainstream prison system. Again,
though, it was not just that this low quality health care added to the
prisoners' debilitation: it was another way of enforcing their helplessness
and through this their own subjection to the prison administration.

Even so, the account of Probyn (1977: 54), as with Rossa on diet and
Houghton on uniform, again illustrates what might happen when
prisoners wandered into some of the more remote, still more secretive and
non-accountable annexes of the prison system: as if the more one became
lost in it, the more dehumanized it could become, with the usual rules
and procedures held in abeyance in these areas. He describes his experience after escaping from Rampton Special Hospital:

> I was eventually caught in a field and the beating and kicking began
> then and did not cease until long after I had arrived back at the institu-
> tion. I was beaten with sticks and kicked as I was dragged to the car.
> This continued in the back of the car. I was dragged out of the car and
> the process continued ... in the refractory ward I was kicked along the
> corridor to the bathroom whilst a doctor followed on behind laughing
> at what was happening.

The chaplains, as the doctors, might only assist in institutionalizing the
prisoners rather than alleviating their pains. Balfour's (1901: 68) advice
from the chaplain on reception was that 'it's lucky for you ... that you
have come just at this time. The governor who has recently left was a
very severe man indeed. Things are bad enough at present, and even now
I would warn you to be very careful of the warders. You are wholly in
their power'. So too, perhaps, was the chaplain himself, as he revealed
when he and Balfour witnessed a beating taking place: 'it's no good ...
there's nothing we can do' (1901: 224), was his response. Again, the
church service might become just another perfunctory task that the chaplains had to perform. As with the provision of medical services, it had
come to be routinized by the administrative structure of prison: 'both
chaplain and criminals were hard-hearted, and no-one, especially the
chaplain, refrained from displaying boredom at the whole business ... the
outstanding features of the services were the cold mechanical method with

which they ran themselves out and the obvious boredom of everybody concerned' (Mason, 1919: 145–6). For Croft-Cooke

> Most of the chaplains of all denominations were little more than a bit-ter joke to the men they were supposed to help … it seems to me deplorable that responsible posts in prison can be filled by men who lack the imagination to realise how much a few heartening words would mean to a prisoner facing them for his initial interview after his first sleepless night in prison. (1955: 62)

Complaints were possible, of course. Indeed, the procedures for which were an inscribed part of the penal arrangements that one would expect to find in any civilized society. Under the existing prison structure, how-ever, it was also most inadvisable. The very act of complaining challenged the legitimacy of the authorities and elevated the prisoners beyond the status that had been assigned to them. As such, they were made aware of what the consequences of any such disruption to the established configu-ration of prison power might be. McCartney observed:

> the desired end of the penal system in regard to the feeding of convicts is not to feed 'em at all, and yet to keep 'em alive, and to stop their grumbling. Therefore, it is stated, in a card hung upon the cell wall, that although the convict may complain about the food, should the complaint be deemed unfounded, or the complaint be frequent, he will be punished by getting no food at all except bread and water. (1936: 122)

In the ordinary course of things, there seemed little point in making a complaint, as Convict 77 affirmed: 'I have over and over again had to complain of the quality of the meat or soup supplied, much of which was unfit for human consumption. But unless the food was absolutely rotten, which was not often the case, no notice was taken of such complaints, and if complaints happened frequently, a prisoner was liable to be reported and punished for giving unnecessary trouble' (1903: 185). Wood (1932: 191) came to the understanding that 'the results of my own small rebellions against authority and the early realisation that resistance was suicidal, led me to adopt the philosophy of passive obedience. I became what is called a "good prisoner"'.

Some complaints did go ahead, nonetheless. Again, though, the theatre of the prison itself could be used to reinforce the prisoner's sense of powerlessness: from the melodramatic, as in the case of Sparks (1961: 143), describing a 'Dartmoor sandwich' at a disciplinary hearing before the visiting justices: 'I was marched in with one screw walking backwards in front of me and holding his stick over my head ready to clout me if I gave any trouble, and another walking behind me ditto'; to the mundane, as when Norman (1958: 28) refers to having to remove his shoes when going before the governor: as if his own place in the prison hierarchy (at the bottom) had to be reinforced in this way. It is hardly surprising that most prisoners passed up the opportunity to complain that had been inscribed for them in them in the prison rules; thus Norman (1958: 78) describing the usual procedure on a commissioner's visit and being asked 'What's the food like?', inevitably replied 'No complaints, sir.' As Croft Cooke put the matter, 'when the [Prison Commissioners' reports] proclaim that "the number of complaints received from prisoners expressed either officially or received indirectly is extraordinarily small", I can well believe it. Prisoners are realists and know the futility of complaints' (1955: 120).

It is necessary, of course, not to overstate the way in which such automotive obedience became the norm in the conduct of prison life. Violence and disorder did occur. From the mid-nineteenth century through to the 1960s, there was periodic rioting (see Adams, 1994). However, on a more individualized day-by-day basis, when violence did take place, at least by prison officers on prisoners, this was likely to be of a highly formulaic nature, with set limits to it and acknowledged only in coded language (violence that took place from officers without such 'authority' was thus likely to be aberrational rather than institutional). It might be provoked by particular breaches of an unwritten code that governed much of the everyday life of prison – one prisoner attacking another, for example. On such occasions, wrote Behan (1959: 209), the attacker would be given 'a clean shirt', which would then be covered up by a code of silence: 'even if the prisoner was ruptured, nobody would know, except prison officials, warders, prison doctors and clergymen'. Such 'disturbing events' were simply excluded from official discourse: we have to look to the prisoners' own accounts to discover their existence.

When this formulaic violence occurred, it was likely to be on those occasions when prisoners were thought to be disrupting the bureaucratic efficiency of the prison (see Boyle, 1977). But, by and large, what we find is that gratuitous violence (by prison officers on prisoners) was usually restricted (at least in the biographical accounts) to the more secret passages and enclaves of the prison: the black hole areas that the punishment blocks and psychiatric wings represented. In these uncharted regions, completely beyond visibility and where the normal threads of accountability were at their weakest, the social distance between the prisoners and the prison establishment was at its greatest: while for the prison officers it was surely the case that those prisoners who ventured into such locations must seem the most outlandish of prisoners, for whom the rules of conduct that regulated most aspects of prison life could be suspended.

Overall, however, accounts of violence in prisoner memoirs are infrequent. Baker (1961: 223), wrote: 'serious violence was so rare at the Scrubs that the problem did not present itself very often'. In reality, to ensure order and obedience, to ensure that the prison remained an unobtrusive, unnoticed institution, there was little need for the authorities to resort to violence. The prisoners internalized their own subjection which was then reinforced daily and constantly by the nature of the prison regime itself – resistance usually being undermined in this way rather than by direct confrontation. As Bidwell (1895: 209) put it, what had been created was 'a vast machine ... [w]ithout passion, without prejudice but also without pity and remorse ... it crushes and passes on'. And while, on this basis, gratuitous acts of violence from individual officers were aberrational, at the same time, acts of kindness were also aberrational rather than institutional. Prison work required neither saints nor sinners to carry it out, but instead, efficient technicians – the kind of prison officers whom Phelan (1940: 27–8) described: 'almost without exception ... the warders were quiet, stolid, decent people ... they were workmen doing a job. Their job was to report any breach of a myriad of regulations. What happened afterwards was no concern of theirs.'[2]

Here, then, was how the sanitized prison that featured in official discourse functioned for its inmates. Its machinery, by and large, from the mid-nineteenth century through to the 1960s operated in a relatively untroubled way because the prisoners came to internalize their own subjection to it. Their memoirs are a testament to this, in addition to the record of continuing deprivation and degradation of prison life that characterized their experiences.

Notes

---

1 The Christmas lunch in prison seems to have been introduced around the end of the nineteenth century in England (although it was already a special event in Canada by 1887, see p 66). Horsley writes as follows: 'Christmas in prison! It does not sound more cheerful than it is, especially to those whose ideas of any feast soar no higher than their stomach. For breakfast, [there is] a six ounce loaf of bread and a pint of gruel or skilly ... for dinner, there is six ounces of potatoes, and three-quarters of a pint of pea soup. For supper, the same as for breakfast' (1887: 62–3).

2 Cf. Wood (1932: 28): 'Warders were cruel and inhuman because the system demanded cruelty and inhumanity in its officers. They were themselves subject to a code of rules every bit as strict as those they had to enforce. They were not only forbidden to talk to prisoners, they were not even permitted to hold conversations with one another while on duty.'

7

Bureaucratization and Indifference

There are two very different versions, then, of 'the truth' about prison life. On the one hand, we have official penal discourse. Here, prisons came to function as they should in a civilized society: there were to be no gratuitous and barbaric punishments – these had been left in the past – the gags, the floggings, even bread and water diets towards the end of this period had been removed from the prison agenda;[1] the sombre, sepulchral atmosphere had been lifted; prisons had become largely conflict-free institutions, the authorities told us; within which they also maintained that food, clothing and hygiene arrangements had been normalized; the prisoners were being encouraged to improve themselves by making use of educational facilities; now, where there were personality problems, there were treatment and rehabilitation programmes available to remedy them. On the other hand, we have the very different story that the prisoners had to tell. In their accounts, continuous themes of deprivation and degradation characterize prison life; reforms might even introduce new privations and torments – the bedlam that association became, for example. If the prisons had indeed become the quiet, orderly, productive institutions the authorities claimed, then this was likely to be because of a habitus of subjection that had become ingrained in prisoner life, rather than some efficient process of reform that the authorities presided over.

Who was telling the truth? The answer to such a question would seem so obvious today that it would almost certainly never even be asked. It is, of course, the authorities. Does not their very status as authorities give validity and credibility to what they are saying? And what happened to all those prisoner-memories, all those shouts not of anger but anguish, not of vitriolic force but of despair? Quite simply: does not the prisoners' very status as prisoners 'automatically' deny any validity to the truth they were trying to tell us in their memoirs? What I want to suggest, here, however, is that there was no necessary inevitability to the credibility that came to be associated with what the authorities said, and the incredibility associated with what the prisoners said. Instead, then, of asking who was telling the truth, a more pertinent question to ask is, what was it that allowed the authorities' accounts to be accepted as the more or less unchallenged truth, notwithstanding the existence of the alternative version to the truth they proclaimed? That there did come to be an inevitability to this was itself the product of two forces specific to the development of civilized societies during the nineteenth and twentieth centuries: bureaucratization on the one hand, public indifference on the other.

Bureaucratization

During this period, the power to punish became the exclusive property of the central state bureaucracies, effectively screening punishment itself from public view in an administrative sense, in addition to the physical separation that now existed. Inevitably, such organizations and the discourses they produced would be a more powerful force than individual prisoners and their writings. Whatever took place in prison, for example, would be shaped, defined and communicated in such a way that it suited their own bureaucratic interests above anything else. A modern penal bureaucracy would thus be able to proclaim its ameliorative, sanitized approach to prison development and at the same time draw a veil of silence across anything that might contradict this. This was the point Behan was making in his reference to 'clean shirts': no one would know of this practice, except prison officials, warders, prison doctors and clergymen. In other words, everybody in the prison would know what was going on, but no one would be prepared to do anything about it. In this way, 'clean shirts' in the Behan context had no formal existence. The bureaucratization of imprisonment that took place in this period would enmesh all those individuals who made up the prison establishment in a dense network of interdependencies which then made it increasingly difficult for them to act as individuals rather than bureaucratic representatives, increasingly difficult for them to go 'out on a limb' and take a stand against the rest of the prison establishment. As a result, the unified penal establishment gained an immense power to define the reality of prison life.

From Local to Central Government Administration

Up to the early nineteenth century in England, there had been no central state bureaucratic management of the prisons. They were administered by local oligarchies, corporations and other local government authorities, and overseen by visiting magistrates. Millbank Prison, opened in 1815, had been the first to be managed by central government. Thereafter, with the decline of transportation and the local punishment carnivals, the development of a systematized, standardized penal system administered through the state's own bureaucratic organizations was increasingly recognized as being part of the broader 'organization of a civilized social life' (Woodward, 1938: 407). Over the course of the nineteenth century, in legislation introduced in 1835, 1865 and 1877, control of the prisons eventually passed from the local to the central state:[2] initially, the latter's convict prisons (Pentonville had been one such institution) operated in conjunction with the local jails, until these were either closed or modified to suit central government specifications and administrative procedures. However, notwithstanding the bureaucratic, monopolistic control of the power to punish that was being established, initially it is not the silence that we now come to associate with prisons that is so striking, but instead the sheer volume, range and weight of differing sources of knowledge that came to be available on this subject: the shift towards bureaucratic centralization, initially at least, did not close down debate about prisons – it stimulated it.

The birth of the modern prison was accompanied by formal processes of inspection, inquiry, accountability and reporting. In England between 1835 and 1877 there were four different inspectorates: that for the centrally administered convict prisons, and those for local prisons in the Northern and Eastern, the Southern and Western and Home (London and the environs) districts.[3] Until the later date, one of the purposes of inspection was to bring about greater uniformity in the prisons and to remove their excesses and inefficiencies. Unlike in the early nineteenth century, when it had been pioneering individuals such as Elizabeth Fry and voluntary organizations such as the Society for the Improvement of Prison Discipline that had campaigned for penal reform, what we find from 1835 onwards is the growing assumption that such matters were now for the state to determine, not local justices or reform-minded individuals and private organizations: the production of the inspectorate's annual prison reports became one aspect of this tendency towards control and direction, setting standards, advising and exposing inefficiencies. Another involved other forms of government inquiry and investigation into the conduct and administration of prison life.

In contrast to the period between 1791 and 1810, when, 'beyond an occasional inquiry into the cost of the hulks and the practicability of penal colonies ... the House of Commons and the Minister of the Crown ... seem to have taken no more interest in prison administration' (Webb and Webb, 1922: 66), between 1850 and 1899, just in relation to prisons, there were three Royal Commissions, six Select Committee reports, three Departmental Committees, and three committees appointed by the Secretary of State.[4] Furthermore, this official discourse was accompanied by a range of other sources of knowledge about prison: the various prisoner biographies, of course, but, in addition, the memoirs of prison officials (see, for example, Burt, 1852; Kingsmill, 1854; Clay, 1861; Griffiths, 1875, 1884), journalistic type investigations (Hepworth Dixon, 1850; Mayhew and Binny, 1862), discussions of penal reform (Symonds, 1849; Hill, 1853; Chesterton, 1856; Cox, 1870; Tallack, 1889); and novels and plays in which the prison played a significant part.[5]

This proliferation and diversity of prison discourse culminated in the early twentieth century, with the opening of John Galsworthy's (1929) play *Justice* in London and Edinburgh in 1910. The hero, Falder, a solicitor's clerk who is sentenced to three years penal servitude, finds its nine-month solitary confinement component difficult to endure.[6] In a swift response, the Home Office reacted to its opening night as follows:

> public attention was called during the year in a forcible way to the alleged horrors and cruelty of the so-called separate system by a dramatic representation which omitted the explanation which would have enabled the public to grasp its meaning and purpose. *So unfamiliar is the public with the history and details of our prison system*, that they learnt for the first time from the stage of a London theatre what has been for sixty years a leading feature in the system of penal servitude. (*Report of the Prison Commissioners*, 1909–10: 14 my italics)

Given the critical nature of the play, it will be of no surprise that the response of the Home Office was to claim that it was based on a fallacious representation of prison conditions: as all bureaucracies will do, it was defending itself. What is also significant, however, is the claim that the public did not have any knowledge of prison life – notwithstanding all the sources of knowledge that had been made available over the previous half – century or so. What this public ignorance represents, I want to suggest, is the triumph of the bureaucratic process: notwithstanding the diversity of discourse that had been produced over this time, the penal authorities were able proclaim their truth as '*the truth*' and by so doing silence or discredit competing versions of this. Here, the claims made by Galsworthy did produce a short-lived scandal: they shocked a public who made connections between solitary confinement as it was represented in the play and medieval punishment and by so doing felt that what was apparently taking place went beyond the boundaries of permissible punishment in the civilized world – a claim which the Home Office was quick to refute: with the effect that the scandal faded away and quiescence returned. There was no inquiry: indeed, the next formal inquiry specific to imprisonment itself was not to take place in England until 1932.[7] And for much of the twentieth century, there also seems to have been a decline in the idea of prison as a theme in popular culture, which it had been for a good part of the nineteenth.[8]

What had occurred to produce, first, this unfamiliarity, despite all the competing sources of knowledge that had been available to the public about prison life, and then, second, the subsequent silence? What was it that had made the public so disinterested in the prison, in contrast to their excitement and enjoyment in all the public punishments that had been in existence up to a few decades earlier? Initially, the new prisons had been highly contested institutions: they had no necessary place in the penal imagination. One of the most significant areas of contestation had been over who should control them. In these respects, the early reports of the prison inspectors were extremely critical of local administration and its inefficiencies they revealed. For example, 'we refer also to the statements of prisoners, from which it appears that many of their more violent fights have taken place on a Sunday afternoon, that the more quiet and inoffensive dare not go to sleep from an apprehension of being made the subject of tricks of a very painful nature' (*Report of the Inspectors of Prisons of the Home District*, 1836: 10). And: 'I visited [Preston House of Correction] ... upon being admitted by the porter I walked into the body of the prison. Not an officer was to be seen. I proceeded to the tread-wheel, and found the prisoners at labour there, amusing themselves with talking and laughing' (*Report of the Inspectors of Prisons of the Northern District*, 1839: 44). Clay (1861, 1969: 177) subsequently wrote that 'the first report in 1836 made no little stir. It consisted mainly of a ruthless exposure of the abominations in Newgate; indeed, it was so plainspoken in one unlucky paragraph that it involved the printers of the House of Commons in a prosecution for libel'.

But against central government criticisms of poor conditions and lack of standardization, there was also a significant popular discourse that was highly critical of the 'luxurious' conditions of the central government's own model convict prisons. Again, Clay provides a summary:

> The controversy about prison-discipline, which revived in 1847, increased next year, grew vigorous in 1849, and culminated in 1850. By degrees, almost the whole press, which had been generally favourable to the plan of separation in 1847, veered round to brisk hostility. Early in 1849 *The Times* began to fulminate; presently *The Daily News*, with other newspapers took part ... in the attack ... *Punch* immediately flung his squibs at the unpopular system. But the journalists had no monopoly of the wrangle. The din stirred up a multitudinous flock of pamphlets, and such a hubbub of philanthropic and anti-philanthropic cawing ensued as has seldom been heard. Many of the great lords of literature shared in the controversial melee. (1861, 1969: 255)

Prisons, as yet, did not have an accepted, automatic, recognizable place in the penal landscape of the civilized world. They were still the subject of claims and counter-claims by central government and its critics about who should run them and how they should be run.

Furthermore, it was as if the very idea of a strong central state and its burgeoning bureaucratic organizations of government was not sufficiently embedded in the social fabric to be trusted by the general public;

such a concept had resonances with popular fears about the spread of 'police' and the expansion of unchecked state power then associated with political developments in Europe (Wiener, 1994). In these respects, the rationality and efficiency underlying the development of the state's convict prisons had to be regularly justified to an uncomprehending and wary general public. The Director of Convict Prisons, Colonel Jebb, for example, was at pains to point out that:

> [Their] cleanliness and good order are not the result of any undue desire to administer to the comfort of a prisoner, but the whole bearing of the daily routine by which they are secured is calculated to thwart the natural tastes and habits of most criminals, and to direct them into new and improved channels. (*Report of the Directors of Convict Prisons*, 1852: 55)

The central state, in its pursuit of bureaucratic efficiency and rationalization, could not move too far in advance of a suspicious public.

At the same time, however, revelations of inefficiencies and brutalities in locally run prisons gave added momentum to the need for the growing centralization of penal power. One such scandal related to ill treatment at Birmingham prison during 1853. The governor had adapted Maconochie's mark system, using the crank as a gauge of labour:

> the daily tasks amounted to the performance of 10,000 revolutions by six o'clock. When this was not carried out, the prisoner was kept in the crank cell until late at night, and if the work was still not done, he was deprived of his supper, receiving no food until eight o'clock the next morning, when he was given only bread and water. (Webb and Webb, 1922: 170)

The Times (29 July 1854: 4) subsequently reported:

> It is not less than a twelvemonth since a very painful sensation was made in this country by the discovery that in one prison, in one of the largest boroughs in England, constructed on the best plan, visited by magistrates, and managed by officers of reputation and experience, there was a systematic practice of atrocities that brought one back to the days before Howard, and beyond even the pale of civilization.

The ineptitude of the visiting magistrates who were meant to oversee local arrangements, but who had failed to do anything more than seek assurances from the governor that all was in order was parodied in Reade's (1856: 258) *It's Never Too Late to Mend*. He argued, instead, for the professionalization of their duties: 'no body of men ever gave nothing for anything worth anything, nor ever will. Now knowledge of law is worth something; zeal, independent judgement, honesty, humanity, diligence are worth something ... yet the state, greedy goose, hopes to get them out of a body of men for nothing.' Central state professional expertise rather than local lay amateurism was the way forward. Not only would this, it was thought, prevent excesses and inefficiencies, but at the same time it was needed to transform the local gaols to meet the demands being placed on the penal system by the presence of the untameable criminal class thought to be at large in England in the early 1860s (*Report from the Select Committee of the House of Lords on Prison Discipline,* 1863: vii).

As such, centralized bureaucratic control was seen as necessary both to bring efficiency to the prison, now the main feature of the penal system and the only defence against the predations of the criminal class; and to bring some standardization to its regimes, putting them on a more deterrent footing, as we saw in relation to prison diet, but at the same time avoiding the aberrational excesses that had taken place in Birmingham. The new administrative structure that was created for these purposes could thus be adjusted towards severity or humanity as suited, with standards for either measurement being carefully checked and calibrated rather than being left to the caprice of local authorities. At this particular time, the shift was towards severity. Under the terms of the Prisons Act 1865, each local prison had to conform to the standards set by central government – these included the provision of separate cells for all the prisoners, duly certified by the Inspector of Prisons as being structurally and in all other respects in accordance with the statutory requirements; and the drawing up of the new dietaries which had to be such as the Secretary of State might approve. Failure to conform to the statutory requirements could lead to central government funding being refused. Apart from encouraging uniformity, what the legislation also meant was that many of the smaller local gaols closed down: 'in the course of fifteen years from 1862, no fewer than eighty out of the 193 prisons of that date, all, of course, the smaller ones which had sometimes no prisoners at all, were entirely discontinued; and with them disappeared the most extreme and the most picturesque of the instances of the lack of uniformity' (Webb and Webb, 1922: 202–3). Public involvement in punishment was being minimized, and central government control strengthened, not just through the architectural design of the prisons and the restrictions placed on visiting, but, in addition, by their reduction in numbers and removal from local communities.

This growth in the penal power of central government was concomitant with a greater uniformity within the prison establishment itself. Up to this time there had been no necessary uniformity of interest between the respective governors, chaplains, doctors and prison officers. The governors were likely to compete with one another over the merits of their particular version of the separate or silent system; the chaplains had initially been regarded as being of the same status as the governors – 'each supreme in his own department: the governor as head of the penal, the chaplain of the religious part of the system' (Griffiths, 1875: 46), notwithstanding the potential for conflict that this might create. And medical officers had been expected to give primacy to the health of their prisoners – having a discretionary power to prescribe invalid diets and so on as they saw fit. For example, the Wakefield surgeon had reported that *'with the discretionary power I have of increasing the diet in individual cases*, I think the food is sufficient' (*Report of the Directors of Convict Prisons*, 1858: 60; my italics). Nor were they hesitant in putting forward their own suggestions as to what the appropriate level of diet *ought* to be, as opposed to what it then was:

> the food tasted by me was of very good quality, and the dietary was generally good and sufficient. There was, however, in my opinion, a serious defect in the supper and breakfast being too scanty – I would strongly advise that 2 oz bread should be added to the supper and breakfast of the men, making the quantity of each of these meals 8 oz. If this change were made, and the quantity of oatmeal in the gruel increased to 2 oz per pint, there would remain, I think, no further complaint and the strength of the sentenced prisoners, which is now decidedly below the healthy average would be greatly improved. (*Report of the Inspector of the Southern District*, 1858: 83)

As regards the prison officers, the direction of their loyalties – to the prisoners (with whom they had more in common) or to the prison authorities – was often uncertain: not only were many of the garnishing practices of the old prison regimes still in existence (see, for example, Chesterton, 1856), but during the 1850s and 1860s, there were suspicions of congenial relationships between prisoners and officers (Thomas, 1972: 57). What authority the prison officers possessed seemed very precarious. *The Times* (26 March 1861: 4) reported that 'there have been mutinous outbreaks ... and there is a vast amount of discontent rife among the inmates, almost ready to burst forth. Several minor instances of insubordination have occurred and more recently information was obtained that a number of inmates intend to seize the wardens and release the prisoners before setting fire to the institution'. Certainly, at the time of the Chatham rioting in 1862, the officers lost control of the prison and three hundred troops were sent for. Part of the problem was that there seems to have been no sense of hierarchy or social distance between the prisoners and prison officers: indeed, with literate prisoners undertaking clerical work, then beyond the capabilities of many officers, some prisoners could actually gain higher status than them within the prison, again confusing its ordering of hierarchies and relationships.

During the 1860s and 1870s, a significant reconfiguration of prison relations took effect, setting in place strong bureaucratic structures, creating a dense web of interdependencies and establishing clear lines of delineation and authority: one which would come to be impenetrable to outsiders, one which would impose restrictions on debate and inquiry. In this way, the discourse produced through its unified central authority would be validated and incontrovertible – at least by other members of the prison establishment, for whom it would be increasingly difficult to step out of line. Public debates between prison governors, for example, about the direction and shape of prison policy effectively came to an end. This would no longer be for a few individuals to determine for themselves and then pursue as they thought fit, but would be determined and made general policy as the result of governmental inquiry, commission and so on, whereby all the appropriate scientific evidence could be assessed. As regards the other prison professionals, their own autonomy was restricted and their status within the prison configuration downgraded and made secondary to efficient bureaucratic management. In this way, the chaplains and doctors were turned into the figures that became recognizable in the prisoner biographies of the late nineteenth century and onwards.[9]

The former were reduced to little more than clerical officers themselves; or they served a merely ornamental purpose: sitting with the governor on adjudications, for example, to provide some dignity and solemnity to what was taking place, but effectively powerless to intervene. They had a lesser status than the chief prison officer to whom they were to report 'any abuse or impropriety' (Prisons Act 1865, Rule 49). Their pastoral duties would be secondary to the disciplinary duties of the officers: the Pentonville chaplain in 1878 reported that 'the visiting [of prisoners] is necessarily very irregular, because we are not allowed to interfere with the discipline in any way so as to interrupt the hours of labour or exercise or rest' (*Report of the Prison Commissioners,* 1878–9: 51). Even their sermons had to be tailored to suit bureaucratic interests: 'as the prisoners are a very mixed class, our desire is to get chaplains who do not have any extraordinary views of any kind, such as might cause bad feelings in the prison'. Religious teachings would not be allowed to stimulate sentiments that might subvert order and discipline.

As regards the doctors, the administrative decision to link diet to discipline placed them in an ambiguous position: if they remained true to their profession – to prescribe a diet that would ensure the health and well-being of prisoners – they would then place themselves beyond the bureaucratic directives to the contrary. The moral dilemma this might pose was largely resolved by the prison authorities removing any discretion the doctors themselves might have in the matter and subjecting them to checks and controls:

> We shall take such steps as are necessary to carry out the recommendation as to the occasional issue of extra bread by desire of the medical officer, adopting the practice recently recommended and followed in the case of local prisons, of having a record kept by the medical officer of his recommendations in these cases, *framed in such a way as to afford the means of judging his mode of proceeding.* This record will be particularly useful in enabling a comparison to be made between the practice of different medical officers, and if the recommendation made by the Commission of the appointment of a medical inspector is carried into effect, will afford a very useful check on the abuse of discretion in this regard. (*Report from the Select Committee of the House of Lords on Prison Discipline,* 1863: xii; my italics)

That the doctors now had to record their decisions even in relation to issuing extra slices of bread to those prisoners they judged to be ill changed the nature of prison medical work: from dispensing medicine to checking for malingerers. With increasing regularity, we find the medical officers having recourse from this time to a stock phrase to describe their work, rather than, as had previously been the case, providing a minutiae of detail, including the local diet and any possible shortcomings they perceived in it: 'provisions are good quality and the general diet is sufficient but not more than necessary for maintaining the health and strength of prisoners' (*Report of the Inspectors of Prisons of the Southern District*, 1870: 28) – exactly as the prison rules had determined it should be.

As for the prison officers, their own place within the prison hierarchy had been raised: there were improvements in their conditions of employment, attempts to recruit a better class of officers with army experience, and, with an extension of their role, much clearer lines of demarcation were drawn between them and the prisoners:

> We have proposed a change in regard to the conduct of the clerical duties of the prisons, which, while it will effect an economy in administering them will be a benefit to the warders, *viz* that of employing discipline officers in the place of clerks. We have reason to believe that both in trustworthiness, intelligence and efficiency we shall find them fully equal to these duties, and as employment of this nature is much sought after, we have no doubt that it will be found a useful stimulus and an additional attraction to induce the better educated soldiers to enter the convict service on discharge. (*Report of the Directors of Convict Prisons*, 1870: xii)

Again, a stock phrase in the annual reports would now be used to describe the performance of this sector of the prison establishment: 'the subordinate officers have performed their duties with intelligence, zeal and fidelity and to my entire satisfaction' (*Report of the Directors of Convict Prisons*, 1872: xiv). In these ways, the various contributors to the prison establishment had been drawn more closely and tightly together. They would increasingly speak with one voice rather than several sometimes contradictory ones, and the distance between themselves and the prisoners would become more rigid.

Now the cohesion of the prison establishment was better placed to give effect to the prison policy of deterrence, in line with the public mood, but carefully fixed by the scientific precepts of experts such as Guy and Smith (see Chapter 4, p. 64–5), in their evidence to the various committees of this period. Even so, the right balance between severity and humanity had to be achieved: deterrence should not lead to inhumanity, as this was not part of the formal penal policy of civilized societies. Complaints that prison policies were indeed inhumane could be taken very seriously, particularly when made by prisoners who had a significant voice and powerful friends beyond the prison. The purpose of imprisonment was to punish according to a carefully calibrated standard, balancing humanity and severity, and thereby avoiding excesses on either side of it. Bureaucratization was intended to bring about the uniformity and standardization of these objectives, not arbitrariness and discretion. The complaints of the Irish prisoners in particular about intolerable conditions led to further commissions of inquiry. With the reputation of these bodies for being 'impartial, expert and representative' (Cartwright, 1975), here was the appropriate way for complaints of systematic ill treatment to be investigated in a civilized society.

The *Report of the Commission of Inquiry into the Treatment of certain Treason-Felony Convicts in English Convict Prisons* (1867) was the first of these. What happened, though, is that not only were the complaints themselves found to be without justification, but by the very act of denying their validity, the legitimacy of what the authorities were doing was itself affirmed:

> of the prison and of the prison arrangements ... We would speak of these emphatically as a perfect model of order, cleanliness and propriety, and as reflecting the highest credit upon ... the Governor and all persons concerned. The cells are sufficiently large and well ventilated, the bedding ample for comfort and health ... the cells are faultless, and contain all that is necessary for comfort (8).

So the report continues on a point-by-point basis, refuting each complaint:

> the prison fare, as far as we saw it, is excellent of its kind, and we do not for one moment believe that we saw anything but the average samples. The bread was in store for the next day's consumption; the soup was in large cauldrons ready to be served out ... Everything was excellent of its kind ... it would be much to be desired that all the labouring population of these islands has as good and wholesome diet as the fifteen hundred convicts now kept to labour on the island of Portland.

As for the prisoners, 'we know that these men have a better diet, sleep in better beds, are more cared for in sickness, have lighter labour than the bulk of the labouring classes in the three kingdoms, and that the stories of their ill-treatment are simple falsehoods'.

In effect, then, notwithstanding the fact that democratic processes of inquiry had been set up to investigate serious claims of mistreatment, and that the prisoners were given access to them (seventeen, in fact, gave evidence to the 1867 Commission), their complaints were not only bound to fail, coming as they did from discredited prisoners, but by the very act of failing they strengthened the truth claims of the authorities, and weakened their own status – by making false complaints they were seen as liars. For example, the *Report of the Directors of Convict Prisons* (1867: 8), written in the aftermath of the Commission's findings: 'grave complaints were made during the year of the treatment of the convicts transferred from the Irish prisons under sentence for treason-felony ... the [subsequent] report went fully into the whole question of convict management, was submitted to parliament and entirely set at rest any doubts as to the treatment of those prisoners'.

We see the same logics of complaint and investigation, followed by denial and reaffirmation of the social distance between the prison authorities and the prisoners in the next formal inquiry into claims of ill treatment (*Report of the Commission of Inquiry into the Treatment of Treason-Felony Convicts*, 1871). Again, notwithstanding the fact that prisoners were able to give evidence to the Commissioners on their own behalf, this had little consequence. There were fairly minor points of detail to which the Committee were sympathetic: 'the tea supplied to certain classes of prisoners also attracted our attention; it appeared to us to be of inferior character, owing to its being kept too long in the cauldron before use' (1871: 8). And, 'the naked search of a prisoner should not take place in the presence of other prisoners and should be conducted by selected officers' (1871: 11). However, any suggestions which seemed to contradict the assumed rationality and circumscribed humanity of prison life, demonstrating instead its irrationality and inhumanity, were simply denied, as if the very suggestion that it could be so was simply unconscionable and unsustainable. The prisoner William Roantree had complained that:

> I have seen small black creatures half an inch in length flow from this tap, wriggling about in the water. Yet the officer said they were young frogs or toads, that the water was sure to be good where they were, that they were good to eat; that he knew one prisoner who would have his hot cocoa poured on top of them into his pint, covered them up for a short time, and so had them stewed for breakfast. A great improvement he said. (1871: 34)

The Commissioners' response was:

> With reference to the allegations that such other foreign substances as a mouse, entrails of a fowl or other refuse, have found their way into the prisoner's diet, we have to observe that if such articles got accidentally into the soup cauldrons even a few hours before the soup was served, they would be boiled down into a condition in which they could not be recognized ... it must be admitted as barely possible that in transition from the kitchen to a prisoner's cell, by accident or design, a foreign object of small size might find its way into a prisoner's ration. (1871: 13)

How could such complaints be believed in the light of the evidence (the laws of science and the word of a prison officer) to the contrary? The subsequent *Report of the Committee appointed to consider and report upon dietaries of local prisons* (1878: 12) again only confirmed the validity of the existing prison arrangements:

> In the course of our numerous visits to local gaols, we have conversed with many prisoners; we have watched them at all hours of the day;

and we cannot avoid the conclusion that, in a large number of cases, imprisonment as now generally conducted, is a condition more or less akin to that of physiological rest ... The struggle for survival is suspended; and the prisoner appears to feel that the prayer for daily bread is rendered unnecessary by the solitude of his custodians. Tranquillity of mind and freedom from anxiety are leading characteristics of his life.

Democratic processes of inquiry and investigation were being applied to the examination of fundamentally non-democratic institutions, where the prisoners had formal, minimal rights but, in practice, virtually no rights. Attacks on the system *per se* were, it seems, almost certain to be dismissed, particularly when the system carried with it the authority of the state itself: only in the case of brutalities inflicted gratuitously on individual prisoners – aberrant behaviour on the part of individual officers for the most part (which, again, the moves to centralized control were designed to check) was a complaint likely to stand much chance of success. On this basis, individual, but not systemic, indiscretions could be acknowledged: it suited the bureaucratic interests of the penal organizations to have such arbitrariness and inefficiency rooted out. What could not be acknowledged was any systemic violence or privation. Nor could irrationality be attributed to the administration of the prisons. Notwithstanding Michael Davitt's assertions that prisoners were so hungry that they would eat candles and poultices, the *Report of the Commissioners Appointed to Inquire into the Working of the Penal Servitude Acts* (1879: xxxviii) concluded: 'It has been stated in evidence that some prisoners eat candles, but we believe this to arise from a desire on the part of a few individuals to eat more fat than the dietary affords, and not from any deficiency in the quantity or quality of the diet'. If it was acknowledged that irrationalities did take place within prison, then this was only because of the irrationalities of the prisoners themselves.

In this particular inquiry, five prisoners as well as Davitt (now a Member of Parliament) had been called to give evidence, confirming, as it were, the openness of such procedures of investigation – the authorities had nothing to hide. Prisoners were given a voice and even Sir Edmund Du Cane was questioned about the charges of abuse made by One who has endured it (1877) in his book *Five Years Penal Servitude*. His response was:

> If there had been any important charge you would have found it exhibited in that book; as a matter of fact, there is nothing, excepting small acts of harshness, it may be, on the part of warders, which are certainly counter-balanced by statements of other acts of kindness; and to my mind it is very remarkable how that book shows that our system of inspection and supervision entirely answers its purpose. There are several cases enumerated in which the prisoner makes his complaint and gets redress as against the warder. (*Report of the Commissioners*

Appointed to Inquire into the Working of the Penal Servitude Acts,
1879: 46)[10]

Here, it was as if Du Cane and One who has endured it were formally
equals before the Committee, each providing a point of view which the
Committee would then impartially adjudicate on. As, indeed, it did so
here, in what had become the usual way: 'after examining a variety of
witnesses, we have come to the conclusion that the system of penal servitude as at present administered is, on the whole satisfactory; that it is
effective as a punishment, and free from serious abuses' (1879: xxi). For
Du Cane, this was a vindication of the entire prison establishment and
confirmation of who was 'telling the truth':

> We have awaited the result of this inquiry with perfect confidence for,
> though we were aware of course, that statements had been made which
> produced an unfavourable impression on those who accepted them
> without inquiry, we were equally aware that they could not stand the
> test of investigation ... the too ready acceptance of such statements and
> the adoption of them as grounds for investigation are not only
> especially unfair to officers who cannot defend themselves against these
> imputations on their character, but are very much against the public
> interest, which cannot be served by undermining the credit and position
> of prison officers. (*Report of the Directors of Convict Prisons,*
> 1879–80: v–vi)

By now, it was as if the process of inquiry had so helped to legitimize the
penal system itself (rather than cast unnecessary aspersions on his staff),
that Du Cane could raise the issue of whether any more inquiries were
necessary: was it not now obvious who told the truth and who did not?

Strengthening the Bureaucracy

The Prisons Act 1877 completed the shift towards central government
control of prisons: the ownership of all the local prisons was vested in the
Secretary of State, to be overseen by a body of Commissioners (maximum
five) whom the Home Secretary would appoint: the Commissioners, with
Du Cane as Chairman, assumed responsibility for the whole prison
administration; of 113 local prisons transferred to it, 38 were promptly
closed. This was a rationalizing measure, which further distanced, in an
administrative sense, local community involvement with the prison:

> Both the inspectors and the justices would be kept, but all would
> perform their duties in a modified form. The inspectors would become
> assistants to the Commissioners, on whose behalf they would visit and
> report upon prisons, while the justices would henceforward act as local
> inspectors with appropriate changes being made to the mode of

appointment and method of reporting, to reflect their new relationship
to the Home Secretary. (McConville, 1995: 474)

The age of formal inquiry that had marked the development of the
modern prison from around 1850 was now drawing to a close. While there
had been eight such inquiries between 1850 and 1879 in relation to
various aspects of prison life, only a further three followed between 1880
and 1899. In effect, as Du Cane had suggested, there was now very little
need for them. The battle for the truth about prisons was virtually over.
And as the public became more distanced from the prison itself, so the
only sources of knowledge available to it were the carefully scripted and
increasingly anodyne annual reports from the authorities themselves. By
the same token, as the idea of imprisonment, and all that this stood for,
became more embedded in the nineteenth-century social fabric, so its
centralized administration came to be more taken for granted, less
contested.

It seems, as well, that the authorities by this stage were becoming
more adept at heading off potential scandals from prisoner revelations
that would otherwise call into question the validity of their own sanitized accounts. For example, after Davitt's claim that bedclothes were
sometimes soiled with faeces (*Report of the Commissioners Appointed
to Inquire into the Working of the Penal Servitude Acts*, 1879: 519) and
that of One who has suffered (1882: 5) that blankets and rugs were
never washed, laundry facilities were improved and elementary personal
cleanliness was facilitated by the issue of bed sheets (*Report of the
Prison Commissioners*, 1883). The authorities were still extremely
anxious not to attract public attention to themselves in such ways and
thereby make more transparent and open to question the power and
prestige that they had been establishing. Hence the concerns of Home
Secretary Cross in 1878: 'while it is commonly admitted that it is better
that ninety-nine guilty persons should escape conviction than one innocent man should suffer, it may also be fairly said that it is better that
any number of prisoners should be somewhat more favourably treated
than they deserve to be, than one man, through any unnecessary prison
treatment, or want of early care should fall sick or die' (McConville,
1995: 309).

Nonetheless, it was impossible to suppress all scandal: there were
reports of suspicious deaths in custody in the 1880s, and further revelations of prison conditions which differed markedly from those to be found
in official discourse. Some of these could still carry considerable weight, as
with the claims made by John Burns, a trade unionist imprisoned for
unlawful assembly and later an MP (see McConville, 1995: 558), and other
energetic individuals with an interest in penal reform such as Michael
Davitt and the Reverend William Morrison, alongside sections of the popular press such as *The Daily Chronicle*. In the early 1890s, their convergence
produced a fierce attack on the prisons. What lay at the heart of the

complaints was the contention that the very process of bureaucratization necessary for the administration of the modern prison *in itself* led to systemic privation and inhumanity: 'across the whole system with its outward cleanliness and smoothness and decorum, lies in a word the hateful trend of torture, torture not so much for the hardened sinner, who can in the end settle down to gaol life, as for the less guilty inmates' (*The Daily Chronicle*, 25 January 1894: 5). Indeed, as Morrison (1894: 461) claimed, the regimes that bureaucratization had made possible were thought to be destroying the spirit of prisoners, leading to their inevitable return to prison on release – and ultimately contributing to the failure of the prison on the deterrence terms that had been set for it from the 1860s. In contrast to the cold, distant, bureaucratized system of administration that had been established, he argued:

> The old local prison administration was a system which kept the ruling classes in touch with social miseries in their acutest form ... Local power created local interest and a sense of local responsibility ... [now] in almost all questions relating to the criminal population ... dilettantism has secured possession of the field. It is from secretaries of benevolent associations and other highly placed officials whose knowledge of criminal offenders is mostly paper knowledge that the public are just now deriving their opinions on criminal matters.

However, Du Cane, in his response to the Gladstone Committee, which had been summoned to address such concerns, was highly sceptical of such possibilities:

> The truth is that when the revival of local interest in the prison is talked of, it assumes that all or most localities alike took such an active and intelligent part in the administration of their prisons as was undoubtedly taken by a few. There were however certainly other samples of local supervision in those days ... Again, the discharged prisoners' aid societies are now locally managed perfectly independent, yet in many cases the work is practically done by the chaplain or some other person, and local interest appears so little to be relied on that the Committee find it necessary to recommend that they should be supervised by the inspectors or officials appointed for the purpose. (Du Cane, 1895: 283)

The point he was correctly making was that one of the inevitable consequences of bureaucratization, in itself a necessity for modernization and standardization, was the exclusion of local bodies and interests from prison involvement. Indeed, it now seemed to be only a very small elite group who did have any interest in such matters, as Laslett-Browne (1895: 233), a defender of Du Cane, intimated: 'outside a narrow circle ... the public believe that our prison system has been conducted with all humanity, with undoubted economy, and with a reasonable amount of success. Progress in such matters is slow, but it is the safest and goes the farthest'.

As it was, the subsequent *Report of the Gladstone Committee* (1895) did not disturb the existing axis of penal power concentrated in the central state and its bureaucratic organizations. If anything, it only strengthened it. Within this framework, but only within it, it acceded that there might now be another shift in the bureaucratically adjustable balance of prison administration with its polarities of severity and humanitarianism – this time towards the latter:

> the centralization of authority has been a complete success in the direction of uniformity, discipline and economy. On the other hand it carried with it some inevitable disadvantages ... while much attention has been given to organization, finance, order, health of the prisoners and prison statistics, the prisoners have been treated too much as a hopeless or worthless element of the community, and the mood as well as the legal responsibility of the prison authorities has been held to cease when they pass outside of the prison gates. (1895: 7)

The Committee were now taking note of the broader role of the state that was beginning to emerge at this time, and its incumbent duty to ensure the well-being of all its subjects – even its prisoners: it was prepared to reduce the social distance between prisoners and the rest of society, and at the same time it acknowledged that their everyday conditions could be enhanced by taking note of the scientific knowledge of experts in these affairs: it would then be left to the central state bureaucracy beyond the purview of Parliament to put any such changes into effect.

This was to be the last major inquiry in England into aspects of prison life for nearly four decades.[11] Not because there were no longer brutalities, hardships and so on, but because the accounts of the authorities in which such matters were denied or ignored had come to be accepted as 'the truth': alternative versions of this – prisoner accounts, or Galsworthy's play – could be simply dismissed or explained away as the product of ignorance and lack of understanding. Such declamations were unlikely to be challenged, so long as the prison seemed proximate to what was expected of it in a civilized society: that it should be hidden from view and not intrude upon public sensitivities. On this basis, the prison authorities would only be challenged when particular scandals erupted (prison was claimed to be too lenient or too severe) or when it seemed incapable of performing the function allotted to it in modern society (removing and safekeeping the undesirable). The subsequent quiescence of the public on prison matters and the absence of inquiry seemed to Du Cane's successor, Ruggles-Brise (1921: 47), confirmation of their satisfaction with the prison system: 'the gloom and mystery which was popularly supposed to envelop the convict system has largely disappeared, and greater public confidence in the administration has taken its place'. Ironically, his book was published in the aftermath of the Official Secrets Act 1920, which further emphasized the secrecy of prison and the power of bureaucratic control by making it an offence for all its employees to disclose information on it without permission. As such, the gloom and mystery he refers to had indeed disappeared – at least from the main sources of knowledge about prison that were now publicly available: for the most part, the annual reports of his own bureaucracy and officially sanctioned memoirs such as his own, where he claimed that 'it is no exaggeration to say that the harshness and abuse of authority are as rare in English prisons as instances and examples of kind and considerate treatment are abundant'. With such assurances and the absence of believable evidence to the contrary, there was no need for any further inquiry: it was the authorities who told the truth – how could it be otherwise?

Indifference

Up to the early nineteenth century, the general public had been centrally involved in the punishment process: from thereon, they had been progressively excluded. However, they were not simply passive onlookers as the newly created penal bureaucracies drew a curtain across these particular 'distasteful scenes'. This certainly did happen but it also happened in conjunction with another of the consequences of the civilizing process. Self-restraint and a desire not to become involved began to repress any inclination for such participation. The sight of prisoners began to provoke feelings of disgust and revulsion. As we know, the prisoners themselves noticed how at least some members of the public would avert their gaze on such occasions; nor did the public want prisons built in their own localities. In addition, it became increasingly clear that they were prepared to eschew any opportunity for involvement in the administration of prisons. The distancing caused by bureaucratization allied to the wish not to become involved generated a sense of moral indifference (Bauman, 1989) to the prisons and what happened within them on the part of the public. As they had become places that should be hidden away, so their prisoners were tainted with the shame associated with these institutions: such ugliness, moral and physical, made the public avoid them. Demonized in this way, the public had little interest in the removal of the prisoners and to what subsequently happened to them.

What had been the initial response of the public to the bureaucratization of penal control? Mary Carpenter had recognized early on what was the crucial issue here. At that time, criminals could no longer be physically expelled, or sent away in some capacity or other, whether by means of death or transportation. Instead, she wrote:

> Convicts are *ours*, and we cannot, if we would, shake off the responsibility, however painful it is. It behoves us to consider the 'treatment'

which 'our convicts' should receive. Here, again, we shall be met by an unwillingness to regard such a subject as a part of our duty, ours as private individuals ... we do not comprehend the principles which guide our legislators. We are quite sure that they wish to do the best they possibly can; *we know that they have built great prisons for these people, on the most new and approved plans; we know that the convicts must be very bad, and we had better leave the management of them in the hands of those who have undertaken the whole thing – what have we to do with their treatment?* (1864: 3: my italics)

As she recognized, not only would the growth of this new form of penal administration shut the public out of any involvement with the punishment process; at the same time, the public themselves would *want* to be shut out of it, would prefer to leave its whole enforcement to the authorities. This would be both a natural product of bureaucratization itself and at the same time a reflection of those growing sensitivities in the civilized world associated with the avoidance of 'disturbing events'. Once the prison itself came to have an institutionalized presence in modern society as the most predominant, most dramatic form of penal control available, what public interest that there had been in the novelty that the new prisons initially represented soon evaporated. There would still, of course, be opportunities to 'scan' the prisoners for those insensitive enough to do so, but as such opportunities came to be restricted, so the attitude of avoidance came to inject itself into the habitus of citizens in the civilized world.

After Carpenter's comments, the public's lack of knowledge and indifference to what was happening behind the prison walls receive regular affirmation from the prison authorities. For example:

> Whereas before 1863 but few years went by without either Parliamentary Committees or Commissions on the subject, and it was continually discussed in one form or another in the popular press, there is now no demand for investigations of that nature, and in fact it is difficult to interest in it any but those who have some special official connection with it, or have taken it up as a special study. (*Report of the Directors of Convict Prisons*, 1871–2: 6)

Again, Sir Edmund Du Cane (1875: 303) told a social science congress that 'I gladly accept the inference that the public interest has decreased in [prison matters]'. If there now seems no doubt that Du Cane welcomed such disinterest, he was not being fanciful. It was becoming a common phenomenon across the civilized world, even in societies where greater public involvement in the absence of less well-developed bureaucratic structures of administration was encouraged.

The same sentiments were recorded in the state of Victoria at this time: 'it seems strange, while so much fault is found with the non-remunerated results of prison labour, that so little interest is taken by the community to facilitate industrial training and to ensure profitable results from the employment of the men and women confined in these establishments'

(*Report of the Inspector-General of Penal Establishments and Gaols*, 1878: 5). And:

> It seems strange that nearly £60000 should be expended annually for the maintenance of criminals, in a new country where so much work has to be done that they might well perform and on which their labour could be made remunerative to the state, and that yet the community should regard the matter with apparent indifference. (*Report of the Inspector-General of Penal Establishments and Gaols*, 1879: 5)

This fledgling bureaucracy actually needed some public involvement to assist in the more efficient management of penal labour – it could be a utility for the colony, a way of rationalizing otherwise expensive and unproductive state resources but, none was forthcoming. If this seemed 'strange' to the authorities, for the general public it was as if once an individual went to prison, they then faced permanent exclusion from the rest of society. Even on release, the mark of imprisonment they carried with them would permanently shut them out. Once they had been designated a criminal, and then removed, the public were indifferent to what subsequently happened to them, and would not allow such distasteful experiences to intrude upon their own everyday existence: why should they make any special effort to help ex-prisoners – were not these the very people who should be shunned and avoided? Such antipathies were seen as frustrating the attempts by the authorities to reduce recidivism, and thereby perpetuating the exclusion of the ex-prisoners:

> despite the more humane view of the treatment of crime nowadays, the previous repugnance to dealing with any who have been in gaol is deeply rooted, and it will be long before the mass of the community are able to dissociate the wrong and the wrongdoer ... an irrational public will not give offenders a second chance. (*Report of the Inspector-General of Penal Establishments and Gaols*, 1912: 7)

Again: 'the greatest hindrance to lasting reform occurs when the prisoner was released as, owing to the attitude of the public, there is a decided loss of status and the ex-prisoner secures recognition only in the original group and with a few philanthropic individuals' (*Report of the Inspector-General of Penal Establishments and Gaols*, 1925: 3).

In New Zealand, Captain Hume, the first Inspector of New Zealand prisons, had been keen to encourage public interest and involvement. With this in mind, he was prepared to keep the prisons open to 'members of both Houses of the legislature and all respectable persons' (*Report of the Inspector of Prisons*, 1884: 2) long after such gratuitous visiting had ceased in England. However, he was soon to report that 'the public are too ready to rest satisfied with knowing that prisoners are properly cared for and not maltreated without thinking whether proper measures are then taken for their reformation' (*Report of the Inspector of Prisons*, 1889: 2). In fact, he shows a complete misunderstanding of the sensibilities of the time. Unsophisticated members of the public (precisely those whom he did not wish to visit) might still have a lurid interest in such matters. Those whom he would have welcomed would increasingly find any such suggestion distasteful. As it was, detachment and disinterest became self-sustaining: 'I am afraid the general public have no idea as to what is being done in prison reform' (*Report of the Controller-General of Prisons*, 1920: 3). We find the same attitudes taking shape in New York. The State Commission of Prisons (1905:10) reported that 'comparatively few people know much about the conditions of jail even in their own countries'. This had now become a familiar claim made by liberals on matters of prison reform – assuming that if the public were more knowledgeable then this would inevitably lead to a greater pressure for humanitarian change – as if this would be their 'natural' sentiment. On this particular occasion, though, this independent inspectorate, established in 1895 for the purpose of making the state prison administration publicly accountable, soon recognized the lack of interest from the public in its own work. The authorities had mistaken indifference for ignorance: it was not simply the case that the general public had no knowledge of what was happening – they did not particularly want to know what was happening. Subsequent revelations of the Commission, for the most part, were met with this disinterest: 'physical conditions [in prison] have ... long been a scandal ... the incredible fact is that public opinion had for over half a century been aware of the barbarity of confining human beings in Sing Sing cells and has let it remain' (*Report of the State Commission of Prisons*, 1913: 12). Here, as elsewhere, only a specific scandal, and not the more general inhumanity that could be found in the prison system, seemed able to spark (temporarily) public interest and create the momentum for change. The removal of the governor of Sing Sing for corruption focussed public attention on this grim old prison with its tomb-like cells. The Grand Jury described them as 'unfit for the housing of animals, much less human beings' - they were 'a scandal to the state of New York' (*Report of the State Commission of Prisons*, 1914: 7). Change was not impossible, then. However, scandals and their momentum are usually short-lived. Lewis (1921: 333) wrote: 'the average American probably knew little of day to day conditions behind penitentiary walls'.

What was clear by the early twentieth century is that imprisonment was seen by the general public as a necessary receptacle for the unwanted or undesirable, but other than this, 'public indifference and neglect is largely responsible for the lack of worthwhile progress in the development and the improvement of our penal and correctional systems ... from time immemorial, the public has been content to send the offender to prison and feels a certain sense of satisfaction and security with the closing of the prison door' (Cass, 1931: 11). It might have seemed like time immemorial, but already the enormous intellectual energy, investment and public interest in prisons during the first half of the nineteenth century had been forgotten as the bureaucratic shroud that had been placed around it gradually cut it off from the mainstream of public life.

The growth of indifference did not mean, of course, that the prison faded altogether from public consciousness. Further scandals would periodically seep out from behind the prison walls and for a short time prison would be headline news. Thereafter, public indifference would again prevail, and the authorities would continue to produce their sanitized official documentation. In these respects, Sir Lionel Fox, Head of the English Prison Commission (1952: 130) was no doubt correct in his observation that 'when all is said and done, responsible publications on penal matters affect the minds of a minimal number of the public'.

It is not the case though, that the public had no interest at all in prisoners as prisoners. For most of them, however – the grey, shuffling, unnoticed shadows of human beings – the processes of bureaucratic enclosure and physical removal allied to public indifference, did indeed make them forgotten and unwanted. But there would always be others who stood out as different and memorable: the hideous nature of their crimes made them so, perhaps, or their superior social standing before going to prison might have the effect of turning them into fabled objects of curiosity. Sightings of such creatures – on railway stations awaiting transportation, or labouring on public works – might lead to a frenzy of excitement. Most civilized societies, in fact, were able to periodically produce heroes or demons of this kind: the unrepentant psychopath, for whom only the most severe privations in prisons were tolerable for the public; against this, there would be the daring frontiersman, eluding escape and preferring some kind of glorious final showdown with the authorities rather than surrender to imprisonment; or the sensitive artist who makes us weep with the anguish of his prison poetry; the murderer who turns out to be a tortured genius, and the escaped prisoner, brave enough to take on and taunt the authorities as they search for him.

In these respects, prisoner memoirs concerning escape, disappearance, the assumption of a new identity and so on – as exemplified above all perhaps, in the English example of Ronnie Biggs[12] – carried far more weight and interest as far as the general public were concerned than accounts of routinized deprivation while inside the prison: as did the memoirs of prisoner-demons – their glorification in crime would be of much greater interest to the public than accounts of the grey, drab mundane rituals that made prison life a chronic privation. But by and large these prisoners were rarities. The public had come to know very little indeed of prison life: they knew that it was not meant to be too lenient – prisoners should certainly not enjoy the experience of prison, nor should they be allowed to gain from it; but on the other hand, there were very clear limits to the extent to which they should suffer in prison: while they should endure all the pangs of a guilty conscience, all the physical and material deprivations of the pains of imprisonment, they were not to be deliberately brutalized. So long as the penal authorities ostensibly conformed to their regime of truth in this way, then it would seem that the general public were satisfied with existing arrangements: prisons protected them from fearsome criminals across whom, every now and again, its bureaucratic curtains might suddenly part to reveal tantalizing glimpses.

Notes

1 The bread and water penal diet, along with corporal punishment, was abolished in English prisons in the Criminal Justice Act 1967.

2 Act for effecting greater uniformity of practice in the government of the several prisons in England and Wales, for appointing inspectors of prisons in Great Britain 1835, Prisons Act 1865, 1877.

3 In 1857, these were reorganized in the form of Northern, Southern and Midland districts; in 1863 changed to Northern and Southern only (McConville, 1981: 488).

4 This voluminous production of penal discourse was not unique to England. Even in the two Australian states and New Zealand with their minute populations and lack of infrastructure compared to England we find inquiries: in Victoria, there was the *Report of the Select Committee of Inquiry into John Price's Administration of the Penal Department* (1857); the *Report of the Royal Commission on Prison and Penal Discipline* (1870) and the *Report of an Enquiry into Brutalities and Corruption at Pentridge Prison* (1885). In New South Wales there was the *Report of a Select Committee on Public Prisons in Sydney and Cumberland* (1861); the *Report of the Board Appointed to Investigate Certain Alleged Irregularities in the Gaol of Paramatta* (1861–2); and the *Report of the Royal Commission to Inquire into and Report on the General Management and Discipline of the Gaol at Berrrima* (1878–9). In New Zealand there was the *Report of the Royal Commission on Prisons* (1868). In New York, the voluntary Prison Association inspected and annually reported on the prisons from 1846 until the State Commission on Prisons was established in 1895. In Ontario, a Board of Inspection was created in 1858; there was also the *Report of the Commissioners Appointed to Enquire into Prisons and the Prison System of the Province of Ontario* (1879); and there were inquires into corruption and brutality at Kingston penitentiary (*Report of the Commissioners Appointed to Inquire into the Conduct, Discipline and Management of the Provincial Penitentiary*, 1849, 1850).

5 In addition to the Dickens novels, there was also Reade's (1856) *It's Never Too Late to Mend*, which was turned into play; there were also plays by Thomas Salt and Thomas Taylor (see Nellis, 1996).

6 Solitary confinement on sentencing had been reduced from its initial eighteen months with the opening of Pentonville to twelve months in 1849, reduced again to nine months in 1854 and then to three months just before the play was opened (see Nellis, 1996; cf. Radzinowicz and Hood, 1986: 502–3).

7 *Report of the Du Parq Committee* (1932). This was then followed, after another gap of more than the thirty years by the *Report of the Inquiry into Prison Escapes and Security* by Admiral of the Fleet, the Earl Mountbatten of Burma (1966). Canada is rather different in these respects, with its *Report of the Royal Commission to Investigate the Penal System of Canada* (1938). There had been no significant inquiries in that country from the late 19th century until then.

8 Galsworthy (1929) wrote one further prison play, *The Fugitive*, and a prison novel, *The Island Pharisees* (1904). Other than these, however, prison literature from the late nineteenth century came to be dwarfed by a much more voluminous literature on police and detection: the detective became glamourized and romanticized, not the criminal, in some of its genres; the police organization rather than the prison was fictionalized in others. The first significant English prison movie was not made until 1954. By that time, Nellis (1988) calculates that around 60 American prison movies had been made. Whatever the overall explanations for this difference, one of them may be the way in which the English public lost interest in them, along with the bureaucratic secrecy that enveloped them; in the United States, the differing standards, particularly in the South, may have galvinized interest: it may also point to more openness in that country.

9 Some of the earlier prisoner biographies (Rossa, 1882: 176–7, One who has suffered it, 1882: 60, Convict 77, 1903: 60), stress both the discretion that medical staff then had and also the kindness and concern of particular individuals.

10 This book, overall, was a fairly mild critique, directed in the main at acts of bullying by individual officers. What Du Cane did not make comment about, nor did the Commissioners pursue, was the institutionalized inequality of social relations within the prison, of which the very process of adjudication on disciplinary matters provides a clear example: 'the prisoner on entry [to the room] is divided from the governor and his clerk by strong iron railings, reaching from the floor to the ceiling. Against these he stands fronting the table at which the governor is seated, having before him not only the particular report on which the man is now brought up, in which is entered the history of man' (One who has endured it, 1877: 218).

11 Report of the Du Parq Committee (1932).

12 Biggs had been one of England's 'Great Train Robbers' in 1963. He escaped from his maximum security prison in 1965 and made his way to Australia. On his identity being uncovered in 1969, he then fled to Rio de Janeiro, where he lived for 30 years, before returning to England in 2001, seriously ill and impoverished. By then, he had become an icon for the modern-day romantic outlaw, periodically (and unsuccessfully) pursued by the police, with his exotic surroundings and lifestyle an attraction for the popular press (see Mackenzie, 1975).

8

The Breakdown of
Civilization

Here, then, were the effects of the civilizing process on penal development in England and similar societies around 1970. It had set in place a framework characterized by a complete absence of punishment to the human body; a largely invisible punishment apparatus; a commitment to the amelioration of penal sanctions; a sanitized formal language of punishment, largely stripped of any emotive vocabulary. This was then presided over by a specific configuration of penal power: the concentrated relationship between the state and its bureaucratic organizations on the one hand, an indifferent, excluded public on the other. Nonetheless, during the 1960s and 1970s something like a breakdown in civilization begins to take place: at least a breakdown of the penal arrangements that had come to be associated with England and similar societies, which at the same time helped to make the existing configuration of penal power unsustainable.

Degrees of Civilization

The effects of the civilizing process on penal development had varied from society to society, in a kind of continuum that stretched across the civilized world. At one end of this, we find the Scandinavian countries and Holland: they were seen as the leaders of the civilized world, the role model for others to follow, at least in relation to the way in which they punished criminals.[1] Such acclaim was based, first, on the rates of imprisonment to be found in these societies – indicators that they punished the least. In 1971, the rate of imprisonment in Holland, for example, was 22.4 per 100,000 of population and that for Norway 37.1. In contrast, that for England was 81.3, for Canada 90 per 100,000, New Zealand 92.7, Australia 128.2, and the United States 109, or, if local jails were included, 200 per 100,000 of population (Waller and Chan, 1974). Second, this acclaim was based on their conditions of imprisonment. In the penal institutions of these countries, described enviously by Austin (1967: 349) as 'homes away from home', it might often be difficult to determine who were prisoners and who were guards (Tollemache, 1973: Franke, 1995), the points of differentiation had become so blurred, the social distance and rigid lines of demarcation characteristic of prisons in England, for example, so reduced.

What had led to the development of such civilized penal arrangements in this part of the world? They were characteristic of the highly developed welfare state commitments of these North European countries, their strong interdependencies and their long histories of tolerance brought about by their geo-political circumstances (Downes, 1982). In addition, there also seems to have been high levels of functional democratization in these societies: everyone was made to feel that they had a role to play and were involved in their country's social and economic development. Notwithstanding the existence of very extensive central state bureaucratic organizations, essential for the administration of their vast welfare networks, these had not become distanced or remote from the general public. Unlike the English model where bureaucratic organizations had become largely closed off to public access and scrutiny, here there was considerably more openness and consultation, less factionalism and division; more collectivism, less indifference, more consensus, less confrontation (Mishra, 1984). The same can be said for penal development in these societies. The bureaucracies were prepared to open up as part of a regular forum of dialogue and discussion to the general public, politicians, the media, reform groups – all those who had some involvement and interest in penal affairs, including prisoners' rights groups: everyone was made to feel they had a point of view which was valued. As Christie (2000: 43) was later to write, 'a general effect of all these meeting places has probably been to establish some kind of informal minimum standard for what is considered decent in the name of punishment, and valid for all human beings'. These same societies invested heavily in scientific expertise (Tollemache, 1973), which again seemed to exemplify their position as leaders of the civilized world, but it was not allowed to occlude inhumanities or to elevate those who possessed such knowledge to some unimpeachable superior status to those who did not, whereby dialogue would become unnecessary and impossible. Overall, these arrangements seemed to allow for the rational, humanitarian penal development that came to be characteristic of these societies.

At the other end of this continuum we find the southern United States.[2] Taking Georgia as an exemplar of this region, in 1971 this state had had the fourth highest rate of imprisonment in the United States (258 per 100,000 of population). In addition, it had executed more than any other state in that country (369) between 1930 and 1967 and the third most (102) between 1950 and 1967, the point when this penalty fell into abeyance. This dramatic difference in the level and character of the way it punished from the leaders of the civilized world reflects the different history of the civilizing process in that region. Prior to the American Civil War, its effect had been minimal in the 'Deep South'. The social structure of these states, cultural values, interdependencies and modes of knowledge were arranged around their identities as slave societies. The consequences of slavery not only flowed through all the tributaries to their social and penal arrangements, but in themselves created extremely short and rigid chains of interdependencies and the most extreme forms of social distance – between slaves and non-slaves, between blacks and whites. It is hardly surprising, then, that punishments to the human body (particularly by whites on blacks) were tolerated in Georgia and the rest of this region when they were fast becoming intolerable elsewhere. There was also a high value on individualism and paternalism and little by way of centralized state authority; it was a region where immediate response to perceived insult or insubordination had become 'second nature', rather than being kept in check by self-restraint. As such, there was little by way of state imprisonment, and in the absence of the state's monopolistic control of the power to punish, a much stronger emphasis on the use of informal methods to resolve conflicts or inflict punishment, such as duelling or other highly ritualized forms of physical combat (Wyatt-Brown, 1982; Greenberg, 1990).

The civil war destroyed this social structure. During the late nineteenth and early twentieth centuries we find a slow shift away from the agrarianism that had been necessary to keep the plantation as its focal point and instead a move towards industrialization and urbanization. However, the war had much less impact on the cultural values of the former slave societies and the myths and prejudices on which these were based. Southern penality began to reflect the new social order, while still carrying the cultural legacy of slavery and its attendant beliefs. This meant that there was, first, a continued tolerance for publicly visible punishments of which the chain gangs became one of the most notorious examples (Steiner and Brown, 1927). Second, there was a continued tolerance of overt brutality and violence. The conditions of chain gang life were no secret in the South – it was just that the public found them and the sight of the chain gang itself entirely acceptable at a time when such sights and conduct had been removed from the rest of the civilized world.

Third, the weak, fragile and largely undeveloped state authority that had been set in place, allowed for the continuity of informal sanctioning practices which now took on new forms specific to the concerns of the dominant social groups in the South: disempowered and dispossessed whites sought to cling on to power and reactivate former glories by terrorizing local black communities in the form of vigilantism and lynching.[3] This would frequently involve the commission of spectacularly vile barbarities on black men before large audiences of white men, women and children.[4] Such activities continued well into the 1930s. It is at this point, however, that the growth and extension of federal power begin to dominate local arrangements and also bolster the authority of the local state. Southern societies became more heterogeneous: populations became more mobile as a result of the modernization of transport systems. Elite groups – newspaper editors, womens' organizations and others – began to speak out against what they now saw as the shamefulness of these and other features of Southern penality; concomitantly, law enforcement processes began to exert greater authority and were able to replace informal extra-legal responses to crime and social problems with the more formal arrangements to be found elsewhere in the civilized world.

For the first time, in the 1930s, state executions exceeded the numbers of unlawful lynchings in Georgia (Clarke, 1998). The establishment of a State Board of Corrections in 1946 marked the beginnings of penal control through a modern bureaucratic organization in that state. This newly established authority expressed its own commitment to a framework of punishment that would be in line with the standards expected of a civilized society. The *Report of the* [Atlanta] *State Board of Corrections* (1961: 4) referred to 'the changes of the last few years: from notorious chain gangs of international disrepute to modern penitentiaries'. Now we can discern a shift in the penal habitus of such societies taking place: from open disregard for suffering and blatant racial prejudice to more scientific objectivity and the pursuit of rehabilitation. The *Report of the State Board of Corrections* advertised the slogan 'Rehabilitation Pays' and referred to 'programs aimed at returning inmates to society as useful and productive citizens – [and] correctional officer training is being provided, so they are not just prison guards' (1965: 5).

Nonetheless, while we might now find the same language and framework of punishment as in other civilized societies, Georgia, like the rest of this region, still punished excessively by comparison:[5] if changes in state formation and the increased sensitivity of elite groups had helped to set in place this modern penal bureaucracy, it was still at a vulnerable, fragile stage of development. Equally, there had been no sudden transformation of the residue of punitive hostility that was part of the local cultural legacy. In effect, the modern penal bureaucracies in this region, instead of insulating themselves from the general public or providing a buffer against their influence on penal development, became, as it were, a funnel for these sentiments, leading to the characteristics of dramatically high levels of imprisonment and execution in Georgia and the rest of the South.

The Unwanted Public

In England and similar societies, the penal bureaucracies had become largely detached from any sense of public accountability and scrutiny during the first half of the twentieth century, steadily becoming more prepared to move in advance of it while placing increasing emphasis on scientific expertise as the driving force of penal policy. Possession of this knowledge only seemed to heighten the divisions between themselves as experts and the unknowledgeable general public, ultimately leading to an unbridgeable gulf between them. In the late nineteenth century, Sir Edmund Du Cane (1885: 172) made the point that prisoners were not paid for their work: 'public opinion demanded that prisoners throughout their sentence should have only the barest necessaries in the way of food and just sufficient money on discharge to enable them to maintain themselves while seeking employment'. At this stage, public opinion was seen as an important referent, even for Du Cane, which the authorities should not move ahead of. When the penal element in prison diet was removed in the early twentieth century, the Prison Commissioners had to defend themselves against public concerns that it had become too generous:

> We feel it necessary to guard against the impression which might be informed from the fact that a small section of the criminal community openly prefers prison to the workhouse, that therefore prison life is unduly attractive ... and that the whole edifice should be reconstructed to meet the special case of a few ne'er do wells who have lost all sense of self-respect, and it is a matter of indifference whether they spend a few nights in a workhouse, a prison or a barn. (*Report of the Prison Commissioners*, 1902: 14)

In making such a defence, however, the authorities were now at least confident enough to concede that there *would* be some who enjoyed a better life in prison than outside – this, though, would no longer compel them to reduce conditions for all, as it had in the second half of the nineteenth century: as if their own position within the axis of penal power had become significantly stronger, and they were less tied to public opinion.

A decade later, the authorities responded to further public concerns about 'pampering':

> We are quite aware that we ally ourselves to criticism in proposing an increased grant of money for the entertainment of prisoners who need it chiefly because of the number of their crimes. But the difficulty in practice is a real one; and since good literature is a reformative influence and we do not think that the hope of eventual reform should ever be abandoned, and since cases do occur of men who after repeated terms of penal servitude take to an honest life and maintain it, we think that that criticism should be faced, and that the slight increase we propose should be made in respect of the convict prisons. (*Report of the Prison Commissioners*, 1911–12: 27)

We begin to see the emergence of a more confident penal bureaucracy, being prepared to introduce reforms, notwithstanding the likelihood of public opposition. Against subsequent complaints that prisons had become too comfortable, the response of the authorities was:

> Our constant effort is to hold the balance between what is necessary as
> punishment ... and what can be condoned in the way of humanizing
> and reforming influences. It is, we hope, quite unnecessary to refute the
> idle statements which contain currency among those unacquainted with
> the system that prisons are made comfortable ... they are only comfort-
> able so far as the laws of hygiene compel cleanliness and wholesome
> food, and decent clothing – all things which are often absent in the lives
> of persons who come to prison. The penalty of crime is not in fantastic
> devices for causing pain or discomfort or cruelty. This was the old
> idea which has long since passed away. (*Report of the Prison
> Commissioners*, 1922: 19)

At least, it had passed away from official discourse. Its production was
now guided by a combination of humanitarian efficiency and scientific
expertise, even if this led to penal regimes that moved ahead of what public
opinion was thought to be on such matters. The authorities still felt that
public opinion was a referent, but a growing distance was now beginning
to open up between themselves and the public, for whom such knowledge
was both beyond them and not open to them. In these respects, public
opinion began to be seen as a bulwark against the ameliorative tendencies
of the authorities, an unnecessary hindrance to penal development, rather
than a legitimate check on it. Hence the frustration the authorities begin to
express over public opposition to the presence of prisons:

> for many years the Commissioners have drawn attention to the unsuit-
> ability of many of our prisons for the development of reforms on
> modern lines ... in recent years the Commissioners have seized every
> opportunity that offered of acquiring land adjacent to existing prisons
> either for cultivation or to enable much needed extensions to be made.
> But this is not everywhere possible since many prisons, though origi-
> nally built on the outskirts of large farms, have long since been engulfed
> by the rising tide of suburban development. (*Report of the Prison
> Commissioners*, 1937: 30)

In the post-war period, as the central state assumed more wide-ranging
powers of intervention and control, so the penal bureaucracy became
increasingly self-serving, increasingly confident of its own abilities and
dismissive of public opinion: 'one cannot be unaware that the body of
assumptions underlying the common talk of common people and direct-
ing their praise and praise alone are not in these matters, the assumptions
on which contemporary prison administration is based' (Fox, 1952: 137).
It was as if public opinion had no right to hold back the more expert-
driven policy development of this period, or even intrude upon it: 'it is
less to purely physical conditions than to methods of treatment and control that the flavour pampering seems nowadays to attack. This can be
ascribed only to a failure to appreciate either the nature or purpose of
the methods of imprisonment'. It is also clear that the authorities no
longer felt constrained by such misconceptions. We can see this in the

discussion of the development of Grendon Underwood psychiatric prison in the 1950s:

> There appears to be misunderstanding in some quarters as to the functions which it is intended this new establishment should serve ... it needs to be emphasized that it is not intended that the institution should become solely or even mainly an establishment for psychopaths. The orientation will be treatment/research, and to weight the clinical climate with the more difficult and often irreversible psychopathic personalities would vitiate the forward looking therapeutic atmosphere which it is hoped will obtain. It is therefore likely that the cases selected will be those with real therapeutic promise, and it may be that those [psychopaths] will not be sent to this establishment at all, and certainly not initially. (*Report of the Prison Commissioners*, 1954: 101)

The prison was built, notwithstanding public wishes to the contrary and 'psychopaths' were not excluded from it. The interests of science, outweighing the concerns of public opinion, made its presence necessary. Overall, the more the authorities were able to rid themselves of the restraints of public opinion on penal development, the more they became condescending and patronizing of it. As Sir John Simon, Under-secretary of the State at the Home Office put it:

> The public should accept something less than one hundred per cent security. Protection of this standard, or something like it, could no doubt be brought about by the strategic confinement of prisoners by loading them with fetters and manacles and irons and so on. No one today would countenance such a thing. It would not only inflict grave injury on the prisoners, but would debase and brutalize the society which perpetrated such infamy ... if society wants to develop the positive and redemptive side of prison work, it must face the fact that the occasional prisoner may escape and do damage. (quoted in the *Report of the Director of Penal Services*, 1957: 8)

In contrast, then, to the functional democratization at work in the Northern European societies, and instead of acting as a funnel for populist cultural values as in the southern United States, in England in particular the penal establishment around 1960 had become a unified, exclusive bureaucratic organization, in which the state itself had confidence.[6] Its particular place in the configuration of penal power had certainly meant that public sentiments had had increasingly less influence on penal development. Indeed, one or two scandals aside, the public had become increasingly indifferent to it. There were none of the shameful associations that popular sentiments had brought about or had allowed to continue in the southern United States. However, if such a configuration was thus able to avoid the excesses of the penal arrangements in the Deep South, it provided none of the momentum to move towards levels and conditions of imprisonment that would be more on a par with the standards set by the leaders of the civilized world. Instead, it was as if the existing arrangements worked adequately enough: punishment, especially imprisonment, had become a largely uncontroversial, non-politicized issue. What the authorities said had become the unchallenged and unchallengeable truth about prison and prison life. Instead of dialogue and discussion with prisoners, members of the penal establishment only warned the public not to be taken in by the prisoners' claims.[7] In ways that were characteristic of organizational myopia and inertia, denial, dismissal, and ridicule were all that were needed from the authorities to uphold the validity of their own proclamations, and for the general public to acquiesce in their untroubling, undisturbing penal administration: 'we have noted with regret that public comment on the state of discipline in prisons has sometimes tended to give the impression that ... there has been a deterioration giving ground for anxiety. This is not the case' (*Report of the Prison Commissioners*, 1954: 1). The same report also acknowledged that there had been disturbances at Wandsworth and a hunger strike at Parkhurst, but dismissed both as follows: 'discontent with the standard of meals was the prime motive, though subsequent investigations failed to reveal anything beyond minor points which could have given grounds for concern' (1954: 3).

There were no inherent difficulties, then; such disorders were the work of troublemakers who would inevitably be found in prison. Or if there were difficulties, then this was simply the prisoners' fault: it was their fault that sanitary arrangements were breaking down, and not 'the faults of plumbing or negligence on the part of the prison staff' (*Report of the Prison Commissioners*, 1958: 8). Equally, the authorities could draw on their own sanitized language of expertise to justify the existing boundary lines and demarcation border between themselves and their prisoners, describing them as being 'of immature personality, [who] exhibit hysterical traits, exaggerate symptoms, are sometimes activated by ulterior motives and from their situations tend to lose a sense of perspective' (*Report of the Prison Commissioners*, 1955: 9). How could these experts conduct any kind of dialogue with such a group as this?

The Breakdown of Civilization

Sir Harold Scott, another former Head of the English Prison Commission (1959: 73–4) wrote that 'mutiny in English prisons is not a serious danger. Our best safeguard against it is the careful selection and training of all ranks, the administration of just rules, and giving every opportunity to every prisoner to make requests or complaints to the Commissioners or the Secretary of State.' It might well have seemed the case, so ensconced had these officials now become, so self-confident of their own abilities to gloss over the inadequacies of their own institutions. It is from this point, however, that a breakdown in the penal arrangements they presided over begins to be set in place – in part at least because of the very effects of the remoteness, isolation and exclusivity of these same bureaucratic organizations. It was a breakdown that upset many of the assumptions associated with penal development in those societies and took the following form.

From the Civilized to the Uncivilized Prison

First, instead of the prison existing as a largely unknown and unknowable site of obedience (and one which the public would be largely indifferent to), it became instead a prominent site of disorder and disruption. Notwithstanding Scott's prognostications, rioting, strikes and escapes were to become a normal feature of prison life in England in the 1960s and 1970s (Fitzgerald, 1977; Adams, 1994), to the point where, when the authorities could note that 'there were no coordinated demonstrations and disturbances ... just sporadic and isolated incidents' (*Report on the Work of the Prison Department*, 1973: 9), this relative peacefulness in itself was seen as worthy of comment. By then, the peacefulness and tranquillity characteristic of the prison reports up to the 1960s had been dissipated by successive scandals that brought the prison back into public prominence. After the escape of the Great Train robber Charles Wilson, *The Times* (13 August 1964: 11) reported: 'this must reduce the general public to despair about the capacity of the forces arrayed against crime to deal with it effectively ... this time the public has the right to demand that the authorities get to the bottom of it. That the need should have arisen is a monumental scandal'. As had come to be the case, scandal provided the prisons with unwelcome publicity for the authorities. It would prize open their monopolistic control, raise questions about what was found in them, when really such matters had been turned by the authorities into issues beyond common-sense scrutiny. Now, however, it was as if scandal had become systemic, symptomatic of the way in which prisons were no longer performing the functions the public expected of them and by so doing, calling into question the authority and expertise of the organizations responsible for their administration.

Nor were such problems confined to England. In New Zealand, there were regular reports of trouble during the 1960s, and then of prisoners going on hunger strike at the new maximum security prison in 1968, after experiencing 'problems of adjustment' with further prison disturbances throughout the prison system. Disturbances had been particularly rife in the United States, with the worst being in Attica in 1971 which left 43 men dead (Wicker, 1975; Adams, 1994). What was it though, that had brought about the change from obedience to confrontation in the prisoners? By now, the social distance between the prison authorities and the prisoners had significantly narrowed, as a result of the succession of ameliorative reforms that had been put in place. As we know, for some prisoners these changes had meant very little, for others, they only brought on new privations. Nonetheless, there was an affectivity to these changes – they were not fictional – and they allowed some prisoners at least to assume a greater confidence and self-respect: they could begin to see themselves as human beings. Their memoirs confirm this, even if they simultaneously still deplore the food, the clothing and so on. Baker (1961: 163) thus writes of his transfer to Leyhill, the first prison in England to let its prisoners wear pyjamas and which had a dining hall like 'a large café'. There was a cricket ground and a new rule book – *Meet Leyhill* – 'a neatly printed pamphlet with a coloured cover'. Even on his later transfer back to Wormwood Scrubs he found 'lawns, flowers, shrubs and an aviary. Scaffolding had already been erected for the installation of showers, baths and a replacement for the old and dreadful lavatory resources' (1961: 191). As such, 'the relationship between officers and prisoners had now altered beyond all recognition' (1961: 192). In such ways, the prisoners' status had indeed been raised, leading to the possibility of providing them with an increased sense of solidarity and a reduction of the gulf between themselves and the prison staff. Yet, notwithstanding these changes, the prisoners themselves remained exactly as they were: prisoners, fixed firmly to the bottom of the prison hierarchy, still outsiders. There was no sense in which the improvement in their conditions reflected some more general blurring of the boundaries between themselves and their guards – and opportunities for constructive dialogue with the penal establishment about their conditions were largely non-existent. The effects of the reforms were thus to increase the prisoners' confidence to challenge the rigid lines of demarcation that marked prison existence, and to express their intolerance of their conditions and demand improvements, notwithstanding the reforms that had been introduced, rather than acquiesce in them. Not having any legitimate channels for this, the illegitimate channel of confrontation and dispute became the only means available to them.

The subsequent escalation in the scale of violence and disorder confirms the changing nature of the configuration of power within the prisons at this time.[8] At the same time, the responses that the authorities were prepared to make to these breakdowns of prison order were circumscribed by their own formal commitment to civilized practices of tolerance and restraint. The formal expectations, at least, were that they would respond to prisoners as human beings, rather than degraded animals: this was the behaviour expected of the penal establishment in the civilized world, even if it may only have demonstrated their own continuing weakness, both to the prisoners and the on-looking public as the mass media made visible these power struggles:

The department's policy was ... to handle demonstrations in a low key so as to avoid unnecessary confrontation, but to make it clear that boundaries must be properly set to the behaviour that could reasonably be tolerated and that firm action would be taken with prisoners who overstepped these limits. This balance was generally achieved. Most of the demonstrations were passive, often taking the form of sit-downs, and remained orderly and good natured ... that such potentially explosive situations as any prisoner demonstration inevitably presents were handled with a degree of professionalism that enabled them to be so effectively contained is greatly to the credit of the prisoners and staff of all the establishments concerned. (*Report on the Work of the Prison Department*, 1973: 45)

By the same token, attempts by the authorities to reassert the essential functions of the prison – effective containment – and thereby prevent disorder may only have helped to bring about the opposite effect. A new emphasis was given to security (*Report of the Inquiry into Prison Escapes and Security*, 1966; *Report of the Advisory Council on the Penal System*, 1968). The architecture of prison began to reflect these new concerns:

[P]ost war training prisons ... had been designed on the assumption that the buildings themselves could be made so secure that a fence sufficient to hinder rather than to prevent escapes could replace the traditional perimeter wall. This assumption, and the buildings designed on it, have since had to be modified ... the prison service now has to contend with a much higher proportion of escape orientated prisoners than it did even a few years ago ... the imposition of more stringent security precautions can be detrimental to the treatment and training of prisoners and many lessons have had to be and are being learned about the reconciliation of tighter security with more constructive regimes and more relaxed and civilized living conditions. (*Report on the Work of the Prison Department*, 1967: 3)

However, the accrued changes that had impacted on prisoner culture could not simply be removed by building stronger walls and fences. Instead, the new security initiatives and classifications could have the effect of enhancing the prisoners' sense of solidarity and self-worth – they were turned into 'special category' prisoners (see McVicar, 1974), as distinct from the shuffling, shambling body of 'grey men' who up to then had been so prominent in much of the prison literature: now, it was as if the authorities no longer pitied them but feared them instead (Cohen and Taylor, 1972).

Furthermore, in the United States, the growing concentration of black prisoners, around 50 per cent of the total population by 1970, contributed to the sense of prisoner solidarity in that country: the cover on the annual prison report in New York State (*Report on the Department of Correctional Services*, 1978) showed a Black Moslem prisoner at prayer.

The continuing resistance of prisoners across these societies led to a growing recognition that even as prisoners they had certain inalienable rights, which even imprisonment could not take away.[9] In the ensuing contestation and determination of these rights, conflict actually worsened. In England, 'the total of thirty-two incidents of concerted indiscipline by groups of inmates including rooftop demonstrations by five or more prisoners was in line with the average for the previous five years' (*Report on the Work of the Prison Service*, 1980: 5). In Victoria there were reports of 'an increase in tension' (*Report of the Director of Penal Services*, 1972, 1973) and 'rioting at Pentridge' and 'serious disturbances' (*Report of the Director of Correctional Services*, 1978). In New South Wales, there were major riots at Bathurst and other prisons in 1974 (*Report of the Director of Corrective Services*, 1975–6). In British Columbia there had been 'a growing number of hostage incidents' (*Report of the Corrections Branch*, 1974). Colvin (1982) noted that there had been a further 39 disturbances between 1971 and 1980 in American prisons.

Increasing Imprisonment, Deteriorating Conditions

Second, levels of imprisonment and prison conditions were beginning to depart from the standards expected of civilized societies. In many ways, this was the product of the very success of the penal bureaucracies in hiding their property away, so that it would not disturb public sensibilities, in remaining closed off from debate and scrutiny, of not wanting to unsettle the arrangements that had made this possible, because they were so well suited to their own interests. However, the retreat of the prison to the margins of the civilized world had also meant that it had been starved of significant resources and was usually placed last in the queue behind more socially desirable and welcomed initiatives when government expenditure was shared around:

> The erection of prisons is a slow and costly business and it would have been completely wrong for the department to have sought to build prisons which may or may not have been needed, particularly at a time when the erection of schools, hospitals and houses could have had a high priority. (*Report of the Comptroller-General of Prisons*, 1956–7: 5)

What resources that had been made available for prison development in the early post-war period were usually spent on high-profile, treatment-oriented services, or on improvements to furnishings or visiting arrangements rather than any straightforward expansion of bed space, or even in elementary improvements to hygiene: 'all progressive prison systems have recognized this responsibility [to reform prisoners] and is shown by the development of educational, vocational, medical, psychological, religious, recreational and social training ... in all these fields, the prison system of this state has made and continues to make advances' (*Report of the Comptroller-General of Prisons,* 1964: 35). In such ways, the prison had remained starved of resources that might increase the possibilities of physical expansion and provide for a significant improvement to material conditions at a time when prison populations across these societies were beginning to increase. In England, for example, while the prison population had stayed relatively stable in the post-war period up to 1957 (around 21,000 at a rate of about 50 per 100,000 of population), by 1972 it had nearly doubled in size to 38,328 and its rate had increased to 77.9 per 100,000 of population. There are remarkable parallels to these increases in corresponding societies. In New South Wales, the daily average prison population increased from 2081 in 1951 to 4163 in 1972. In Victoria, it had increased from 1335 in 1955 to 2318 in 1972. In New Zealand, it had increased from 1138 in 1954 to 2452 in 1973. These increases, it would seem, were a natural outgrowth of changing demographic trends: aside from general increases in the overall population of these societies in the post-war period, by the late 1950s, there had been a particular growth in the population of young male adults – those whom the criminal statistics always illustrated were the most criminogenic social group.[10] These changes were likely as a matter of course to have an impact on the upward growth of prison numbers. Indeed, crime rates also increased significantly over the same period.[11] As Scull (1977: 57) put it: 'the absolute size of the prison population (and even its size relative to the total population) may continue to rise even as the proportion of convicted criminals being imprisoned falls'.

The position in the United States did differ to a degree, however. The prisoner population had increased from 166,165 in 1950 to 220,149 in 1960; from then up to 1970 it declined to 196,429 in that year (producing rates of 109.5, 120.8 and 96.7 respectively).[12] Emphasis had been given to the development of community alternatives to the prison during the 1960s, particularly probation and parole. These provisions had had a much longer and significant history in North America than elsewhere: in Australia and New Zealand, for example, up to the 1950s, probation had been minimally developed, usually involving only a handful of part-time officials in each jurisdiction (Pratt, 1991); in England, parole was only introduced to the penal system in 1967. Furthermore, in the United States, these provisions had been closely associated with a long history of scientific expertise and the language and treatment of rehabilitation (see Denison, 1937/8; Burgess, 1937), perhaps thereby attributing to them a quite high status in the sentencing structure, at a time when these forms of knowledge they were particularly associated with dominated penal thought and language. As a result, they were allowed to play a more significant role than in corresponding societies at that time in arresting the growth of imprisonment. Nonetheless, the transfer of resources from the prison to community sanctions that this also involved (Scull, 1977) led to a worsening of conditions within them, as elsewhere (Mitford, 1975). In England in 1969, for example, 30 per cent of prisoners were sharing a cell (Fitzgerald and Sim, 1982).

The increasing visibility of the prison made these uncivilized conditions a matter of public knowledge: 'overcrowding in British prisons has become an affront to the efficiency of the penal system ... the degrading conditions in which some prisoners are forced to live ... must be disturbing to any civilized community' (*The Times*, 14 October 1970: 8). The response of the state and the penal establishment was again to try and return the penal system to some demonstrably efficient humanitarian basis. The way to do this was by trying to further restrict the use of prison by developing ostensible alternatives to it as was being done in North America – using these for the inadequate grey men, rather than the expensive and inhumane prison. There was no desire to be seen by the rest of the world as 'uncivilized' as a result of the exposure being given to the prisons. The 1967 Criminal Justice Act imposed restrictions on the powers of magistrates to send fine defaulters to prison; under the terms of the Criminal Justice Act 1972, the use of imprisonment for the first time for an offender under 21 was restricted in various ways. Meanwhile, the courts themselves showed a growing reluctance to send petty recidivist property offenders to prison (Pratt, 1997). From the early 1970s, a range of new community sanctions such as suspended sentence supervision orders, parole, community service orders, day training centres, detoxification centres, bail hostels, probation homes and hostels would be organized. The bifurcation (Bottoms, 1977) between those who should go to prison and those who should not, between those who could be released early and those who had to be detained longer, could thus be solidified through the introduction of these new measures.

In these respects, prison, it was thought, could increasingly be discarded, so that it would ultimately become a 'last resort' penal option. The breakdown in 'civilization' had provided an opportunity to re-establish and affirm the state's commitment to its values and expectations. As the Home Secretary (*Hansard*, 21 November 1971, 826, 972) commented, 'those who need not be sent to prison, those who are not guilty of violent crimes, should be punished in other ways in the interests of relieving the strain on the prison service and in the interests of the community ... people who have committed minor offences would be better occupied doing a service to their fellow citizens than sitting alongside others in a crowded jail.' The reorganization of the separate probation and prison departments in New South Wales in 1970 into the Department of Corrective Services (similarly Victoria in 1977) reflected the shift in emphasis and priorities that were taking place in the penal bureaucracies that would preside over the new community arrangements.

Notwithstanding this commitment to return the levels of imprisonment to those more closely identifiable with the standards of the civilized world, these initiatives proved to be largely ineffectual. Prison numbers continued to rise during the 1970s. In England, from 39,280 to 43,109 between 1975 and 1980 (with the use of imprisonment as against all other sanctions increasing from 13.4 to 14.8). In the United States, the

1960s' decline was arrested: the adult male prisoner population increased from its 1970 level to 304,256 in 1980. In New York State, the population increased from its low point of 12,577 in 1970 to 29,251 in 1982. Growth such as this led to a further deterioration of prison conditions. By 1980 in England around 40 per cent of the prisoner population were now having to share a cell with one or two others (Fitzgerald and Sim, 1982). The seemingly inexorable growth in crime across these societies during the 1970s[13] inevitably contributed to this increase but so too did the inefficiency of the penal establishment itself, due to the misuse of some of the alternatives to custody provisions that had been introduced, which added to the prisoner population rather than reduced it.[14]

A Fragmented Penal Establishment

Third, instead of a unified, univocal penal establishment, we find an increasingly fragmented and despairing body, as the various groups within it begin to assert their own interests, or jockey for new positions within its hierarchy, often turning on each other in the process. The prison authorities, unable to conceal the deficiencies of their own prison standards, and powerless to arrest the growing use of imprisonment, became more prepared to acknowledge inherent difficulties rather than issue blanket denials: 'one has a penal system operating largely in walled prisons which are too small, which were built fifty to 120 years ago, with inadequate or inappropriate provisions for work, education or leisure and other activities' (*Report of the Department of Prisons*, 1965–6: 3). However, the growth of prison numbers over the same period meant that prison buildings now considered unsuitable or 'uncivilized' by contemporary standards still had to be used with further deleterious consequences: 'the quality of life at the older Victorian prisons and many of the hutted camps has continued to be of major concern' (*Report on the Work of the Prison Department*, 1972: 4); 'overcrowding still prevails in too many institutions ... we know from experience that prisoners cannot be compelled, nor should they be expected to submit without protest to living in the cramped, squalid, and unsanitary conditions that still prevail in older prisons' (*Report on the Work of the Prison Department*, 1974: 13); 'the essential development of the [nineteenth-century] prison estate seemed in 1977 more remote than at any time' (*Report on the Work of the Prison Department*, 1977: 3). These acknowledgements reached their apex in the *Report on the Work of the Prison Service* (1981): prevailing conditions had become an 'affront' to a civilized society. It was not simply the case, though, that official discourse representations of the prison had changed – from seeing them as one of the emblems of the civilized world in the nineteenth century to one of the shameful stains on it in the late twentieth. In addition, by being prepared to acknowledge this themselves, even to the point of siding with prisoners, the authorities' position reflected the changing balance of power within the prison itself; and beyond this, it reflected the growing conflict between themselves and the central state – the cornerstone of penal power itself in these societies.

At the same time, the cloak of therapeutic, scientific expertise on which so much of the penal establishment's prestige and status had been based in the post-war period came to be discredited and, to a point, discarded. Their own technocratic evaluative procedures only showed ineptitude and inefficiency, rather than the expected degree of success in terms of reforming prisoners and reducing reconviction (Martinson, 1974). Indeed, it was now accepted that therapeutic penal intervention could be 'inappropriate and harmful for many offenders for whom it is used' (Home Office, 1970: 68). The Home Office (1976: 32) recognized that 'neither practical experience nor the results of research in recent years have established the superiority of custodial over non-custodial methods in their effect upon renewed offending'. This did not mean that the sanitized language associated with this expertise would disappear overnight: it was too deeply ingrained in the formal culture of the penal establishment for this to happen.[15] However, in reflection of the changing emphasis within prison regimes, the authorities now found themselves speaking its language to blandly sanitize and legitimate the introduction of stark new security initiatives: 'control units' were introduced in 1974 'to provide deliberately spare – though not spartan – regimes – for the hard core of intractable troublemakers whose behaviour had been found seriously and persistently to disrupt the prisons' (*Report on the Work of the Prison Department*, 1973: 45). Other therapeutic initiatives – the use of drugs, for example – also began to be associated with oppression within the prisons (Sim, 1990). But with their expertise tarnished, and with no other available body of expert knowledge that suited their professional aspirations, it was as if the authorities found themselves steering a rudderless, out-of-control ship.[16]

The growing gulf between between prison management, increasingly prepared to acknowledge the legitimacy of prisoner grievances and prison officers, increasingly involved in the new form of prison expertise – security – contributed to this sense of helplessness. The latter – perhaps in part because of the elevation of their own status that their involvement with the enforcement of security now gave them – were becoming detached from the rest of the prison establishment, and by so doing were becoming part of the prison problem rather than the solution to it. Among evidence of growing brutalities by prison officers which were becoming increasingly difficult to conceal or deny,[17] the prison managers variously found themselves in conflict with them in the 1970s over their recourse to strike action, abuse of overtime payments, more general time abuse, as well as clashes they were engineering with white-collar prison workers.[18]

Official investigations and other forms of exposure uncovered not some rational, sanitized penal programme, but only the irrationality and ugliness of prison life. New channels of communication had been opened up at this time between prisoners and the public, through the work of prisoners' rights groups and sympathetic individuals (see Fitzgerald, 1977; Cohen and Taylor, 1978). It thus became possible to reveal the new tactics of security and control, on the basis that these exceeded the parameters of the 'civilized'. The scandal that broke over the sensory deprivation aspects of the control units was one example of this and forced their closure in 1975.[19] Again, the use of the MUFTI squad in 1978 and 1979 – a specialist prison officer unit, whose members wore no form of identification and were not tied to a given prison and were therefore unrecognizable by the prisoners they came into contact with – raised public concerns about such non-accountable, indiscriminate use of state power and force.

The growth of governmental inquiries into various aspects of prison life in the 1960s and 1970s (after the silence that had prevailed for most of the twentieth century until then) was symptomatic of the decline in the authority and ability of the penal establishment to define the reality of prison life and to offset the need for any formal investigation beyond this. The second half of the nineteenth century had been an era of inquiry only until the authorities had been able to establish their monopolistic control over penal arrangements and silence their critics, or at least become powerful enough to ignore them. The new inquiries indicated that this era was coming to an end. Furthermore, they departed from the blinkered inheritance of their predecessors. In New South Wales, it was acknowledged that 'the Department of Corrective Services as a whole is inefficient, disorganized and badly administered. It has become demoralized. It must be revitalized' (*Report of the Royal Commission on New South Wales Prisons*, 1978: 20). And in England, that 'all is not well in our prisons' (*Report of the May Committee*, 1979: 1).

From Public Indifference to Public Anxiety

In these societies, the idea that the public should be kept away from penal development begins to change around 1970: not so much as some discernible shift in the axis of penal power to actively include them within it but, instead, as a series of attempts to appeal to them as rational, sensitive citizens and thereby elicit their support for the new penal initiatives that were being introduced (*Report on the Work of the Prison Department*, 1967). Community alternatives to prison would expose the public to the punishment apparatus to a degree that they had become unused to: hostels might be built in their locality, community service orders might involve them working alongside offenders in some capacity. In a bid to offset any inherent reservations that the public might have about such proximities, there is a growing emphasis on the need to establish community links in the annual prison reports of the 1970s: 'every prison has made contacts of one kind or another with the community. This is invaluable for the social health of a prison and promotes a better understanding outside the prison of the problems and aims of the establishment' (*Report on the Work of the Prison Department*, 1973: 6). In this way, it was thought, alarm and trepidation would be overcome as the public weighed up and approved the economic and humanitarian benefits of the new initiatives to all concerned. There seemed to be an assumption among the authorities and the liberal elites that an increasingly broad base of public opinion, on being appraised of the reality of prison conditions, of their expense and inhumanity, would support the drives to reduce prison levels and provide more cost effective, humane community based punishments (see Briggs, 1975). *Time* (18 January 1971: 53) reported on 'The Shame of the Prisons':

> It is not just the riots, the angry cries of 426,000 invisible inmates from the Tombs to Walla Walla, that have made prisons a national issue. Public concern is rooted in the paradox that Americans have never been so fearful of rising crime, yet never so ready to challenge the institutions that try to cope with it. More sensitive to human rights than ever, more liberated in their own lives and outlooks, a growing number of citizens view prisons as a new symbol of unreason, another sign that too much in America has gone wrong.

By channelling this discontent and anti-authoritarianism towards a rational, enlightened penal policy, it was thought that the prison could be pushed back to the marginal place it should have in the civilized world. Again, those societies with the lowest rates of imprisonment were still looked upon as its leaders, setting the example for others to follow: 'the first priority must be a commitment to develop non-custodial methods and to reduce the use of prisons, borstals and other custodial methods to a minimum ... the fact that within Western Europe there are wide variations in the rates of imprisonment gives grounds for thinking that much more could be done in Britain' (Haxby, 1978: 151).

However, at exactly the same time as the door to the axis of penal power is opened a little in this way, so the public's threshold of tolerance and self-restraint was being progressively lowered, further adding to the instability of the existing configuration of penal power. Alongside the tense, creaking relationship between the state and its bureaucratic organizations, the public indifference that had been a connecting lever in this axis was changing to increasing anxiety and alarm at the growing evidence of its failure to provide penal arrangements that were untroubling for them, scandal-free and invisible – what they had taken to be some of the most important characteristics of punishment in the civilized world. The disjuncture that now existed between the penal programme of the state and its bureaucracies and the concerns of the general public had been recognized as early as 1967 in the United States:

> on the local, state and national levels there is growing concern among both private citizens and public officials about an alarming general increase in crime, for example, nationally an increase of sixteen per cent over the year. Paradoxically, at a time when the country is faced with not only an apparent, but a real increase in crime, the Department of Corrections is witnessing a continuing drop in its inmate populations. (*Report of the Department of Correctional Services*, 1967: 7)[20]

Indeed, this very growth in public alarm to policies that seemed to make no sense to them – crime was rising as prison numbers declined – surely helps to explain the way in which imprisonment began to grow again in that country: the much greater electoral accountability of its penal officials meant that this alarm and anxiety more quickly began to find direct political expression which the non-publicly accountable bureaucracies in England and elsewhere were protected against. It meant that, in the United States, from having a bureaucratic structure that was flexible enough to restrict the growth of imprisonment in the 1960s, it then became the first to accelerate it when the public mood changed in the 1970s.

There was no popular support for the initiatives designed to reduce the prison populations, only growing concern at the apparent inability of the state and its authorities to bring order to prisons, and its inability to address crime problems; no demands for less punishment, only increasing demands for more. Opinion polls regularly revealed concerns over public safety and beliefs that the courts were not punitive enough. In Canada in 1980, 63 per cent of the public believed this, only 4 per cent did not; in England, the results to a similar poll in 1981 were that 64 per cent thought the courts were not sufficiently punitive, with only 4 per cent disagreeing – findings also replicated in the United States in the same year.[21] In other words, there was a growing sense of public dissatisfaction with the way in which the axis of penal power was then operating. As the mood of the public changed from indifference to anxiety, so it seemed that it was no longer sufficient for punishment just to be hidden away – there had to be some more forceful, ostentatious, repressive measures of punishment as well, as if in a bid to re-establish the damaged authority of the state and the security that came with this.

Notes

---

1 See, for example, *Report of the Department of Justice* [New Zealand] (1968); *New York Times*, 30 October 1970: 9.

2 Georgia was one of twelve such states, the others being Alabama, Arkansas, Florida, Kentucky, Louisiana, Missouri, Oklahoma, North Carolina, South Carolina, Tennessee, Texas and Virginia (Myers, 1998).

3 Johnston (1996) provides a helpful outline of the term. It involves planning and premeditation; voluntary involvement of private citizens; 'autonomous citizenship' that constitutes a new social movement; the possible use of force; a perceived threat to the established order; it provides assurance to its participants.

4 See, for example, Raper (1933); Williams (1959); Hall (1979); Bartley (1983).

5 By 1972, all these states had imprisonment levels of over 158 per 100,000 of population and were in the highest twenty of all the United States (Waller and Chan, 1974).

6 See, for example, Lodge (1975).

7 For example, Horsley (1887: 49); Quinton (1910: viii); Page (1937: ii); Rose (1960: 279).

8 Cf Mennell (1992: 138): 'where the balance of power is becoming more equal, expect to find symptoms of rebellion, resistance, emancipation among the outsiders'.

9 Cf Report of the Department of Correctional Services (1976: 6): 'the major emphasis in the management of correctional facilities is the promotion of due process for inmates – justice means governance by rules applying to all. It means the preservation of all rights save those inherently inconsistent with incarceration'. On the general issue of prisoners' rights, see Jacobs (1980).

10 In Australia, for example, the population of New South Wales grew from 3,092,621 in 1949 to 4,047,700 in 1963; in Victoria, from 2,142,986 to 3,040,450, with the biggest increase in the 17–24 age group (Mukherjee, 1988).

11 In Canada, the rate of criminal code incidents increased from 2,771 per 100,000 of population in 1962 to 5,212 in 1970; in Australia, charges brought before the Magistrates Courts increased from 825,334 in 1960 to 1,089,655 in 1970; in England, the level of recorded crime increased from 743,713 offences in 1960 to 1,555,995 in 1970; in New Zealand, recorded crime increased from 102,792 offences in 1960 to 165,859 in 1970; in the United States from 3,384,200 in 1960 to 8,098,000 in 1970.

12 In relation to Canada, McMahon (1992) illustrates the relative stability of the rate of imprisonment in that country from 1955 to 1977 (95.9 to 98.4 per 100,000 of population). This is attributed to the importance given to community rehabilitation in that country.

13 In Canada, the rate of criminal code incidents increased from 5,311 per 100,000 of population in 1971 to 8,343 in 1980. In Australia, the number of offences reported to the police increased from 462,158 in 1975–6 to 820,399 in 1981–2; in England, by 1980 recorded crime had increased to 2,688,235 offences in 1980; in New Zealand to 349,193; in the United States it had increased to 13,408,300.

14 See, for example, Bottoms (1981) on the use of suspended sentences in England; more generally and theoretically, Cohen (1985).

15 For example, *Report of the Department of Correctional Services* (1975: 6): 'At a time when correctional systems throughout the nation are under public scrutiny concerning their ability to produce effective rehabilitation services, New York state is intensifying its efforts to offer educational, counselling and training programs'.

16 Cf *Report of the Department of Justice* [Wellington] (1975: 4), 'the human warehousing approach ... is one of the most serious obstacles to the policy of dealing with each person as an individual.'

17 See, for example, *Report of the Board of Inquiry into Several Matters Concerning HM Prison Pentridge and the Maintenance of Discipline in Prisons*, 1973.

18 See *Report of the Royal Commission on New South Wales Prisons, 1978*; *Report of the Director of Corrective Services*, 1980–1, 1981–2, *Report of the Department of Correctional Services*, 1980–1.

19 The Home Secretary claimed that prison officers were now working so efficiently in mainstream prison that the units were no longer necessary; furthermore, he was 'satisfied that allegations of sensory deprivation, cruelty and brutality ... were completely unfounded' (*Report on the Work of the Prison Department*, 1975: 5).

20 Its prison population declined from 20,000 in 1965 to 14,564 in 1968.

21 Source: Hastings and Hastings (2000).

9

The Gulag and Beyond

These anxieties contributed greatly to the subsequent electoral success of political parties that closely identified themselves with neo-liberalism. During the 1980s and 1990s this philosophy was able to establish itself as a hegemonic force across all these societies, to varying degrees, irrespective of which political party won power. What then began to take shape as a result of its impact was a realignment of the existing social structure that had been characteristic of the development of the civilizing process during the nineteenth and twentieth centuries. Instead of the incremental growth of the state and the axis of power vested in the relationship between it and its bureaucratic organizations, we find the development of a new axis of power – between the central state and the general public, with the state's own seemingly ineffective bureaucratic organizations left on one side. In practice, it meant that the state would be prepared to address popular concerns over matters such as the growth of crime and the perceived leniencies in punishment rather than appearing aloof and above them. Nonetheless, this populist punitiveness (Bottoms, 1995) was not the only influence on penal development during the 1980s and 1990s. For a good part of this period, it was to be secondary to an enhanced bureaucratic rationalism, presided over by the state, which attempted to affirm most of the existing standards and assumptions associated with the civilizing process. Nonetheless, as the authority of the state became progressively weaker and public anxieties more clamorous, so we find that populist punitiveness became increasingly influential, running in tandem with bureaucratic rationalism, sometimes overriding it altogether, with the overall effect of pushing the boundaries of punishment in the civilized world into new, uncharted regions.

Bureaucratic Rationalism

Notwithstanding the prominence given to law and order issues in the electoral success of Conservatives in Britain and Republicans in the United

States in the late 1970s and much of the 1980s, there was to be no wholesale 'turning the clock back', no complete reversal of all the expectations of what punishment should be like in the civilized world. The very power of the concept of civilization itself – its embeddedness as a defining *leitmotif* of Western development – still seemed to make any deliberately designed departures from its standards threatening and unwelcome to social stability: if no longer solely on humanitarian grounds, then most certainly economic. Indeed, economic rationalism had been another important feature of the political successes of neo-liberalism, and in the ensuing period played a significant role in penal development.[1] Instead, then, of dramatically altering the existing penal framework, the state largely pursues a policy of enhanced bureaucratic rationalism to solidify and stabilize it. However, distrustful of its own organizations' ability to put such objectives into effect, these bodies are to be given much closer direction by the state itself and are also to be made more publicly accountable across the criminal justice and penal systems.

Thus, in an attempt to ensure that alternatives to custody would make inroads into the prison population and function as they were intended to do, judicial autonomy would be curtailed to ensure that its idiosyncrasies did not contravene the state's penal purposes. Increasingly, the state itself decides who should be available for such sanctions and who should not. The serious (violent, sexual crime)/non-serious (property crime) distinction that had emerged during the 1970s, was given legislative prescription in, for example, the 1982 Criminal Justice Act in England and its 1985 counterpart in New Zealand. The same legislation in England systematized parole procedures, stripping away authority from its own parole board, making this form of early release unavailable for some, mandatory for others. At the same time, parole boards began to abandon their increasingly flawed modes of clinical diagnosis which had been used to inform the decision to release and instead look to the seemingly more efficient, scientific form of actuarial prediction to achieve this (Feely and Simon, 1992).

Probation and other community-based penal organizations would no longer be allowed to develop their alternatives to prison on an ad hoc basis; instead these would be systematized and thereby function more efficiently as the state directed. A 1988 Action Plan (Home Office, 1988) 'called on every local probation area to develop its own complementary strategy for targeting more intensive forms of probation supervision on young adult offenders in particular, with a view to reducing the use of custody for this age group' (Cavadino and Dignan 1997: 23). Systems management then became a new form of expertise, whereby such specialists would strive to block loopholes in the penal system to prevent policies malfunctioning or having unintended consequences, as had characterized the 1970s' introduction of these alternative to custody sanctions.

Assaults were made on union power in the prisons. It had been recognized in New South Wales that 'one of the greatest challenges which faced the Corrective Services Commission was overcoming the "closed shop" approach adopted by the former administration' (*Report of the Director of Corrective Services*, 1979–80: 1). During the 1980s, there were further indicators of the disruption and instability the officers were capable of causing to the prisons: undermining the authority of the governors by trying to impose their own prison musters, industrial action, continuing revelations regarding abuse of their employment privileges (see, for example, *Report of the Director of Corrective Services*, 1985–6), and claims of systemic violence in attempting to assert control within the prisons (Coggan and Walker, 1982; Woolf and Tumin, 1991). In recognition of the way in which the officers were threatening to destabilize the functioning of the prisons, the Fresh Start initiative was launched in England in 1987, redrawing the officers' conditions of service in a bid to neutralize the corrosive effect of existing working practices. Furthermore, the subsequent ruling that from 1 April 1993 all new staff should wear badges identifying them by name carried great significance. Five decades earlier, it had been the prisoners who were allowed to stop wearing the cell badge – now it was the officers' turn to put a badge back on: not just to make themselves known to the prisoners (an extension of their accountability to them) but, as well, to reaffirm where their status should be in the prison hierarchy: above the prisoners, certainly, but, in addition, well below the badgeless management.

As the state began to more directly determine prison policy and set targets and guidelines for each prison to follow, the prison authorities found themselves increasingly circumscribed. Their annual reports become more likely to take the form of assurances of efficient compliance with the basic functions of imprisonment. General comment or discussion of prisons in their broader context is steadily reduced and is replaced by frequent references to 'missions' and 'goals' with graphs and flowcharts illustrating inputs, throughputs and outputs. The bureaucracies become more autopoietic, protecting themselves with their own managerialist concerns, using these new forms of expert knowledge to demonstrate greater efficiency in completing the directives set them by the state:

> the task of the prison service is to use with maximum efficiency the resources of staff, money, building and plant made available to it by parliament in order to fulfil in accordance with the relevant provisions of the law the following functions: keeping offenders in custody; to provide for prisoners as full a life as is consistent with the facts of custody, in particular making available the physical necessities of life; care for physical and mental health; advice and help with personal problems; work; education; training, physical exercise and recreation; and the opportunity to practise their religion; to enable prisoners to retain links with the community and where possible assist them to prepare for their return to it. (*Report on the Work of the Prison Service*, 1989–90: 3)

At the same time, the prisons are to be made more open and accessible. In England, there was a new section in the *Report on the Work of the Prison Department* – 'the prison service in society':

the prison service would benefit from and public sentiment requires that as many aspects of government which includes the prison service should be opened up to as wide an audience as possible ... the service needs support from an informed and interested public. British society has become much more sceptical and less willing to accept without question the actions of those responsible for public administration. The prison service has a reputation for secrecy. That reputation is in my view unjustified ... nevertheless we have accepted that more could be done. (1980: 8)

This 'openness', continuing the trend that emerged during the 1970s, would generally involve a greater accessibility of prison to the mass media, in the hope that this would focus 'public attention on the realities of the prison system instead of purely sensational myths of which perhaps the most persistent belief is that prisons are holiday camps' (1981: 1). In pursuance of this policy:

the department issued guidance to governors which significantly extend their freedom to communicate directly with the local media about their establishments. Many of them are already making use of their freedom to increase awareness of their communities of the prisons in their midst ... we remain convinced that the prison service has nothing to lose and a great deal to gain from greater public knowledge of prisons and we intend to seek further opportunities of improving that knowledge. (1983: 6)

Openness would be accompanied by accountability. To this end, a prison inspectorate was (re)introduced in 1981, the Home Secretary explaining its purpose as follows: 'I have made clear on many occasions in the past that I am committed to opening up the prisons to the public gaze as far as is consistent with the need to protect privacy and security ... the establishment of an Inspectorate is a ... vital part of the process of increasing public understanding of the prison system' (*Report of the Chief Inspector of Prisons*, 1982: iii). The prison would no longer be able to hide behind the closed door of its governing bureaucracies. Poor conditions and irregularities were regularly exposed in the subsequent reports: 'deplorable sanitary arrangements' (1984: 17); 'the physical conditions in which many prisoners had to live continued to border on the intolerable' (1987: 3); 'we were dismayed to find in prison after prison kitchens that were either unsanitary or unsafe, or both ... kitchens were frequently dirty, greasy and littered with food scraps' (1988: 8). The reports were not always critical, but such exposure was necessary, the Chief Inspector reflected, given that the Home Secretary had told him that 'he wanted me to help him make the British prison service the best in the world' (1991–2: 33). The way to achieve this standard once again, it would seem, would be to encourage the prisons to reform themselves on pain of shameful exposure if they did not do so. At the same time, the unfavourable sights that were revealed may further convince the general public of the difficulties and expense of the prison system and the necessity to restrict its use. It was as if political parties, while being prepared to exploit public misconceptions about prison conditions to win power (see Hall, 1980; Taylor, 1981), then wanted to continue the public education programme that had been set in place, on the assumption that rational thought and knowledge would inevitably triumph over emotive, common-sensical myths.

Again, to put the prisons on a more efficient basis, limited privatization was introduced to the penal system in the early 1980s. After a cautious start (since it seemed to be undermining the monopolistic control of the state's power to punish), it was only a few steps to the introduction of private prisons themselves. In contrast to the decrepit antiquity of the nineteenth-century institutions and even the inadequacies of more recent prison development, the private sector quickly came to be seen as being able to provide a new benchmark for civilized prison arrangements. For example, in England, in contrast to the shared cellular confinement that was increasingly becoming the norm of prison life,

> the regime at the Worls [private prison] is based on prisoners being out of their cells for a minimum of twelve hours on weekdays and ten and a half hours per day over the weekend. Prisoners have an entitlement to six hours per week for education, another six for physical education, two and a half hours each for visits to the library, and the prisoners' shop, and twenty one hours a week for meals, showers etc. (*Report on the Work of the Prison Service*, 1990–1: 12)

However, there was no need for full-scale privatization of the prisons to achieve efficiencies and modernization:[2] this would have been inefficient in itself – too politically controversial, for example. Instead, a limited injection of the private sector would provide new standards for the public prisons to strive towards – and at the same time would act as a reminder to the public sector of what the state was prepared to do if it failed to achieve them. As such, it seemed that a revitalized prison service was emerging from its nineteenth-century shadows in the late twentieth, one suited again to the standards of the civilized world: no more talk of inefficiencies and inability to manage, instead, talk of achievements and success: '[this has been] a very successful year for the Victorian prison service. The organization will continue to make improvements which contribute to successful outcomes for both the Department of Justice and government policy and will continue to address the needs of the public, prisoners and staff by providing contemporary and forward looking correctional services' (*Report of the Correctional Services Commissioner*, 1995–6: 18). No more talk of prisons that had to be shamefully hidden away; instead talk of prisons that once again conformed to the highest standards associated with punishment in the civilized world: 'Beechworth is a "jewel in the crown" of the Office of Corrections. To see is to believe. If you have never visited Beechworth, you have really missed half of the magic of the Office of Corrections' (*Report of the Correctional Services Commissioner*, 1996–7: 31).

In such ways, it became possible to change the image of the prison: from one associated with decrepitude and disorder to one of productivity and efficiency: an ostensibly modern, rationally administered institution rather than one trapped in the inefficient past, with all the accoutrements and identifiers associated with its new standing: 'the bulk of the publicity section's work during the year concerned development work on the implementation of the corporate identity introduced in 1985 ... new stationery has been introduced and work was undertaken on an integrated sign system. A corporate identity manual will be introduced toward the end of 1986' (*Report on the Work of the Prison Service*, 1985–6: 7). In accordance with these changing associations, and assisted by both a new technology of construction (Rutherford, 1985) and the promise of a more efficient private sector, it became economically possible to launch new prison building programmes. In New York, the first new prison in 29 years was built in 1977; the *Report of the Department of Correctional Services* (1985–6: 19) referred to 'the largest [prison] expansion in its history'. In England, a new building programme began, 'the biggest this century' (*Report on the Work of the Prison Service*, 1985–6: 3). In New South Wales, 'the largest prison capital works budget in the states history is now under way ... a new facility is to be built at Junee ... in line with minimum economy units currently being built in the United States – maximum cost efficiency is to be achieved' (*Report of the Director of Corrective Services*, 1990–1: 9). However, it is important to stress that prison, in most of these jurisdictions, was still intended to be used as a last resort penal option: the new prisons were intended to replace old ones, not to add to them.

Frustrations over the futility and expense that had come to be associated with imprisonment were reiterated by the Home Secretary in 1988:

> For over a hundred years, penal policy in this country has appeared to focus on custody. If a fine is not enough, custody is said to be the only adequate penalty. Other orders are described as non-custodial penalties and assessed as alternatives to custody. All this reinforces custody in a central position. Why we do this? [Prison] should not be the final solution to which all persistent criminals progress, however minor their offences. It will be a long haul, but we want to make out of date the notion that the only punishment that works is behind bars. (Home Secretary, 1988, quoted by Whitfield, 1991: 16)

New prisons were being built, but it was intended that they be used sparingly. This was affirmed in *Crime, Justice and Protecting the Public* (Home Office, 1990). If its title illustrated the way in which public protection had now been elevated to a significant role in crime and penal policy development, reflecting the new political relationship between the state and the general public, it was still envisaged that the way to achieve this was by a commitment to existing penal rationalities and through ensuring maximum efficiency of existing resources. It stipulated that 'punishment in proportion to the seriousness of the crime ... should be the principal focus for sentencing decisions'. The distribution of offenders between prison and non-prison should still be determined by the serious/non-serious *offence* axis. Furthermore, citizens themselves were to be given a more active role in crime prevention. This had begun informally during the 1980s with the growth of local neighbourhood watch committees. A decade later, it was to be seen as a normative activity for every citizen – a form both of empowerment and social responsibility, intervening to reduce crime which the inefficient state bureaucracies had been unable to do:

> There are doubtless some criminals who carefully calculate the possible gains and risks. But much crime is committed on impulse, given the opportunity presented by an open window or unlocked door, and it is committed by offenders who live from moment to moment ... it is unrealistic to construct sentencing arrangements on the assumption that most offenders will weigh up the possibilities in advance and base their conduct on rational calculation. Often they do not. (Home Office, 1990: 8)

The post-war emphasis on societal responsibility for an individual's criminality had changed. Crime was no longer the product of society's unfairness but, instead, of an individual's irrationality. However, as it then seemed, the penal system could not be constructed on the basis of accommodating such irrationalities: it would lead only to what was still conceived of as another irrationality – a massive increase in imprisonment. Instead, a more active role was sought for the public to participate in preventing crime in the first instance. Indeed, as the very idea of some realms of state responsibility and provision of services became progressively squeezed out of the political agenda of the neo-liberal state, so this was to become both a political and practical necessity.

Continuities

For much of the 1980s and into the 1990s, the parameters of punishment in England and most similar societies remained largely unchanged. There was still violence and disorder in the prisons – and on occasions it seemed only to worsen (see Woolf and Tumin, 1991), in spite of the commitment to openness and accountability. There were still the legions of 'grey men' populating the prisons, in spite of the systematized alternatives to custody:

the mailbag shop, Wandsworth. I cannot think of a place more like the grave; or a cemetery, fenced in and guarded, whose tombs have delivered up their grey corpses. Zombies sit and cut the cloth, zombies stitch and sew. Grey men, with long skull heads; balding. They had mangled mouths, chipped and broken teeth; haunted red eyes. (Hill, 1991: 123).

In these respects, the efficiency drives and the reforms had had minimal impact. But in other respects, although prison populations had been pushed upwards in some of these societies, they were not as high as might have been expected, given all the law and order rhetoric during the 1970s and much of the 1980s. Indeed, in some, it appeared that they had achieved a certain stability, even a decline. In England, after an increase to 46,000 in 1985, between 1986 and 1991 the prison population declined to 43,000 and then remained at that level. In New South Wales there was a decline from 4,163 in 1977 to 3,417 in 1984. In New Zealand, the prison population declined from 2,786 in 1972 to 2,333 in 1986. Furthermore, what these significant falls in both New South Wales and New Zealand illustrated was the way in which it was possible to bring about changes in the flow of prisoners by state decree, by simply ordering the right switches to be pressed on the punishment machinery that it had increasingly taken charge of. In both these countries, the state had changed the rules for parole eligibility and early release in the 1980s to bring these declines. Overall, right across these societies, for the time being at least, the flow was still intended to be away from prison (Chan, 1992). Certainly, the rate of imprisonment in the United States was now beginning to accelerate exponentially – from just below 100 per 100,000 of population in 1973 to around 150 in 1979 and then to 200 in 1983, but not yet to the point where these were unrecognizable, impossible, irretrievable levels, on a par only with levels in societies beyond the civilized world. It was as if they were still within the same cluster of imprisonment rates as similar societies, if at the far end of this. And it was as if the same logics and rationalities were at work in the analytical frames of reference of the period: they were thus seen as aberrational levels of imprisonment, but levels that might be pulled back, if the punishment machinery was made to function as efficiently as it should (Rutherford, 1986). They were certainly not seen as a normal, acceptable feature of penal arrangements in the civilized world.

In these respects, then, the state's own commitment to bureaucratic rationalism had largely shackled the emotive public sentiments that had become a potent political force. Certainly, there had been localized developments which indicated that bureaucratic rationalism could become harnessed to the influence of populist punitiveness, or might give way to it altogether. The reintroduction of the death penalty in the United States in 1976 was an example of the former.[3] In that country, its abandonment had only been fragile and partial. Unlike similar societies in the civilized world, it had never been democratically voted out of existence but had only been placed on hold by the United States Supreme Court in its ruling that, as it had been practised in 1972, it constituted a 'cruel and unusual punishment'. Once the technology of punishment could incorporate death by lethal injection (now the predominant mode of execution in that country) then, as it were, the death penalty could be 'civilized' and made acceptable again. What had been needed to make such a sanction tolerable was the sanitization and efficiency associated with the civilizing process in conjunction with the hostile public sentiments which supported executions: the balance of the two could now achieve precisely this.

The new model extra-punitive detention centres in England, and their boot camp counterparts in the United States were examples of the latter. The detention centres were quickly revealed to be ineffective deterrents to crime, which had been the reason for their introduction in 1981 (Home Office, 1984). It was as if such knowledge then only confirmed the irrationality of penal sanctions such as these which did not correspond to the established values of the civilized world. And armed with it, it was as if any further departures from these values would be inconceivable, would defy rationality. Or, at least, the prevailing rationality, the rationality of using prison as little as possible, of humanizing its conditions, and so on. Instead, it was as if the brutalizing detention centres and boot camps and the death penalty in the United States were aberrations, the price that liberal establishments had had to pay with the election of neo-liberal governments who were prepared to open up penal development to popular sentiments. Yet, for the most part, all the dark forces of punishment that law and order rhetoric at election times had hinted at seemed to be little more than this, kept largely in check by the driving force of bureaucratic rationalism, and the more deeply embedded standards and values of the civilizing process itself. These hallmarks thus continued to be seen in penal development. For example:

The Disappearance of Prison

Public opposition to the proximity of prison buildings was still in evidence: 'the community has been slow to accept the need for new prison department buildings ... it has always to be remembered that urban sites tend to be unwelcome both to local residents and to local authorities with pressing housing requirements' (Home Office, 1977: 115–19). There are the same attempts to hide the appearance of the prison. A Home Office (1985: 34) study of trends in North American prison design noted: 'there are no watchtowers as are found on the older, higher security penitentiaries'. It went on to report on the building of

Fort Sasketchewan Correctional Centre, Alberta, Canada: 'the site is located in an area south of two highways, within city boundaries. Trees and berms effectively screen the centre from view ... [it is] a campus-like facility intended to create as normal an environment as possible' (1985: 47).

These trends continue today. Who, for example, would think that the Baltimore Central Booking and Intake Facility (Kessler, 2000: 92) refers to a prison? At the same time, urban renewal becomes possible in some of those urban ghettos which housed nineteenth-century prisons – on condition that the prison which contributed to their blight is closed; or in some cases, it leads to a reinvention of the prison as, say, a museum, or a hotel and restaurant complex (where it has a kind of daring, exotic appeal to the public as it is at last opened up to them, on condition that it is in this new guise) confirming that the right place for these institutions is in the past, not the present. This is no longer the way in which imprisonment is administered in the civilized world, where such distasteful, offensive sights are avoided.

The Amelioration of Prison Conditions

Diet

Improvements to the quality and quantity of the diet continued, in line with broader social trends. For example, in New South Wales, 'menus are planned to add up to 3,200 calories per day ... orange, cereal, toast for breakfast; three sandwiches and fruit for lunch; savoury rissoles, potato, beans, fruit salad and ice cream for dinner' (*Report of the Director of Corrective Services*, 1983: 54). Prisoners in England were to be given an increased role in designing their own menus and in food preparation (*Report on the Work of the Prison Service*, 1989–90), in line with their status as rational, thinking subjects with rights – they did not need to have every decision made for them by the authorities anymore. Furthermore, it was recognized that:

> food is one of the most important basic needs of prisoners – and one of the most likely areas to provoke unrest. A new approach to catering which increases the dietary allowance by ten per cent gives caterers greater flexibility in the choice of menu ... we are using insulated metal trays to improve appearance, keep food hot and give better portions. (*Report on the Work of the Prison Service*, 1992–3: 16)

In reflection of the increasingly heterogeneous nature of modern society and the diversity of food preferences, 'there is a diversity of menus to reflect the ethnic and cultural mix'. The latest advances in nutritional science are brought to bear: 'the menus are tested and approved by a consultant nutritionist'.

Clothing and Personal Hygiene

Here, again, prisoners are to be given more choice in clothing, reflecting the higher expectations of personal hygiene and broader changes in fashion:

> Following last year's review of inmate clothing, the supply of underpants is being increased to allow a minimum of four changes a week. This is being phased in over 1991. All inmates serving three months or more now get their own shoes and gym shoes. Boxer shorts and a range of coloured T shirts and sweatshirts are being introduced and new styles of shoe and gym shoe are being developed. (*Report on the Work of the Prison Service*, 1990–1: 15)

They may even be allowed to wear their own clothing:

> prisoners can feel more responsible for their own lives if they have more choice about what to wear and if they know they can be held accountable for keeping their clothes in reasonable condition. The prison service has sought to tackle this latter issue by introducing personal kit systems for longer term sentence prisoners ... there is currently a major programme to increase the choice and quantity of underwear, and to improve the design of footwear. The government intends to go further in providing opportunities for convicted male prisoners to exercise responsibility for and choice in what they wear. Accordingly the government aims to progressively allow these prisoners to wear their own clothes if they so wish. (1990–1: 63)

Internal sanitation in all prison cells began to be put into effect in England in 1982 and was completed in 1996.

The Sanitization of Penal Language

In addition to the rational, objective language which recognizes the limits to imprisonment and the need to develop alternatives to it, we find a continuation of the humanitarian approach to prison conditions: '[these are] improving to allow families and friends to visit inmates in pleasant and relaxed surroundings; new vehicles will ensure a more humane and efficient transport system' (*Report of the Director of Corrective Services*, 1983: 32).

The New Punitiveness

Punishment in the civilized world, it would seem, would stay within familiar territory, but would be presided over by a more efficient, streamlined administrative machinery. And yet it was then, as if at some point during the 1980s and the early 1990s, the state begins to press a different set of switches on the machinery it had constructed: as if a flick of these switches, moving from stop to go, became all that was necessary to push back the existing boundaries of punishment to much more unfamiliar regions, even to conjure up new possibilities of punishing which previously seemed to have no place in the civilized world.

As regards the prison, instead of trying to restrict and stabilize its populations, the state embarks on a process of accelerated growth: the controls that had been put in place to restrict this are progressively taken off, to a point where this acceleration reaches a level of unparalled 'hyper-activity' in the United States (Simon, 2000). In that country, the rate of imprisonment leapt to 304 per 100,000 of population by 1991 and then to 500 in 1999; when gaols are included with prisons, the overall rate has increased from 230 per 100,000 in 1979 to 709 in 1999 (Christie, 2000). This means that around two million adult males now are likely to be incarcerated in that country at any given time. In New York state, the rate of imprisonment increased from 195 per 100,000 of population in 1985 to 398 in 1998. In Georgia, the rate reached 342 per 100,000 in 1991, 502 in 1999, or 956 per 100,000 when gaols and prisons are counted together (Garland, 2000).

While countries such as England, New Zealand, Canada and Australia cannot match this pace, there has still been significant growth in imprisonment in all of them. In England, the rate of imprisonment increased from 93 per 100,000 of population in 1986 to 130 in 2001 and an increase in the numbers of those imprisoned from 46,981 to 66,700 over the same period. In New Zealand, the rate of imprisonment increased from 75 per 100,000 in 1986 to 150 in 2000: the prison population has more than doubled from 2,654 to 5,679 over the same period. In New South Wales, the rate of imprisonment increased from 70 per 100,000 of population in 1982 to 120 in 1998 (3,719 to 7,697 in total). The rate of imprisonment for Australia as a whole increased from 65 per 100,000 to 106 (9,826 to 19,906 in total, Carcach and Grant, 1999). In Canada, the rate of imprisonment increased from 111 per 100,000 in 1989 to 135 in 1999 (Christie, 1993; Canadian Centre for Justice Statistics, 2000). Furthermore, all the indications are that the growth of prison will not only continue, but is being actively planned for.[4]

In these respects, the continuing hallmarks of the civilizing process (which anyway become fainter in the 1990s' reports) are matched by a series of discontinuities, or reversals to it (which gather force over the same period). These take the form of the following features.

The Reappearance of Prison

It becomes clear that among some communities at least, the old resistance to the presence of prisons is breaking down. Prison, in fact, can be accepted as a valuable source of employment, which replaces more traditional but now redundant industries ('more than a dozen communities lobbied for the [new prison] facilities that ultimately went to Elmira and Napanoch', *Report of the Department of Correctional Services*, 1985–6: 18). In other words, prison may be tolerated because it has the potential to be a valuable community resource, rather than an encumbrance to economic development and investment, as was previously the case. At the same time, its appearance may be tolerated because of changing cultural attitudes – it becomes a sign of reassurance that the state is trying to protect its worthy citizens. In Georgia, there are now opportunities for citizens to phone and book a place on one of the guided tours of its prisons that the authorities provide (*Report of the Department of Corrections*, 1997).

The Deterioration of Prison Conditions

In some respects, we see deliberate reversals to the ameliorative trajectory of prison policies. In England, in the aftermath of the Learmont Report (1995), prisoners would no longer receive general privileges. Instead, they would begin their sentence in 'basic regimes', from which they could work their way upwards and enhance their conditions. Thus from 2000, four levels come into existence which the prisoners have to move through to gain improvements to everyday essentials of prison life, such as visits, clothing, television, association, and so on. The state's relationship with them has been redefined and restricted: their well-being is dependent on their own self-improvement.

In Georgia, inmates' heads are shaved on arrival. They must maintain a clean appearance, they must wear pressed uniforms labelled 'state prisoner' (*Report of the Department of Corrections*, 1995). Any sensitivity that there may once have been to such stigmatization seems to have evaporated. In addition, they are to 'keep their spartan cells immaculate'.

In contrast to the high quality benchmarks of improved conditions that the private sector had been intended to set for subsequent prison development, across the United States we find the rise of the super-max prisons:

> correctional staff were no longer directly involved in the supervision of inmates because inmates were locked in cells for twenty-three hours or more per day and thus were no longer in situations where supervision was required. Staff entered living units only for periodic checks and counts, to enquire about inmate needs, and deliver food and other

services to inmates and to escort prisoners who had been first placed in handcuffs, and often also leg restraints and waist chains, one at a time to exercise, showers, the telephone and so on. (King, 1999: 172)

The Severity of Penal Language

The authorities no longer need show reticence or shame about the size of their prison populations, or even the unpleasantness of their conditions. Instead, these features may be relished and proclaimed. The authorities in New York state seem to have been amongst the first to speak this new language of punishment: 'Tough but enlightened correctional system: caught, convicted, canned. That's the scenario awaiting those who break New York's laws' (*Report of the Department of Correctional Services*, 1985–6: 3). The same report goes on to illustrate how the length of prison terms there compared favourably with other states. That is to say, they were longer in New York: 'felons released in 1985 had spent an average of twenty-eight months behind bars in New York; by comparison, the average length of incarceration that year was sixteen months in the federal system, twenty in California, and twenty-four in Texas'. They were also keen to affirm that they followed the trend to punish more rather than less: 'New York locks up felons at the nationwide average of 195 per 100,000 residents'.[5]

Georgia, too, was quick to abandon its commitment to rehabilitation: in its place, it asserts that 'correctional facilities should be operated in a humane but severe, disciplined manner' (*Report of the Department of Corrections*, 1986: 3). The severity of its prison regimes include a forbearance on gym activities. Instead, for the purposes of exercise, 'all inmates are to walk four and a half miles per day ... we have substituted a cold sandwich for lunch – there is no hot lunch' (*Report of the Department of Corrections*, 1996: 4). At the same time, the social distance between the authorities and the prisoners is extended again. The practice whereby inmates came to be addressed as 'Mr' is reversed: the rules now state that they must address the staff with 'Sir' or 'Ma'am' as a sign of respect for them (*Report of the Department of Corrections*, 1995). Furthermore, the authorities no longer speak of 'correctional institutions' but instead of 'state prisons' (*Report of the Department of Corrections*, 1996).

In England, the emphasis that prison should be used as a last resort has gone: 'I am not as concerned about the size of the prison population as some. It should be driven by the decision of the courts to send people to prison' (Home Secretary, *The Guardian*, 13 May 1993: 3). This shift away from the careful restrictive controls of bureaucratic rationalism to open-ended use of prison as an outlet for overflowing public sentiments was most famously affirmed when Michael Howard became Home Secretary in 1993: 'Let us be clear – prison works. It ensures that we are protected from murderers, muggers and rapists – and it makes many who are tempted to commit crime think twice' (Cavadino and Dignan 1997: 38).

In comments such as these, we see a quite dramatic reversal of one of the main assumptions of penal policy from the late nineteenth century onwards: that prison should be used sparingly. This had been why those countries where this was most apparent were looked on as leaders of the civilized world. It is very hard now to find envious glances being cast in their directions. Prisons have always been intended to 'work', of course: for much of the nineteenth and twentieth centuries bureaucratic expertise had been harnessed to prison development to try to ensure that they would do exactly that – as this term was understood by the penal authorities: they were to work in terms of bringing about rehabilitation through reform and treatment, thereby reducing the likelihood of a prisoner's reconviction on release. They never really did work in this way of course, but now they are to work in a very different way: they are to work by simply keeping their predatory populations away from the rest of society – if prisons can achieve little else, then at least they can achieve this.

Protecting the Public (Home Office, 1996) represented another abrupt departure from the sanitized penal language associated with punishment in the civilized world. It was the successor to the 1990 *Crime, Justice and Protecting the Public* document. Now, it seemed that any connection to crime and justice to bring about such protection was unnecessary. In contrast to the previous reaffirmation of the need to restrict the prison population, it was premised instead on the assumption that this would significantly expand if there was indeed to be public protection, as Howard had previously intimated:

> model prisoners should get a little time off for good behaviour ... every-one else should serve their sentence in full ... five years should mean five years. It's time to get honesty back into sentencing ... No more automatic early release, no more release regardless of behaviour, and no more half time sentences for full time crimes. (Cavadino and Dignan, 1997: 198)

These commitments, in varying degrees, to reverse some of the central assumptions of penal policy for most of the nineteenth and twentieth centuries, are made possible by new, previously inconceivable tolerances of prison levels and conditions.

Beyond the prison itself, new beacons have been lit in the outlying reaches of the penal world by the reintroduction of sanctions from previous eras: chain gangs in the Deep South again, and judicially ordered shaming penalties in other parts of the United States and Australia. These can compel offenders to wear stigmatic clothing and/or perform menial labour before a public audience, or otherwise give off warning signs about themselves: one offender was thus required to post a sign outside his home and in his car saying 'Dangerous Sexual Offender – No Children Allowed' (Karp, 1998: 29). As the Northern Territory [Australia] Attorney-General explained the matter, when introducing the legislation for the Punitive Work Order in that state in 1996, 'those serving a punitive work order will be clearly obvious to the rest of the community. They will be identifiable as Punitive Work Offenders either by wearing a special uniform or some other label. It is meant to be a punishment that shames the guilty person' (*Ministerial Statement on the Criminal Justice System and Victims of Crime*, 20 August 1996). Shame as a penal tactic had never disappeared from the civilized world, even if shaming punishments for individual offenders had long since faded away. However, while considerable attempts had been made to reduce any residual shaming components of punishment for them, it had been used as an indicator of disapproval of those societies whose penal systems seemed out of line with civilized values.[6] Now, though, in another shift in the moral economy of shame, it can be used once again against individual offenders. This does not of necessity mean that shame has to be debasing and humiliating. Alongside these forms, we also find reintegrative shaming practices (Braithwaite, 1989), designed to allow for conscience formation in the offender and forgiveness from their local community gaining momentum, principally through the restorative justice movement: instead of the state being prepared to make these gestures, as it was supposed to do for much of the post-war period, these, like many other of its responsibilities, have been devolved. Furthermore, whatever the differences in terms of their intended effects, these divergent forms of shaming seem to arise out of the same conditions of existence: a greater public, rather than bureaucratic, involvement in the process of punishment, greater emotional release at the expense of bureaucratic efficiency, greater visibility of punishment rather than invisibility.

The New Axis of Penal Power

How do we explain the impact of this new punitiveness? The answer is to be found in the new axis of penal power that was established between the central state and the general public, a key feature of the neo-liberal political programme. Notwithstanding the restraints and restrictions that the state was trying to police more efficiently to keep the boundaries of punishment within recognizable limits during much of the 1980s, public anxieties about crime, disorder and ineffective responses to these problems only increased. The indifference of the general public was further eroded, giving way to intolerance and demands for still greater manifestations of repressive punishment. This occurs in conjunction with the seeming inability of the state to resolve some of the most pressing manifestations of these anxieties. There was a virtual recognition that it no longer had the answer to spiralling crime problems during the 1980s and 1990s (Garland, 1996), and its own authority progressively weakens.[7]

The strong state of neo-liberal polity increasingly becomes the ineffectual, discredited state. Ultimately, instead of the central state educating the public and leading them along a rational, reasoned path of development, it is as if the position comes to be reversed, with the axis of penal power significantly shifted away from the dominant bureaucratic rationalism of the state and towards the emotive punitiveness of the general public.

There seems little doubt that the public mood became more sharply punitive from around 1980 onwards (Walker and Hough, 1988) than had been the case in the previous twenty years. From there on, opinion polls continue to reveal increasing concerns over public safety and exponential complaints that the courts were not being punitive enough. In comparison with the level of responses to this question in 1980, in 1992 in Canada, 85 per cent thought that the courts were not punitive enough, only 3 per cent disagreeing with the suggestion; in the United States in 1990, the responses were 82 per cent for, 3 per cent against; in England in 1993, the responses were 77 per cent for, 2 against.[8]

These concerns might then be typically connected to broader undercurrents of worry, insecurity, fear of the future, lack of concern for others and a heightened concern for one's own security, amidst a general sense of powerlessness and foreboding. For example,

> sixty-five per cent of the public [in Britain] reject the idea that there will be less crime in the future as a result of politicians' promises about getting tough on crime. In addition, eighty-seven per cent say that their concern over crime has increased in the last decade or so. The same poll revealed that sixty three per cent of British adults think that Britain is less caring than a decade ago, and forty per cent believed it will get worse over the next ten years. Half the public now agree that many of those on state benefit do not genuinely need such help, an increase of sixteen percentage points on 1989; eighty eight per cent feel that people should be encouraged to stand on their own two feet.[9]

It is then as if the new levels of punitiveness that had been established as a result of these concerns might be periodically tested on specific issues and brought to a point, thereby establishing the groundwork for still further explorations in punishment which push back its boundaries to increasingly unrecognizable horizons. Life imprisonment must mean exactly that, for example: in New Zealand, 67 per cent agreed with this, with only 11 per cent supporting the possibility of parole (*National Business Review*, 3 March 1997: 8). Another poll in England indicated that 76 per cent felt that the public should have the right to be notified about the release of sex criminals from prison, with 58 per cent agreeing that they should be 'named and shamed'.[10]

Some of the reasons for this increasing anxiety are due to the effects of the civilizing process itself. The civilized world becomes increasingly cosmopolitan and pluralistic from the 1970s: this brings with it the possibilities for new interdependencies and tolerances through transnational trade arrangements, treaty alliances, greater mobility of labour, and so on, but at the same time, state sovereignty seems under threat from international treaties and alliances that override territorial boundaries and national characteristics. And within each state, the growing prominence of new social movements seem to challenge the legitimacy of the more long-established foundations of the civilized world (the nuclear family, police, church, trade unions, class solidarity, and so on). New possibilities of everyday existence and experience are opened up, but which at the same time seem fraught with new risks and dangers. New sources of crime information – university-organized crime surveys, independent victim surveys, self-report studies, telephone surveys, surveys for women's magazines – designed to make our understandings of crime levels and risks more exact, may now supersede the inaccurate official crime statistics as the most reliable source of knowledge we have on the subject. While, for the state authorities, these are seen as evidence of the minimal crime risks that most of us face (see Hough and Mayhew, 1983), through the reporting and publicizing of this knowledge in the mass media and other sources, they only seem to enlarge the risks we face and increase our sense of unease and insecurity. In such ways danger is made to seem more omnipresent and incalculable. We become consumed by worry about what can happen to us today, rather than what is likely to happen, and we conjure monsters that seem to be lying in wait for us in the shadows of everyday existence. The fact that recorded crime at least seems to have stabilized or is even in significant decline across some of these societies, is not sufficient to put a brake on these fears which all our most significant and influential sources of knowledge on this matter seem to construct.[11]

In so doing, they have reshaped the habitus of citizens in the civilized world in the late twentieth and early twenty-first centuries. It changes from certainty and stability, characteristic of the first two decades or so of postwar social development, to uncertainty and insecurity. Cultural values change from tolerance and forbearance to animosity and hostility to those who seem to threaten an ever more precarious security.[12] Here, then, are the circumstances for Bauman's heterophobia to take effect on penal development. New problems emerge to threaten the stability of everyday existence, which seem beyond both the capacity of the state and its citizens to address – at least in a way which corresponded to the previously established values and assumptions of the civilized world. A weakened central state is prepared to follow an increasingly punitive public and thereby allow public anxieties to make their stamp on penal policy. One of the first manifestations in this shift in the axis of penal power is seen in a speech made by Mario Cuomo, Mayor of New York in 1983, and later quoted by the prison authorities as the course that had been preset for them to follow:

> Where does the system go from here ... it will go where it is sent ... if we follow the logic that says getting tough on crime means incarcerating

all felons, you will see this system grow to around fifty thousand inmates. We can handle that ... do we as a society really believe that non-violent felons – the petty check forgers, the small time embezzlers – belong behind forty feet walls? Do we really believe that it is a better alternative than a lengthy sentence of community service? Because if we do, you had better get out your checkbooks. Because you are going to have to write me a check to build ten thousand more cells. The choice is the people's. You tell us how. You tell us where. The choice has always been the public's to make. (*Report of the Department of Correctional Services*, 1985–6: 18)

Nearly twenty years later, we now know the choices the public have made – for the prison authorities to put into effect. From a level of custody of 30,000 when Cuomo made his speech, the prison population of New York state had climbed to around 70,000 in 1997.

Towards the Gulag

This new configuration of penal power still does not mean, by and large, a full reversal of the effects of the civilizing process. Instead, it is much more the case that the efficient, modernized machinery of punishment that had been put into effect now runs in conjunction with the punitive mentality of the general public, rather than suppressing it, or holding it off with one or two tokenistic gestures. The reintroduction of the death penalty in the United States had been a precursor of what such a conjunction might allow to happen. Now, with its growing influence, public punitiveness steadily pushes the boundaries of permissible punishment outwards – ensuring that its forms remain familiar, even though the boundaries themselves keep arriving at more distant horizons. Only where these boundaries are particularly fragile, are these public sentiments able to burst entirely through them, constructing penal forms previously out of place in the civilized world. When this happens, and in a bid to shore up its own weakened authority, the state is prepared to revisit the possibilities of punishing that give out more obvious signs of reassurance to the public ('I recall seeing chain gangs as a child ... the impression I had was one of hard labour and a law-abiding state. That's the image Florida needs today – instead of innocent citizens being robbed and raped everyday', Crist, 1996: 178): similarly the self-shaming techniques that have returned to the penal repertoire in some parts of the civilized world. The revival of interest in indigenous justice in New Zealand and Canada stems from this weakness of the central state. It no longer retains monopolistic control of the power to punish, but allows local non-western practices to run alongside its own authority.

The collapse of faith in the state's own ability to provide security can also lead to demands for an increased public involvement in the administration of punishment. This provided the driving force for the introduction of Megan's Law (Simon 1998) and subsequent derivatives in the United States and elsewhere. Here, a child was sexually assaulted and murdered by an ex-convict with a history of sexual offending who had moved, unknown and unannounced into the local community. The subsequent trauma of the child's parents was the trauma of all parents who have ever been involved in such cases. What has changed, though, is the way such concerns now have the force to be translated into penal policy as 'the right to know': this right to know, the right of local communities to be informed of the release of those with predatory inclinations – where they are to reside and what prohibitions and restrictions have been placed on their behaviour – has now been inscribed in law in various ways. There is to be no forgiveness, no end to the suspicion of those who constitute such demonic others. As President Clinton said when signing Megan's Law, 'we respect people's rights but today in America there is no greater right than a parent's right to raise a child in safety and love ... America warns – if you dare to prey on our children, the law will follow you wherever you go, state to state, town to town' (Office of the Press Secretary, The White House, 25 July 1995).

Again, the new axis of penal power may lead to the state putting into effect penal policies that reflect the public's common sense, rather than the scientific rationalities of its own experts. The introduction of three strikes laws and other forms of mandatory sentences continue the trend set in the early 1980s to curb the sentencing discretion of the judges and the parole discretion of the prison authorities. Now, however, this is done with the knowledge that this will increase the prison population, rather than reduce it. Such trends represent a breakdown of the serious/non-serious distinction as the point of distribution to differing modalities of punishment for these two groups. Instead, in addition to the seriousness of one's crime, one can now be punished for the kind of person one is thought to be: 'it is not good enough that there is no guarantee at present that a persistent offender will receive a more severe penalty when he appears before the court for the fifth time than on his second appearance ... persistent offenders need to know that if they persist in their crimes they will receive increasingly severe punishment' (Home Secretary, *The Guardian Weekly*, 7 May 2001: 2). Such irrationalities can now be met by prolonged imprisonment. Under the terms of the new axis of penal power, this has become the rational, not the irrational response to such unreasoning criminals. Hence, as well, the reference to 'prison works' in England: for most of the public, prison no doubt always has worked in the sense that it removes those who are unwanted or cannot be tolerated; now, rather than excluded from influencing penal development, it becomes an important aspect of it, as common sense is increasingly allowed to override expert knowledge.[13] By the same token, why let out of prison those whom we know are certain to offend again – can we not just detain them indefinitely? Again, the United States led the way here, with its sexually violent predator statutes.[14] On completion of the original sentence, a civil trial takes place before a judge and jury to determine whether these sexual predators are still 'dangerous': if so, they remain in confinement indefinitely. In England, recent proposals would mean that there is to be no release at all for those judged to be psychopaths, only the opening up of further proceedings against them designed to ensure their further detention on completion of a finite term of imprisonment.[15]

It should be no surprise, however, that the United States has moved down this route so far in advance of the other comparable societies, and was also the first of them to start off on it: and it should be of no surprise that the most blatant reversals to the trajectory of the civilizing process are in those regions that came latest to it. Not only might it be thought the anxieties and concerns of everyday life are more pronounced there – with correspondingly less by way of state support to provide security and solutions – but, in addition, the necessity to win public approval by judges, prosecutors and the like when being elected to office means that these public sentiments are likely to have considerably more political purchase in the United States than elsewhere (Zimring and Hawkins, 1991). Indeed, the pace of imprisonment in that country, vastly outstripping the growth in the rest of the civilized world has led to the formation of 'Western style gulags' (Christie, 1993): imprisonment in the United States is now on a par with levels previously associated only with the former Eastern bloc, one of the characteristics which had seemed to set that region so far apart from the civilized world. Now, in the United States, a new kind of gulag is being constructed: high levels of imprisonment are no longer simply an aberration that can be reversed or defeated by rational arguments, but instead are one of the very conditions of existence of its social structure; a natural product, a characteristic of the firm relationship between the weakened central state and the forceful general public. Here, the crime control industry, rather than acting as a marginal supplement to bring order and security to the main purposes and business of everyday life, becomes itself one of the main purposes of the business of everyday life. Gulags become a possibility in Western societies under the very specific conditions to be found in the United States: a conjunction between an enhanced bureaucratic rationalism associated with the civilizing process itself which streamlines the penal system and allows it to cope with the demands that the new punitiveness now places on it, on the one hand; and, on the other, a central state that seems to have minimal insulation from the demands of populist punitiveness. Rather than assume leadership itself, it is prepared to be led by public opinion which, because of the heightened sense of risk and the lack of state-provided security in other respects, seems able to tolerate higher levels of penal repression and deprivation than in most other civilized societies.

The position has been rather different in the rest of the civilized world: the pace of imprisonment accelerates (the same efficient, streamlined machinery of punishment has been constructed and is pushed outwards by the influence of an anxious public) but not at the same pace. Elsewhere, the state has not been so prepared to relinquish control of the steering mechanism of punishment. The deeply embedded, non-electable penal authorities, officials and administrators, while capable of mendaciously camouflaging their own inhumanities, at the same time seem able to provide a buffer against the outright domination of popular sentiment on penal development. This is also reflected in penal trends beyond the prison: judicially ordered shaming sanctions are, as yet, confined to the United States and the more remote parts of Australia; elsewhere, the penal bureaucracies still preside over most community sanctions (with the public excluded), simply tightening up enforcement procedures or otherwise to take account of the new punitiveness (Cavadino and Dignan, 1997).

The less the bureaucratic organizations of punishment have been pushed to one side in the new axis of penal power, the less the influence of populist punitiveness is likely to be and the more likely that there will still be significant voices that worry about prison levels and insist on 'civilized' conditions within the prisons. In some of these societies, the new deluxe private prisons are still the way forward in prison development, not the American super-max model. In England, the Chief Inspector of Prisons still produces reports that are critical of any lapses from 'civilized standards' (1996: 26). And still attempts to have these standards affirmed, as with the proposals put forward for 'healthy prisons':

> the weakest prisoners feel safe, all prisoners are treated with respect as individuals; routines can ensure that there is a chance of a daily shower and that clothing and bedding are clean. Arrangements for cooking and serving food should be hygienic and it should be possible to eat meals in the company of others. The standard of cleanliness should be high ... all of the prisons which are contracted out and a few of the prisons in the public service have adopted the practice of addressing prisoners by the title of 'Mr' or by the use of a first name. (1996: 26)

Here, the emphasis is still on trying to provide respect for the prisoners, rather than demonstrably eliciting their respect for the staff.

Individual prison governors have been prepared to speak out against conditions in their own prisons, and in the last decade especially, its more senior figures have assumed a directly confrontational role against their political overseers.[16] However, if these are indicators of opposition to any further steps that the central state might be prepared to take along the route to the gulag in England, they may also be seen as a sign of the weakness of such opposition – such figures can speak out because the state is no longer particularly interested in what they have to say. It is these representatives of the penal establishment who have become the outsiders. The state can now ignore them, in much the same way that their own bureaucracies came to ignore public sentiments. The retiring Chief Inspector of Prisons' comments on his five years work were that 'I have never received ministerial acknowledgement of, or response to, any of these reports or their contents, or their recommendations' (*The Weekly Telegraph*, 27 July 2001–31 July 2001: 10). It is as if such authority figures, even when they have been introduced to expose and make accountable the penal bureaucracies, are themselves simply another part of the same penal establishment that the state turns away from. What is it that the public wants, and how can this be given effect is the more potent force on penal development? Expressions of public mood, caught in opinion polls and other sources, increasingly drive penal policy rather than rationalized, authoritative judgement.

To give effect to these sentiments, there is no great need to worry about the cost of imprisonment anymore: previous references to 'cost-effectiveness' and 'economic restraints' in the mission statements of the penal authorities are more difficult to find now (see *Report of the Director of Corrective Services*, 1989–90; *Report of the Director of Corrective Services*, 1992–3). The efficiencies and reforms associated with bureaucratic rationalism seem to have taken care of most of these restraining factors. There is no sense of anxiety about increases in imprisonment whether this be on economic or humanitarian grounds: they have become manageable and acceptable.

Limits or No Limits?

What happens, though, should the state insist that there are still limits, nonetheless, beyond which it is not prepared to move? Such a refusal may then generate inflammable, sporadic *ad hoc* strikes by the general public directed at whichever groups of the undesirable or unwanted are unfortunate enough to come to their attention. In England, a young child, Sarah Payne, was raped and murdered in July 2000. The most popular Sunday newspaper in that country, the *News of the World*, campaigned for nearly two months afterwards for the government to introduce sex offender registers in the manner of Megan's Law in the United States, with headlines such as 'Does a Monster Live near You?':

> we have begun the biggest public record of child sex offenders ever seen in this country ... There are 110,000 proven paedophiles in the United Kingdom, one for every square mile of the country. We have started identifying these offenders and made a pledge that we will not stop until all 110,000 are named and shamed. Week in, week out, we will add to our record so that every parent in the land can have the right to know where these people are living. (*News of the World*, 31 July 2000: 2)

The paper went on to insist that this was not a charter for vigilantism. It did not need to provide a charter for this to happen – what it had done was to act as the catalyst for an outpouring of emotional turmoil, which burst through the strait-jacket of self-restraint and indifference that might once have held such sentiments in check. An increasingly unusual nexus of social work professionals, academic experts and government ministers combined against the weight of popular sentiment and refused to go beyond the existing notification procedures (to the police and penal professionals) of the Sex Offenders Act 1997. The response was the formation of nationwide vigilante groups, with a view to hunting down and driving out such monsters. Where the state had refused to take action, members of the public would be prepared to do so themselves.

These, though, have been only the most widespread and visible of a range of similar activities in recent years.[17] There are clear resonances here with the origins of the vigilante groups that once roamed the Deep South. Then and now, their emergence reflects a dissatisfaction with the existing criminal justice and penal systems, which seem too remote and non-responsive to the interests of ordinary people; a sense of vulnerability, and perceptions that the state's own penal solutions to crime and social problems cannot keep them in check. The difference today, however, is that these new forms of vigilantism are more class-specific, a reflection of social arrangements where security becomes a market-driven commodity, which some can purchase, but others are unable to (Garland, 1996).[18] Those living on the fragile borders of respectability, most at risk from the approaching demons that threaten us, but without the material resources to insulate themselves from them, are those most susceptible to involvement in such activities (Girling et al., 1998). What also seems clear, however, is that when state power is removed or weakened – the prerequisite for the emergence of these more emotive, public participatory forms of justice – it is just as possible that new social movements based on the rule of the mob will emerge, alongside some humane form of community or restorative justice. Indeed, it is not the case that restorative justice acts as an alternative to such possibilities; these possibilities are the price that has to be paid for its own emergence, and whatever its effectivity.

Does this mean that the penal boundaries of the civilized world are likely to be inexorably pushed back altogether and the civilized world moves into completely unfamiliar penal territory, to the point where all its hallmarks will completely disappear? First, it has to be said that there are likely to be natural limits to this process of expansion and growth. In America, 'after growing explosively for three decades, the nation's prison population has begun to stabilize … for the first time in years, the overcrowding that has plagued state prisons and local jails alike is beginning to ease, as a result of falling crime rates and a decade of new construction' (*New York Times*, 9 June 2001: 8). If fear of crime was so responsible for the acceleration in public anxieties in the 1980s and 1990s, its levelling off now may put a brake on them and their concomitant influence on penal development. Again, if public anxieties can be attributed to the great social and economic upheavals of the last three decades, the way in which these changes have now become embedded in the social fabric may provide some sense of assurance and stability. If, for most people, what has been happening to penal development in the last two decades has been perfectly tolerable – untouched by it themselves, the removal of various unwanted groups has so far been welcomed – this may nonetheless help to define the limits to current trends. It is only when ordinary people begin to be touched by the penal apparatus that any sustained questioning of what is happening begins to take place. As Holocaust researchers (Gellatly, 1990; Johnson, 1999) remind us, a crucial feature of the Nazi regime in Germany was to ensure as far as possible that it was only 'Others' – Jews, homosexuals, gypsies, and so on – who were targeted, not normal, ordinary citizens: so long as they remained as such, they had nothing to fear.

There are also moral limits to the process of expansion. The repugnance among the rest of the civilized world to the use of the death penalty in the United States may have the effect of conscience raising in that society.[19] Indeed, in the aftermath of the publicity given to the execution of Oklahoma bomber Timothy McVeigh in June 2001, support for the death penalty in that country (at 65 per cent all the same) fell to its lowest level in twenty years. Despite high levels of public support for the reintroduction of the death penalty in England, successive attempts to do so between 1982 and 1994 were resoundingly defeated in Parliament.[20] In such societies it has ceased to be a penal option.

By the same token, against the acceleration of prison levels in the rest of the civilized world, some of its members still stand out as exceptions. Governments in such societies can still make choices, of course: they can still ensure that the boundaries of punishment remain within recognizable limts; or they can take a few further steps along the route towards the gulag. In Victoria, a different choice seems to have been made by successive governments in that state from most other civilized societies: the rate of imprisonment is 61 per 100,000 of population. And individuals have choices: for every judge who invents some new way to publicly shame and humiliate offenders in the United States, there is another who refuses to enact mandatory sentencing laws by finding loopholes in them (Freiberg, 2000). In other words, there is no reason to think of some naturally expanding universe of punishment. There are likely to be natural limits to it, there are likely to be moral limits to it.

However, it also needs to be recognized that it is most unlikely that there will be any simple, sudden retraction to what has been happening in the last two or three decades: as if this has all been an aberration, some sort of prolonged, irrational nightmare, which we can somehow wake from, and through a combination of rational argument and human goodness begin the work of rebuilding and restoring our societies to what had been the previous limits to punishment in the civilized world. To return to these levels and expectations of punishment would only be possible if the social structure and cultural values that were their preconditions were also in existence. For most people, what has been happening over the last two decades has indeed been entirely tolerable. Save for one or two scandals, one or two awkward conscience-raising moments, there is no pressure on governments to punish any less, only to punish more. And we have seen what can happen when the state seems to renege on the axis it has forged with populist punitiveness. This may bring into existence, in sweeping, unpredictable forms, a twilight world that lies beyond the gulag itself. In the aftermath of Sarah Payne's murder, the leaders of one vigilante group claimed to possess a self-constructed, self-styled 'list of power' – the names and addresses of local people whom they suspected of paedophile activities, as if participation in a hunt such as this in itself became a form of empowerment, an extension of what they had been encouraged to do for two decades, but with all the restraints and limits that had been set for them pushed out of the way. One woman who was later interviewed about her involvement with this group seemed to scarcely believe what she had found herself doing – but showed at the same time how easy it is to become involved in such activities once the conditions for them are set in place. She said, in the report:

> There is no list. I asked for it when I discovered that they were going to target someone in my sister-in-law's road. They said to me the list's all mental. I said no way, you could not have a mental list, that you know every house and every road that has a paedophile. The [woman] ... feels ashamed because she enjoyed walking up the street with a gang of women, all shouting to get the paedophiles out. 'I can't help it but this is how I felt. Walking the streets with all the noise, I got a buzz out of it. I know it sounds really childish. But when I came back here I thought, what have I done'. (*The Observer*, 13 August 2000, p. 4)

What we see from this woman's comments is how fragile the thin veneer of civilization which has been pasted across the modern world has become in recent years: how much of the restraints and inhibitions against such involvement, how the safeguards designed to relegate such disturbing scenes to a distant memory or to have them assigned, as its exclusive property, to the uncivilized world, are capable of fragmenting and allowing them to overrun our weakened defences. Let us not close our eyes to such possibilities, as has been our practice as citizens in the civilized world towards disturbing events and rest on the assumption that, because we live in the civilized world, 'it could not happen here'. It can happen here, under the particular circumstances and conditions that we find in existence today.

It seems to be one of the characteristics of modern, civilized societies that there always has to be a happy ending to any story: even fairy tales now have to have happy endings, as George Steiner has pointed out to us. Our belief in reason, justice, science, human nature, will ultimately prevail, we assure ourselves. We have the capacity to find a reasoned solution to all that which troubles us. I am certain that this can be the case. But it is not necessarily the case. Usually, the very act of thinking in this way means that we also have a tendency to ignore or disbelieve or dismiss the dark side that these propensities carry with them. In this book, I have tried to redress the balance.

Notes

1 See, for example, *Report of the Director of Corrective Services* (1992–3).

2 Victoria seems to have been the jurisdiction that became most committed to privatization: there was a 47/53 split between the private and public sector in the mid-1990s.

3 As in the ruling of Gregg v Georgia 1976 (428 US 153); see also *New York Times*, 15 August 1992 D: 20.

4 See Home Office Statistical Bulletin (1998), Department of Corrections [New Zealand] 2000.

5 Nor have the leaders of the civilized world been immune to these increases: in Norway, the rate of imprisonment in 1999 was 56 per 100,000 of population; in Holland it was 85 per 100,000 of population (Christie, 2000: 27).

6. See, for example, the 1932 movie, *I Am a Fugitive from a Chain Gang*; also, in relation to Georgia's prisons, *Time Magazine* 13 September 1943: 23; Hall (1979).

7 In Canada, the rate of recorded crime had increased to 10,342 by 1991. In England, recorded crime had increased from its 1980 level to 5,276,173 in 1991. In New Zealand, from its 1980 level to 525,622 in 1991. In the United States, to 14,872,900 in 1991. In New South Wales, crime reported to the police increased from 243,266 in 1980–1 to 481,874 in 1990–1; in Victoria, from 224,514 to 440,323 over the same period.

8 Source: Hastings and Hastings (2000).

9 Source: http://www.mori.com/polls/1999/rd990913.htm.

10 Source: http://www.mori.com/polls/2000/noname.htm.

11 During the 1990s, recorded crime in England fell from 5,591,717 in 1992 to 4,598,327 in 1997. In New Zealand, from 525,622 in 1991 to 455,552 in

1999. In the United States, from 14,872,900 in 1991 to 12,475,600 in 1998. In Canada, the rate of recorded crime per 100,000 of population fell from 10,342 in 1991 to 7,733 in 1999. Changes in recording procedures in Australia over the same period make such a comparison unreliable; however, the indicators in that country are upwards (Australian Bureau of Statistics, 1999) and therefore against this trend.

12 In New Zealand, a growing majority (63 per cent) now favour of a return of the death penalty, with support most strongly felt by 18–24 year olds (76), reflective of the views of those in the forefront of the social, economic and cultural changes of the last two decades (*National Business Review*, 3 March 1997: 8).

13 Cf. Zimring (1996) on the passage into law of the Californian 'Three Strikes' proposals.

14 The first such law was introduced in Washington State in 1990.

15 See *The Independent International*, 28 July 1999: 11.

16 Compare the memoirs of former Director General of Prisons Derek Lewis (1997), with the politically neutral accounts of his predecessors such as Du Cane (1885), Ruggles-Brise (1921), Fox (1952).

17 See also Rose (1994), Dawes and Hil (1998), Girling et al. (1998). There are various less direct means of local community disapproval also in existence: for example, in New Zealand, the distribution of 'naming and shaming' leaflets by individuals or local citizen groups.

18 So far, the levels of violence in current vigilante activities do not even begin to compare to what used to take place in the Deep South. (See Southern Commission on the Study of Lynching 1931)

19 Cf. *The Australian* (13 June 2001: 1) 'Europe calls on US to ban executions'.

20 The focus of opposition was again concentrated around the need for governments to lead public opinion, not to follow it, and that the death penalty had no place in the civilized world (see *Hansard*, for example, 7 June 1988 [134] 764, 785).

Bibliography

Adams, R. (1994) *Prison Riots in Britain and the USA*. Basingstoke: Macmillan.

Ainsworth, W.H. (1838) *Jack Sheppard*. Philadelphia: Lea and Blanchard.

Allen, W. (1847) *The Life of William Allen*. Philadelphia: H. Longstreth.

Austin, P. (1967) *The Swedes: How They Live and Work*. Newton Abbott: David and Charles.

Australian Bureau of Statistics (1999) *Recorded Crime*, Canberra: Government Printer.

Babyak, J. (1994) *Bird Man*. Berkeley, CA: Ariel Vamp Press.

Baker, P. (1961) *Time out of Life*. London: Heinemann.

Ball, B. (1956) *Prison was my parish*. London: Heinemann Ltd.

Balfour, J. (1901) *My Prison Life*. London: Chapman and Hall.

Bartley, N. (1983) *The creation of modern Georgia*, Athens, GA: University of Georgia Press.

Bauman, Z. (1989) *Modernity and the Holocaust*. Cambridge: Polity Press.

Beattie, J. (1986) *Crime and the Courts in England 1660–1800*. Oxford: Clarendon Press.

Behan, B. (1959) *Borstal Boy*. London: Hutchinson.

Bender, J. (1987) *Imagining the Penitentiary*. Chicago: University of Chicago Press.

Bidwell, A. (1895) *From Wall Street to Newgate*. London: Macmillan.

Booth, W. (1890) *In Darkest England and the Way Out*. London: Salvation Army.

Bottoms, A.E. (1977) 'Reflections on the renaissance of dangerousness', *Howard Journal*, 16: 70–96.

Bottoms, A.E. (1981) 'The suspended sentence', *British Journal of Criminology*, 21: 1–26.

Bottoms, A.E. (1995) 'The politics and philosophy of sentencing', in C. Clarkson and R. Morgan (eds), *The Politics of Sentencing*. Oxford: Clarendon Press, pp. 170–90.

Boyle, J. (1977) *A Sense of Freedom*. London: Pan Books.

Braithwaite, J. (1989) *Crime, Shame and Reintegration*. Cambridge: Cambridge University Press.

Briggs, D. (1975) *In Place of Prison*. London: Temple Smith.

Brocklehurst, F. (1898) *I Was in Prison*. London: T. Fisher Unwin.

Brodie, A., Croom, J. and Davies, J. (1999) *The Prison Experience*. Swindon: English Heritage.

Broome, D. (1988) 'The stigma of Pentridge', *Journal of Australian Studies*, 22: 3–18.

Burgess, E. (1937) 'Protecting the public by parole and by parole prediction', *Journal of the American Institute of Criminal Law and Criminology*, 27: 491–502.

Burnett, J. (1966) *Plenty and Want*. London: Scolar Press.

Burns, R. (1932) *I am a Fugitive from a Georgia Chain Gang*. New York: Vanguard Press.

Burt, J. (1852, 1969) *Results of the Separate System of Confinement*. Montclair: Paterson Smith.

Canadian Centre for Justice (2000) *Statistics 2000*. Ottawa: Statistics Canada.

Carcach, C. and Grant, A. (1999) *Imprisonment in Australia*. Canberra: AIC.

Carlyle, T. (1850) *Latter Day Pamphlets*. London: Chapman and Hall.

Carpenter, M. (1864, 1969) *Our Convicts*. Montclair: Paterson Smith.

Cartwright, T.J. (1975) *Royal Commissions and Departmental Committees in Britain*. London: Hodder and Stoughton.

Cass, E. (1931) 'American prisons today', *Annals of the American Academy of Social and Political Science*, 157: 612–16.

Cavadino, M. and Dignan, J. (1997) *The Penal System: An Introduction*. London: Sage.

Chadwick, E. (1842, 1965) *The Sanitary Conditions of the Labouring Population of Great Britain*. Edinburgh: Edinburgh University Press.

Chan, J. (1992) *Doing Less Time*. Sydney: Institute of Criminology.

Chapman, P. (1984) *Madame Tussaud's Chamber of Horrors*. London: Constable.

Chesterton, G. (1856) *Revelations of Prison Life*. London: Hurst and Blackett.

Chinn, C. (1995) *Poverty Amidst Plenty*. Manchester: Manchester University Press.

Christie, N. (1993) *Crime Control as Industry*. London: Routledge.

Christie, N. (2000) *Crime Control as Industry*. London: Routledge.

Clarke, J. (1998) 'Without fear or shame: lynching, capital punishment and the subculture of violence in the American South', *British Journal of Political Science*, 28: 269–89.

Clay, W. (1861, 1969) *The Prison Chaplain*. Montclair: Paterson Smith.

Clayton, G. (1958) *The Wall is Strong*. London: Longmans.

Coggan, G. and Walker, M. (1982) *Frightened for my Life*. London: Collins.

Cohen, S. (1985) *Visions of Social Control*. Cambridge: Polity Press.

Cohen, S. and Taylor, L. (1972) *Psychological Survival*. London: Penguin.

Cohen, S. and Taylor, L. (1978) *Prison Secrets*. London: NCCL.

Collins, P. (1962) *Dickens and Crime*. London: Collins.

Colvin, M. (1982) 'The New Mexico prison riot', *Social Problems*, 29: 444–63.

Convict 77 (1903) *The Mark of the Broad Arrow*. London: R.A. Everett.

Cox, E. (1870) 'Habitual criminals'. *Law Times*, 49: 158–64.

Crawford, W. (1835, 1968) *Report on the Penitentiaries of the United States*. Dublin: Irish University Press.

Crist, C. (1996) 'Chain gangs are right for Florida', *Corrections Today*, 58: 178.

Croft-Cooke, R. (1955) *The Verdict of You All*. London: Secker and Warburg.

Cronin, H. (1967) *The Screw Turns*. London: Longmans.

Crook, J.M. (1971) 'A most classical architect: the architecture of Thomas Harrison', *Country Life*, 22 April: 941–7.

Crookston, P. (1967) *Villain*. London: Jonathan Cape.

Cumming, E. (1933) 'Sports and games', in A. Turberville (ed.), *Johnson's England*. Oxford: Oxford University Press.

Cunningham, H. (1980) *Leisure in the Industrial Revolution*. London: Routledge.

Darwin, C. (1859) *On the Origin of Species by Means of Natural Selection*. London: Murray.

Davison, G., Hirst, J. and Macintyre, J. (1998) *The Oxford Companion to Australian History*. Melbourne: Oxford University Press.

Davison, R. (1931) 'Prison architecture', *Architectural Record*, 67 (30): 69–100.

Davitt, M. (1886) *The Prison Life of Michael Davitt*. Dublin: Lalor.

Dawes, G. and Hil, R. (1998) 'Racialised vigilantism', paper presented at the Australian and New Zealand Criminology Conference, Brisbane.

Defoe, D. (1722, 1970) *The Fortunes and Misfortunes of the Famous Moll Flanders*. Oxford: Oxford University Press.

Defoe, D. (1726, 1970) *Memoirs of the Life and Times of Jonathan Wild*. Oxford: Oxford University Press.

Delacy, M. (1986) *Prison Reform in Lancashire 1700–1850*. Stanford: Stanford University Press.

Dendrickson, G. and Thomas, F. (1954) *The Truth about Dartmoor*. London: Gollancz.

Denison, G. (1937/8) 'Psychiatry and the conditions of criminal justice', *Yale Law Journal*, 47: 319–40.

Dennis, R. (1984) *English Industrial Cities of the Nineteenth Century*. Cambridge: Cambridge University Press.

Department of Corrections (2000) *Penal Policy Today*. Wellington: Department of Corrections.

Dickens, C. (1836/7, 1969) *The Pickwick Papers*, London: Oxford University Press.

Dickens, C. (1837, 1959) *Nicholas Nickleby*. London: Thames Publishing Company.

Dickens, C. (1838, 1959) *Oliver Twist*. London: Thames Publishing Company.

Dickens, C. (1841a, 1959) *Barnaby Rudge*. London: Thames Publishing Company.

Dickens, C. (1841b, 1969) *The Letters of Charles Dickens*. Oxford: Clarendon Press.

Dickens, C. (1850, 1959) *David Copperfield*. London: Thames Publishing Company.

Dickens, C. (1859, 1993) *A Tale of Two Cities*. London: Wordsworth Classics.

Dickens, C. (1860, 1959) *Great Expectations*. London: Thames Publishing Company.

Dixon, W.H. (1850) *The London Prisons*. London: Jackson & Walford.

Dostoyevsky, F. (1860, 1985) *The House of the Dead*. London: Harmondsworth.

Downes, D. (1982) 'The origins and consequences of Dutch penal policy since 1945', *British Journal of Criminology*, 22, 325–57.

Drummond, J. and Wilbraham, A. (1939) *The Englishman's Food: A History of Five Centuries of English Diet*. London: Cape.

Du Cane, E. (1875, 1876) 'Address on the repression of crime', *Transactions of the National Association for the Promotion of Social Science*. London: Longmans Green, pp. 271–308.

Du Cane, E. (1885) *The Punishment and Prevention of Crime*. London: Macmillan.

Du Cane, E. (1895) 'The Prison Committee Report', *The Nineteenth Century* 38, 278–94.

East, W.N. and Hubert, W. (1939) *Report on the Psychological Treatment of Crime*. London: HMSO.

Elias, N. (1939, 1984) *The Civilizing Process*. Oxford: Blackwell.

Elias, N. (1994) 'Notes on a lifetime', in N. Elias, *Reflections on a Life*. Cambridge: Polity Press.

Elias, N. (1996) *The Germans*. Cambridge: Polity Press.

Elias, N. and Scotson, J. (1965) *The Established and Outsiders*. London: Sage.

Elsam, R. (1818) *A Brief Treatise on Prisons*. London: J. Taylor.

Evans, R. (1982) *The Fabrication of Virtue*. Cambridge: Cambridge University Press.

Faucher, L. (1844, 1969) *Manchester in 1844*. London: Cass.

Feely, M. and Simon, J. (1992) 'The new penology', *Criminology*, 30, 449–70.

Field, J. (1848) *Prison Discipline*. London: Longmans.

Fielding, H. (1743, 1992) *Tom Jones*. London: Wordsworth Classics.

Fitzgerald, M. (1977) *Prisoners in Revolt*. London: Penguin.

Fitzgerald, M. and Sim, J. (1982) *British Prisons*. Oxford: Basil Blackwell.

Fletcher, J. (1997) *Violence and Civilization*. Cambridge: Polity Press.

Fox, L. (1952) *The English Prison and Borstal System*. London: Routledge and Kegan Paul.

Foucault, M. (1978) *Discipline and Punish*. London: Allen Lane.

Franke, H. (1995) *The Emancipation of Prisoners*. Edinburgh: Edinburgh University Press.

Febvre, L. (1930) 'Civilisation: Evolution of a Word and a Group of Ideas', reprinted in Rundell, J. and Mennell, S. (eds) (1998) *Classical Readings in Culture and Civilization*, London: Routledge.

Freiberg, A. (2000) 'Guerillas in our midst? Judicial responses to governing the dangerous', in M. Brown and J. Pratt (eds), *Dangerous Offenders*. London: Routledge, pp. 51–69.

Galsworthy, J. (1904) *The Island Pharisees*. London: Heinemann.

Galsworthy, J. (1929) *The Plays of John Galsworthy*. London: Duckworth.

Garland, D. (1990) *Punishment and Modern Society*. Oxford: Oxford University Press.

Garland, D. (1996) 'The limits of the sovereign state', *British Journal of Criminology*, 36: 445–71.

Garland, D. (2000) 'The meaning of mass imprisonment', paper presented at the British Society of Criminology Conference, Leicester.

Gatrell, V. (1994) *The Hanging Tree*. Oxford: Oxford University Press.

Gay, J. (1712, 1923) 'The Mohocks', in *The Plays of John Gay*. Oxford: Oxford University Press.

Gay, J. (1716, 1923) 'Trivia; or, the art of walking the streets of London', in *The Plays of John Gay*. Oxford: Oxford University Press.

Gay, J. (1728, 1973) *The Beggar's Opera*. Edinburgh: Oliver and Boyd.

Gellatly, R. (1990) *The Gestapo and German Society*. Oxford: Clarendon Press.

Giddens, A. (1990) *The Consequences of Modernity*. Cambridge: Polity Press.

Girling, E., Loader, I. and Sparks, R. (1998) 'A telling tale: a case of vigilantism and its aftermath in an English town', *British Journal of Sociology*, 49: 474–90.

Glover, E. (1956) *Probation and Re-education*. London: RKP.

Graham, J. (1992) 'Settler society', in G. Rice (ed.), *The Oxford History of New Zealand*. Auckland: Oxford University Press.

Greenberg, K. (1990) 'The nose, the lie and the duel in the antebellum South', *American Historical Review*, 95, 57–74.

Grew, B. (1958) *Prison Governor*. London: Jenkins.

Griffiths, A. (1875) *Memorials of Millbank*. London: Chapman and Hall.

Griffiths, A. (1884) *The Chronicles of Newgate*. London: Chapman and Hall.

Guy, W. (1863) 'On sufficient and insufficient dietaries – with special reference to the dietaries of prisoners', *Journal of the Statistical Society*, XXVI, 239–80.

Hall, J. (1979) *Revolt against Chivalry*. New York: Columbia University Press.

Hall, S. (1980) *Drifting into a Law and Order Society*. London: Cobden Trust.

Hansard, references as shown in text.

Hardy, T. (1886, 1994) *The Mayor of Casterbridge*. London: Wordsworth Classics.

Hart-Davis, R. (ed.) (1962) *The Letters of Oscar Wilde*. London: Rupert Hart-Davis.

Hastings, E. and Hastings, P. (eds) (2000) *Index to International Public Opinion (1979–1999)*. Westport, CT: Greenwood Press.

Haxby, D. (1978) *Probation: A Changing Service*. London: Constable.

Healy, W. and Alper, B. (1941) *Criminal Youth and the Borstal Systems*. New York: Commonwealth Fund.

Heckinstall-Smith, A. (1954) *Eighteen Months*. London: Wingate.

Hignett, N. (1956) *Portrait in Grey*. London: Muller.

Hill, F. (1853) *Crime: Its Amount, Causes and Remedies*. London: John Murray.

Hill, P. (1991) *Stolen Years*. London: Corgi.

Hill, R. and Hill, F. (1875) *What We Saw in Australia*. London: Macmillan.

Hindus, M. (1980) *Prison and Plantation*. Chapel Hill: University of North Carolina Press.

Hobhouse, S. and Brockway, F. (1923) *The English Prison System*. London: Macmillan.

Hole, C. (1949) *English Sports and Pastimes*. London: Batsford.

Holt, W. (1934) *I was a Prisoner*. London: Mills.

Home Office (1843) *Report Relative to the System of Prison Discipline*. London: PP XXV (457).

Home Office (1945) *Prisons and Borstals*. London: HMSO.

Home Office (1959) *Penal Practice in a Changing Society*. London: HMSO.

Home Office (1960) *Prisons and Borstals*. London: HMSO.

Home Office (1970) *Non-custodial and Semi-custodial Penalties*. London: HMSO.

Home Office (1976) *Review of Criminal Justice Policy*. London: HMSO.

Home Office (1977) *Prisons and Prisoners*. London: HMSO.

Home Office (1984) *Tougher Regimes in Detention Centres*. London: HMSO.

Home Office (1985) *New Directions in Prison Design*. London: HMSO.

Home Office (1988) *Punishment, Custody and the Community*. London: HMSO.

Home Office (1990) *Crime, Justice and Protecting the Public*. London: HMSO.

Home Office (1996) *Protecting the Public*. London: HMSO.

Home Office Statistical Bulletin (1998) *The Prison Population in 1997*. London: HMSO.

Hopkins, A. (1930) *Prisons and Prison Building*. New York: Architectural Book Publishing Co.

Hornung, E.W. (1899, 1984) *The Complete Short Stories of Raffles*. London: Souvenir Press.

Horsley, J. (1887) *Jottings from Jail*. London: T. Fisher Unwin.

Hough, M. and Mayhew, P. (1983) *The British Crime Survey*. London: HMSO.

Houghton, H. (1972) *Operation Portland*. London: Rupert Hart-Davis.

Howard, D. (1960) *The English Prisons*. London: Methuen.

Howard, J. (1777, 1929) *The State of the Prisons*. London: Dent.

Howitt, W. (1840) *The Rural Life of England*. London: Longmans.

Ignatieff, M. (1978) *A Just Measure of Pain*. London: Macmillan.

Jackson, G. (1971) *Soledad Brother*. New Jersey: Cape.

Jacobs, J. (1980) 'The prisoners' rights movement and its impacts', in N. Morris and M. Tonry (eds), *Crime and Justice*. Chicago: University of Chicago Press, pp. 429–70.

Jock of Dartmoor (1933) *Dartmoor from Within*. London: Readers Libraries Publishing Co.

Johnson, C. (1734, 1926) *A General History of the Lives and Adventures of the Most Famous Highwaymen, Murderers and Robbers*. London: Navarre Society.

Johnson, E. (1999) *Nazi Terror*. New York: Basic Books.

Johnston, L. (1996) 'What is vigilantism?', *British Journal of Criminology*, 36, 220–36.

Johnston, N. (1960) 'John Haviland', in K. Mannheim (ed.), *Pioneers in Criminology*. Montclair: Paterson Smith, pp. 107–28.

Jones, H. (1965) *Crime in a Changing Society*. London: Penguin.

Jones, H. and Cornes, P. (1973) *Open Prisons*. London: Routledge.

Karp, D. (1998) 'The judicial and judicious use of shame penalties', *Crime and Delinquency*, 44, 277–94.

Kessler, J. (2000) 'Prisons in the USA', in L. Fairweather and S. McConville (eds), *Prison Architecture*. Oxford: Architecture Press, pp. 89–97.

King, R. (1999) 'The rise and rise of supermax', *Punishment and Society*, 1, 163–86.

Kingsmill, J. (1854) *Chapters on Prisons and Prisoners*. London: Longmans.

Laqueur, T. (1989) 'Crowds, carnival and the state of English executions 1604–1868', in A. Beir, D. Cannadine and J. Rosenheim (eds), *Modern Society: Essays in English History in Honour of Lawrence Stone*. Cambridge: Cambridge University Press, pp. 305–55.

Laslett-Browne, H. (1895) 'Common-sense and crime', *Fortnightly Review*, 64, 224–33.

Learmont, J. (1995) *Review of Prison Service Security*. London: HMSO.

Lee, J. (1885, 1985) *The Man They Couldn't Hang*. Devon: Devon County Council.

Leigh, J. (1941) *My Prison House*. London: Hutchinson.

Lenci, S. (1978) 'The future of prisons', in P. Dickens, L. Fairweather and S. Mc Conville (eds), *Penal Policy and Prison Architecture*. Chichester: B. Rose, pp. 21–9.

Levenstein, H. (1988) *Revolution at the Table*. New York: Oxford University Press.

Lewis, D. (1997) *Hidden Agendas*. London: Hamish Hamilton.

Lewis, O. (1921) *The Development of American Prisons and Prison Customs*. New York: Prison Association.

Locke, T. (1990) *New Approaches to Crime in the 1990s*. London: Longmans.

Lodge, T. S. (1975) 'The founding of the Home Office Research Unit', in R. Hood (ed.), *Crime, Criminology and Public Policy*. New York: Free Press, pp. 11–25.

London, J. (1903) *People of the Abyss*. New York: Literary Classics.

Lovett, W. (1876) *The Life and Struggles of William Lovett*. London: Trubner.

Mackenzie, C. (1975) *Biggs: The World's Most Wanted Man*. New York: W. Morrow.

Malcomson, R. (1973) *Popular Recreations in English Society 1700–1850*. Cambridge: Cambridge University Press.

Manderville, B. (1725) *An Enquiry into the Causes of the Frequent Hangings at Tyburn*. London: J. Roberts.

Markus, T. (1993) *Buildings and Power*. London: Routledge.

Martinson, R. (1974) 'What works? Questions and answers about prison reform', *The Public Interest*, 35: 22–54.

Mason, E. (1919) *Made Free in Prison*. London: Allen and Unwin.

Masur, L. (1989) *Rites of Execution*. Oxford: Oxford University Press.

Matthews, R. (1999) *Doing Time*. London: Macmillan.

Maxwell, A. (1942) 'Foreword', in W.N. East, *The Adolescent Criminal*. London: J. & A. Churchill.

Mayhew, H. and Binny, J. (1862, 1968) *Criminal Prisons of London*. London: Frank Cass.

McCartney, W. (1936) *Walls Have Mouths*. London: Gollancz.

McConville, S. (1981) *A History of English Prison Administration*. London: RKP.

McConville, S. (1995) *English Local Prisons 1860–1900*. London: Routledge.

McGuire, J. (1988) 'Judicial violence and the civilizing process', *Australian Historical Studies*, 23: 187–209.

McMahon, M. (1992) *The Persistent Prison?*, Toronto: Toronto University Press.

McVicar, J. (1974) *McVicar by Himself*. London: Hutchinson.

Mennell, S. (1985) *All Manners of Food*. Oxford: Basil Blackwell.

Mennell, S. (1990) 'Decivilizing processes: theoretical significance and some lines of research', *International Sociology*, 5: 205–33.

Mennell, S. (1992) *Norbert Elias: An Introduction*. Oxford: Blackwell.

Mennell, S. (1995) *Civilizing and Decivilizing: Civil Society and Violence*. Dublin: University of Dublin.

Mill, J.S. (1811) 'On the penal law of England', *The Philanthropist*, 1: 66–73, 143–56.

Mill, J.S. (1836, 1977) 'Civilization', in J. Robson (ed.), *Collected Works*, XVIII, 119–47.

Mishra, R. (1984) *The Welfare State in Crisis*. New York: St Martins Press.

Mitford, J. (1975) *The American Prisons Business*. London: Allen and Unwin.

Morris, P. and Morris, T. (1963) *Pentonville*. London: Routledge and Kegan Paul.

Morrison, W. (1894) 'Are our prisons a failure?', *Fortnightly Review*, 61: 459–69.

Mukherjee, S. (1988) *Sourcebook of Australian Criminal and Social Statistics*. Canberra: AIC.

Myers, M. (1998) *Race, Labour and Punishment in the New South*. Columbus: Ohio State University Press.

Neild, J. (1812) *The State of the Prisons in England, Scotland and Wales*. London: John Nichols and Son.

Nellis, M. (1988) 'British prison movies: the case of "Now Barabas"', *Howard Journal*, 27: 2–31.

Nellis, M. (1996) 'John Galsworthy's "Justice"', *British Journal of Criminology*, 36: 61–84.

Nevill, W. (1903) *Penal Servitude*. London: Heinemann.

Norman, F. (1958) *Bang to Rights*. London: Secker and Warburg.

O'Connell, S. (1999) *The Popular Print in England*. London: British Museum Press.

O'Malley, P. (1999) 'Volatile and contradictory punishments', *Theoretical Criminology*, 3: 175–96.

One who has endured it (1877) *Five Years Penal Servitude by* .... London: Richard Bentley.

One who has suffered (1882) *Revelations of prison life by* .... London: Richard Bentley.

Oxford English Dictionary (1992) Oxford: Oxford University Press.

Page, L. (1937) *Crime and the Community*. London: Faber and Faber.

Peterson, A. (1961) 'The prison building programme', *British Journal of Criminology*, 1: 307–16.

Phelan, J. (1940) *Jail Journey*. London: Secker and Warburg.

Plint, T. (1851) *Crime in England*. London: Charles Gilpin.

Potter, H. (1997) *Hanging in Judgement*. New York: Continuum.

Poynter, B. (1969) *Plenty and Want*. London: Routledge and Kegan Paul.

Pratt, J. (1991) 'Punishment, history and empire', *Australia and New Zealand Journal of Criminology*, 24: 118–38.

Pratt, J. (1992) *Punishment in a Perfect Society*. Wellington: Victoria University Press.

Pratt, J. (1997) *Governing the Dangerous*. Sydney: Federation Press.

Probyn, W. (1977) *Angel Face*. London: Allen and Unwin.

Quinton, R. (1910) *Crime and Criminals*. London: Longmans Green.

Radzinowicz, L. (1948) *A History of English Criminal Law*, Vol. 1, London: Stevens and Sons Ltd.

Radzinowicz, L. and Hood, R. (1986) *A History of English Criminal Law*, Vol. 5, London: Butterworths.

Raper, A. (1933, 1969) *The Tragedy of Lynching*. Montclair: Paterson Smith.

Reade, C. (1856) *It's Never too Late to Mend*. Leipzig: Tauchnitz.

Report from the Select Committee of the House of Lords on Capital Punishment (1856) London: PP VII.

Report from the Select Committee of the House of Lords on Prison Discipline (1863) London: PP IX.

Report of the Advisory Council on the Penal System (1968) London: HMSO.

Report of the Board Appointed to Inquire into and Report on the General Management and Discipline of the Gaol at Berrima (1861/2) Sydney: V and P (1862), 2.

Report of the Board Appointed to Investigate Certain Alleged Irregularities in the Gaol of Parmatta (1862) Sydney: Government Printer.

Report of the Board of Inquiry into Several Matters Concerning HM Prison Pentridge and the Maintenance of Discipline in Prisons (1973) Melbourne: Government Printer Victoria.

Report of the Chief Inspector of Prisons (1982) London: HMSO.

Report of the Chief Inspector of Prisons (1984) London: HMSO.

Report of the Chief Inspector of Prisons (1987) London: HMSO.

Report of the Chief Inspector of Prisons (1988) London: HMSO.

Report of the Chief Inspector of Prisons (1991–2) London: HMSO.

Report of the Chief Inspector of Prisons (1993) London: HMSO.

Report of the Chief Inspector of Prisons (1996) London: HMSO.

Report of the Commissioners on the Treatment of the Treason Felony Convicts in the English Convict Prisons (1867) London: PP XXX.

Report of the Commission of Inquiry into the Treatment of Treason-Felony Convicts (1871) London: PP XXXII.

Report of the Commissioner of Penitentiaries (1953) Ottawa: Canada Sessional Papers (1952–3) 2.

Report of the Commissioner of Penitentiaries (1960) Ottawa: Canada Sessional Papers (1960–1) 3.

Report of the Commissioner of Penitentiaries (1961) Ottawa: Canada Sessional Papers (1960–1) 3.

Report of the Commissioners Appointed to Enquire into Prisons and the Prison System of the Province of Ontario (1879) Toronto: Government Printer Ontario.

Report of the Commissioners Appointed to Enquire into the Conduct, Discipline and Management of the Provincial Penitentiary (1849) Montreal: Government Printer.

Report of the Commissioners Appointed to Enquire into the Conduct, Discipline and Management of the Provincial Penitentiary (1850) Montreal: Government Printer.

Report of the Commissioners Appointed to Inquire into the Workings of the Penal Servitude Acts (1879) London: PP XXXVII.

Report of the Commissioners on the Conditions and Treatment of the Prisoners Confined in Birmingham Borough Prison (1854) London: PP XXXI.

Report of a Committee Appointed to Consider and Report upon Dietaries of Local Prisons (1878) London: PP (95) XLIII. 53.

Report of a Committee Appointed to Consider Certain Questions Relating to the Employment of Convicts in the United Kingdom (1882) London: PP XXXIV.

Report of a Committee Appointed to Inquire into the Dietaries of Convict Prisons (1864) London: PP XLIX.

Report of the Committee Appointed to Inquire into the Operation of the Acts Relating to Transportation and Penal Servitude (1863) London: PP XXI.

Report of the Committee of Inquiry on Prison Rules and Prison Dress (1889) London: PP LXI.

Report of the Committee on the Dietaries of County and Borough Prisons (1864) London: PP XLIX.

Report of the Comptroller-General of Prisons (1883) Sydney: V & P LA (1883/4) 6.

Report of the Comptroller-General of Prisons (1885) Sydney: V & P LA (1885–6) 4.

Report of the Comptroller-General of Prisons (1893) Sydney: V & P LA (1894) 3.

Report of the Comptroller-General of Prisons (1896) Sydney: V & P LA (1897) III.

Report of the Comptroller-General of Prisons (1904) Sydney: V & P LA (1905) III.

Report of the Comptroller-General of Prisons (1926) Sydney: V & P LA (1927) III.

Report of the Comptroller-General of Prisons (1956–7) Sydney: V & P LA (1957) III.

Report of the Comptroller-General of Prisons (1963–4) Sydney: V & P LA (1964) III.

Report of the Controller-General of Prisons (1920) Wellington: Government Printer.

Report of the Controller-General of Prisons (1922) Wellington: Government Printer.

Report of the Controller-General of Prisons (1926) Wellington: Government Printer.

Report of the Controller-General of Prisons (1927) Wellington: Government Printer.
Report of the Controller-General of Prisons (1934) Wellington: Government Printer.
Report of the Controller-General of Prisons (1937) Wellington: Government Printer.
Report of the Controller-General of Prisons (1938) Wellington: Government Printer.
Report of the Controller-General of Prisons (1947) Wellington: Government Printer.
Report of the Controller-General of Prisons (1950) Wellington: Government Printer.
Report of the Controller-General of Prisons (1960) Wellington: Government Printer.
Report of the Controller-General of Prisons (1961) Wellington: Government Printer.
Report of the Correctional Services Commissioners (1995–6) Melbourne: Government Printer.
Report of the Correctional Services Commissioners (1996–7) Melbourne: Government Printer.
Report of the Corrections Branch [British Columbia] (1974) mf 75–0770.
Report of the Department of Correction (1967) Albany: Department of Correction.
Report of the Department of Correctional Services (1967) Albany: Department of Correctional Services.
Report of the Department of Correctional Services (1975) Albany: Department of Correctional Services.
Report of the Department of Correctional Services (1976) Albany: Department of Correctional Services.
Report of the Department of Correctional Services (1978) Albany: Department of Correctional Services.
Report of the Department of Correctional Services (1978–9) Albany: Department of Correctional Services.
Report of the Department of Correctional Services (1980–1) Albany: Department of Correctional Services.
Report of the Department of Correctional Services (1985–6) Albany: Department of Correctional Services.
Report of the Department of Corrections (1986) Atlanta: Department of Corrections.
Report of the Department of Corrections (1995) Atlanta: Department of Corrections.
Report of the Department of Corrections (1996) Atlanta: Department of Corrections.
Report of the Department of Corrections (1997) Atlanta: Department of Corrections.
Report of the Department of Justice (1967) Wellington: Government Printer.
Report of the Department of Justice (1968) Wellington: Government Printer.
Report of the Department of Justice (1975) Wellington: Government Printer.
Report of the Department of Prisons (1965–6) Sydney: Government Printer New South Wales.
Report of the Departmental Committee on Corporal Punishment (1938) London: HMSO.
Report of the Director of Correctional Services (1978) Melbourne: Victoria (1980–1) pp. 11.
Report of the Director of Corrections (1962–3) Ottawa: Canada Sessional Papers (1962–3) 2
Report of the Director of Corrective Services (1969) Sydney: Government Printer NSW.
Report of the Director of Corrective Services (1975–6) Sydney: Government Printer NSW.
Report of the Director of Corrective Services (1979–80) Sydney: Government Printer NSW.
Report of the Director of Corrective Services (1980–1) Sydney: Government Printer NSW.
Report of the Director of Corrective Services (1981–2) Sydney: Government Printer NSW.
Report of the Director of Corrective Services (1983) Sydney: Government Printer NSW.
Report of the Director of Corrective Services (1985–6) Sydney: Government Printer NSW.
Report of the Director of Corrective Services (1987) Sydney: Government Printer NSW.
Report of the Director of Corrective Services (1989–90) Sydney: Government Printer NSW.
Report of the Director of Corrective Services (1990–1) Sydney: Government Printer NSW.

Report of the Director of Corrective Services (1992–3) Sydney: Government Printer NSW.

Report of the Director of Penal Services (1957) Melbourne: Victoria V and P (1958–9) 2.

Report of the Director of Penal Services (1961–2) Melbourne: Victoria V and P (1963–4) 2.

Report of the Director of Penal Services (1972) Melbourne: Victoria V and P (1972–3) 3.

Report of the Director of Penal Services (1973) Melbourne: Victoria V and P (1973–4) 3.

Report of the Directors of Convict Prisons (1852) London: PP (1853) LI.

Report of the Directors of Convict Prisons (1858) London: PP (1859) XIII.

Report of the Directors of Convict Prisons (1860) London: PP (1861) XXX.

Report of the Directors of Convict Prisons (1867) London: PP (1867–8) XXXIV.

Report of the Directors of Convict Prisons (1870) London: PP (1871) XXXI.

Report of the Directors of Convict Prisons (1871) London: PP (1872) XXXI.

Report of the Directors of Convict Prisons (1872) London: PP (1873) XXXIV.

Report of the Directors of Convict Prisons (1879–80) London: PP (1880) XXXVI.

Report of the Du Parq Committee (1932) London: HMSO.

Report of an Enquiry into Brutalities and Corruption at Pentridge Prison (1885) Melbourne: Government Printer Victoria.

Report of the Gladstone Committee (1895) London: PP LVII.

Report of the Inquiry into Prison Escapes and Security (1966) London: HMSO cmd 3175.

Report of the Inspectors of Penitentiaries (1880) Ottawa: Canada Sessional Papers 1880–1, 14, 9.

Report of the Inspectors of Penitentiaries (1881) Ottawa: Canada Sessional Papers 1882, 15, 7.

Report of the Inspectors of Penitentiaries (1887) Ottawa: Canada Sessional Papers 1888, 21, 11.

Report of the Inspectors of Penitentiaries (1897) Ottawa: Canada Sessional Papers 1898, 32, 13.

Report of the Inspectors of Penitentiaries (1915) Ottawa: Canada Sessional Papers 1916, LI, 26, 34.

Report of the Inspectors of Penitentiaries (1921) Ottawa: Canada Sessional Papers 1922, L, 8.

Report of the Inspectors of Penitentiaries (1922) Ottawa: Canada Sessional Papers 1923, LIX, 5.

Report of the Inspectors of Penitentiaries (1929) Ottawa: Canada Sessional Papers 1928–9, III, 5.

Report of the Inspectors of Penitentiaries (1945) Ottawa: Canada Sessional Papers 1944–5, III, 5.

Report of the Inspector of Prisons (1881) Wellington: Government Printer.

Report of the Inspector of Prisons (1884) Wellington: Government Printer.

Report of the Inspector of Prisons (1889) Wellington: Government Printer.

Report of the Inspector of Prisons (1890) Wellington: Government Printer.

Report of the Inspector of Prisons (1900) Wellington: Government Printer.

Report of the Inspector of Prisons and Reformatories (1933) Toronto: Ontario Sessional Papers (1934) 66, 5.

Report of the Inspector of Prisons and Reformatories (1938) Toronto: Ontario Sessional Papers (1939) 71, 4.

Report of the Inspectors of Prisons of the Home District (1836) London: PP XXXV.

Report of the Inspectors of Prisons of the Home District (1837) London: PP XXXII.

Report of the Inspectors of Prisons of the Home District (1839) London: PP XXI.

Report of the Inspectors of Prisons of the Home District (1845) London: PP XXIII.

Report of the Inspectors of Prisons of the Home District (1851) London: PP XXVII.

Report of the Inspectors of Prisons of the Northern District (1839) London: PP XXI.

Report of the Inspectors of Prisons of the Northern District (1848) London: PP XXV.

Report of the Inspectors of Prisons of the Southern District (1858) London: PP (1859) XXIX.

Report of the Inspectors of Prisons of the Southern District (1870) London: PP XXXVII.

Report of the Inspectors of State Prisons (1862) Albany: New York (State) Inspectors of State Prisons.

Report of the Inspectors of State Prisons (1866) Albany: New York (State) Inspectors of State Prisons.

Report of the Inspectors of State Prisons (1870) Albany: New York (State) Inspectors of State Prisons.

Report of the Inspector-General of Penal Establishments and Gaols (1878) Melbourne: Victoria (1878) PP II.

Report of the Inspector-General of Penal Establishments and Gaols (1879) Melbourne: Victoria (1879–80) PP II.

Report of the Inspector-General of Penal Establishments and Gaols (1887) Melbourne: Victoria (1887) PP II.

Report of the Inspector-General of Penal Establishments and Gaols (1902) Melbourne: Victoria (1902) PP II.

Report of the Inspector-General of Penal Establishments and Gaols (1910) Melbourne: Victoria (1910) PP III.

Report of the Inspector-General of Penal Establishments and Gaols (1912) Melbourne: Victoria (1912) PP III.

Report of the Inspector-General of Penal Establishments and Gaols (1925) Melbourne: Victoria (1926) PP 2.

Report of the Inspector-General of Penal Establishments and Gaols (1943) Melbourne: Victoria (1944–5) PP II.

Report of the Inspector-General of Penal Establishments and Gaols (1944) Melbourne: Victoria PP (1945–7) PP II.

Report of the Joint Committee of the Senate and House of Commons on Capital and Corporal Punishment and Lotteries (1954) Ottawa: Queen's printer.

Report of the May Committee (1979) London: HMSO cmnd 7673.

Report of the New York State Prison Department (1898, 1899) Albany: Department of Corrections.

Report of the New York (State) Prison Department (1891) Albany: NY State Prison Department.

Report of the New York (State) Prison Department (1900) Albany: NY State Prison Department.

Report of the New York (State) Prison Department (1901) Albany: NY State Prison Department.

Report of the New York (State) Prison Department (1904) Albany: NY State Prison Department.

Report of the New York (State) Prison Department (1907) Albany: NY State Prison Department.

Report of the New York (State) Prison Department (1917) Albany: NY State Prison Department.

Report of the New York State Prison Inspectors (1862) Albany: NY Prison Inspectors.

Report of the New York State Prison Inspectors (1874) Albany: NY Prison Inspectors.

Report of the New York State Prison Inspectors (1875) Albany: NY Prison Inspectors.

Report of the Prison Commissioners (1878–9) London: PP (1879) XXXIV.

Report of the Prison Commissioners (1883) London: PP (1883) XXXI. 445.

Report of the Prison Commissioners (1887–8) London: PP (1888) XLI. 203.

Report of the Prison Commissioners (1889) London: PP (1889) XLI.
Report of the Prison Commissioners (1890) London: PP (1890)XXXVII.
Report of the Prison Commissioners (1895) London: PP (1895) LVI.
Report of the Prison Commissioners (1899) London: PP (1900) XL. 1.
Report of the Prison Commissioners (1900–1) London: PP (1902) cmd. 804.
Report of the Prison Commissioners (1902) London: PP (1902–3) XLVI.
Report of the Prison Commissioners (1908–9) London: PP (1909) cmd 4847.
Report of the Prison Commissioners (1909–10) London: PP (1910) cmd 5360.
Report of the Prison Commissioners (1911–12) London: PP (1912–13) XLIII.
Report of the Prison Commissioners (1918–9) London: PP (1919) XXVII cmd. 374.
Report of the Prison Commissioners (1922) London: PP (1922–3) cmd. 1761.
Report of the Prison Commissioners (1924–5) London: PP (1924–5) cmd. 2307.
Report of the Prison Commissioners (1926) London: PP (1927) cmd. 2597.
Report of the Prison Commissioners (1935) London: PP (1936–7) XV cmd. 5430.
Report of the Prison Commissioners (1936) London: PP (1937–8) cmd. 5430.
Report of the Prison Commissioners (1937) London: PP (1937–8) cmd. 4308.
Report of the Prison Commissioners (1942) London: PP (1946–7) cmd. 7010.
Report of the Prison Commissioners (1945) London: PP (1946–7) XIV cmd. 7146.
Report of the Prison Commissioners (1946) London: PP (1947–8) XV cmd. 7271.
Report of the Prison Commissioners (1947) London: PP (1947–8) cmd. 7475.
Report of the Prison Commissioners (1949) London: PP (1950–1) cmd. 8080.
Report of the Prison Commissioners (1950) London: PP (1950–1) cmd. 8356.
Report of the Prison Commissioners (1951) London: PP (1952–3) cmd. 8692.
Report of the Prison Commissioners (1952) London: PP (1952–3) cmd. 8948.
Report of the Prison Commissioners (1954) London: PP (1955–6) cmd. 9547.
Report of the Prison Commissioners (1955) London: PP (1956–7) cmd. 10.
Report of the Prison Commissioners (1956) London: PP (1957–8) cmd. 322.
Report of the Prison Commissioners (1958) London: PP (1958–9) cmd. 825.
Report of the Prison Commissioners (1960) London: PP (1960–1) cmd. 1467.
Report of the Royal Commission on Capital Punishment (1956) London: PP VII cmd. 8932.
Report of the Royal Commission to Inquire into and Report on the General Management and Discipline of the Gaol at Berrima (1878–9) Sydney: V and P (1879) III.
Report of the Royal Commission to Investigate the Penal System of Canada (1938) Ottawa: Queen's Printer.
Report of the Royal Commission on New South Wales Prisons (1978) Sydney: Government Printer NSW.
Report of the Royal Commission on Prisons (1868) Wellington: Government Printer.
Report of the Royal Commission on Prison and Penal Discipline (1870) Melbourne: Victoria PP (1870) 2.
Report of a Select Committee on Public Prisons in Sydney and Cumberland (1861) Sydney: V and P (1861) 1.
Report of the Select Committee of Inquiry into John Price's Administration of the Penal Department (1857) Melbourne: Government Printer.
Report of the Select Committee on Andover Union (1846) London: PP V (633) 3–10.
Report of the Solicitor-General of Canada (1971–2) Ottawa: Canadian Sessional Papers (1972) 3, 41–60.
Report of the State Board of Corrections (1961) Atlanta: Department of Corrections.
Report of the State Board of Corrections (1965) Atlanta: Department of Corrections.
Report of the State Board of Corrections (1967) Atlanta: Department of Corrections.
Report of the State Commission of Corrections (1931) Ossining: New York State Commission of Corrections.

Report of the State Commission of Prisons (1905) Albany: New York (State) Commission of Prisons.

Report of the State Commission of Prisons (1913) Albany: New York (State) Commission of Prisons.

Report of the State Commission of Prisons (1914) Albany: New York (State) Commission of Prisons.

Report of the State Commission of Prisons (1917) Albany: New York (State) Commission of Prisons.

Report of the Superintendent of Police Respecting the Prisons of British Columbia (1891) Victoria, BC: Government Printer.

Report of the Royal Commission to Investigate the Penal System of Canada (1938) Ottawa: Queen's Printer.

Report on the Operation of the Department of Prisons (1949/50) Sydney: Government Printer.

Report on the Work of the Prison Department (1963) London: PP (1963–4) cmnd. 2381.

Report on the Work of the Prison Department (1964) London: PP (1964–5) cmnd. 2708.

Report on the Work of the Prison Department (1965) London: PP (1965–6) cmnd. 3088.

Report on the Work of the Prison Department (1967) London: PP (1967–8) cmnd. 3774.

Report on the Work of the Prison Department (1968) London: PP (1969–70) cmnd. 4186.

Report on the Work of the Prison Department (1969) London: PP (1970–1) cmnd. 4486.

Report on the Work of the Prison Department (1972) London: PP (1972/3) cmnd. 5375.

Report on the Work of the Prison Department (1973) London: PP (1974/5) cmnd. 5767.

Report on the Work of the Prison Department (1974) London: PP (1974/5) cmnd. 5767.

Report on the Work of the Prison Department (1975) London: PP (1975/6) cmnd. 6523.

Report on the Work of the Prison Department (1977) London: PP (1977–8) cmnd. 6877.

Report on the Work of the Prison Department (1980) London: PP (1980/1) cmnd. 8228.

Report on the Work of the Prison Service (1981) London: PP (1981/2) cmnd. 8543.

Report on the Work of the Prison Service (1983) London: PP (1983/4) cmnd. 9306.

Report on the Work of the Prison Service (1985–6) London: PP (1986/7) cm. 11.

Report on the Work of the Prison Service (1989–90) London: PP (1990/1) cm. 1302.

Report on the Work of the Prison Service (1990–1) London: PP (1991/2) cm. 1724.

Report on the Work of the Prison Service (1992/3) London: PP (1992/3) cm. 2385.

Rich, C. (1932) *Recollections of a Prison Governor*. London: Hurst and Blackett.

Rickards, C. (1920) *A Prison Chaplain on Dartmoor*. London: Arnold.

Roberts, H. (1850) *The Dwellings of the Labouring Classes*. London: Savill and Edwards.

Rockwood, C. (1834) *The Life and Adventures of that Notorious Robber and Murderer Richard Turpin*. London: Arnold.

Rossa, J. O'D. (1882) *My Years in English Jails*. New York: D. J. Sadleir & Co.

Rose, D. (1994) *In the Name of the Law*. London: Vintage.

Rose, G. (1960) *The Struggle for Penal Reform*. London: Stevens.

Rothman, D. (1971) *The Discovery of the Asylum*. Boston: Little, Brown.

Ruck, S.K. (ed.) (1951) *Paterson on Prisons*. London; F. Muller.

Ruggles-Brise, E. (1921) *The English Prison System*. London: Macmillan.

Runyon, T. (1954) *In For Life*. London: Andre Deutsch.

Russell, C. (1973) *Everyday Life in Colonial Canada*. London: B.T. Batsford.

Rutherford, A. (1985) 'The new generation of prisons', *New Society*, 73: 408–10.

Rutherford, A. (1986) *Prisons and the Process of Justice*. Oxford: Oxford University Press.

Scott, H. (1959) *Your Obedient Servant*. London: A. Deutsch.

Scull, A. (1977) *Decarceration*. London: Prentice-Hall.

Sim, J. (1990) *Medical Power and the Prison*. London; Routledge.

Simon, J. (1998) 'Managing the monstrous: sex offenders and the new penology', *Psychology, Public Policy and Law*, 4: 452–67.

Simon, J. (2000) 'The "Society of Captives" in the era of hyper-incarceration', *Theoretical Criminology*, 4: 285–308.

Smith, E. (1858) 'On the principles involved in a scheme of prison dietary', *Transactions of the National Association for the Promotion of Social Science*, 293–306.

Smith, E. (1864) 'Gaol dietary: the operations of the recent Committee', *The Social Science Review*, 2 (NS): 85–120.

Smollett, T. (1757, 1930) *The Adventures of Peregrine Pickle*. London: Dent.

Society for the Improvement of Prison Discipline (1826) *Remarks on the Form and Construction of Prisons: with Appropriate Designs*. London: SIPD.

Southern Commission on the Study of Lynching (1931), *Lynchings and What they Mean*, Atlanta: The Commission.

Sparks, R. (1961) *Burglar to the Nobility*. London: Arthur Baker.

Sparks, R. (1996) 'Penal austerity: "less eligibility" reborn?', in R. Matthews and P. Francis (eds), *Prisons 2000*. London: Macmillan.

Sparks, R., Bottoms, A.E. and Hay, W. (1996) *Prisons and the Problem of Order*. Oxford: Clarendon Press.

Spearman, E. (1895) 'Prisoners on the move', *The Fortnightly Review*, CCCXLVIII (NS): 717–22.

Spierenburg, P. (1984) *The Spectacle of Suffering*. Cambridge: Cambridge University Press.

Steiner, J. and Brown, R. (1927, 1969) *The North Carolina Chain Gang*. Montclair: Paterson Smith.

Stephen, J. (1883) *History of the English Criminal Law*. London: Butterworths.

Strange, C. (2001) 'The Undercurrents of Penal Culture-Punishment of the Body in Mid-Twentieth century Canada, *Law and History Review* 19, 343–385.

Strutt, J. (1830) *The Sports and Pastimes of the People of England*. London: Thomas Tegg and Son.

Symonds, J. (1849) *Tactics for the Times: As Regards the Condition and Treatment of the Dangerous Classes*. London: John Olliver.

Tallack, W. (1889) *Penological and Preventive Principles*. London: Wertheimer, Lea.

Taylor, G. (1824) 'Prisons and penitentiaries', *The Quarterly Review*, 30: 404–40.

Taylor, I. (1981) *Law and Order: Arguments for Socialism*. London: Macmillan.

Taylor, R. (1960) 'The habitual criminal: observations on some of the men sentenced to preventive detention', *British Journal of Criminology*, 1: 21–36.

Teeters, N. and Shearer, C. (1957) *The Prison at Philadelphia Cherry Hill*. New York: Random House.

Thackeray, W. (1840) 'Going to see a man hanged', *Fraser's Magazine*, 20: 150–8.

Thomas, K. (1983) *Man and the Natural World*. London: Allen Lane.

Thomas, T. (1972) *The English Prison Officer since 1850*. London: Routledge.

Thomson, B. (1907) *The Story of Dartmoor Prison*. London: Heinemann.

The Times, varions editions as shown in the text.

Tollemache, R. (1973) 'Crisis agencies and the treatment of offenders in the Netherlands', *Howard Journal*, 13: 397–410.

Turner, B. and Skinner, T. (1784) 'An account of some of the alterations and amendments attempted in the duty and office of the Sheriff of the County of Middlesex and London', *Gentleman's Magazine*, 2: 21–32.

Vassall, J. (1975) *Vassall: The Autobiography of a Spy*. London: Sidgwick and Jackson.

Wakefield, E. (1832) *Facts Relating to the Punishment of Death in the Metropolis*. London: Wilson.

Walker, N. and Hough, M. (eds) (1988) *Public Attitudes to Sentencing*. Aldershot: Gower.

Waller, I. and Chan, J. (1974) 'Prison use: a Canadian and international comparison', *Criminal Law Quarterly*, 47–71.

Walvin, J. (1978) *Leisure and Society*. London: Longman.

Warden (1929) *His Majesty's Guests*. London: Jarrolds.

Webb, B. and Webb, S. (1922) *English Prisons under Local Government*. London: Longmans, Green and Co.

Whitfield, D. (1991) 'Maidstone Prison, England', in D. Whitfield (ed.), *The State of the Prisons 200 Years on*. London: Routledge, pp. 13–29.

Wicker, T. (1975) *A Time to Die*. New York: New York Times Book Co.

Wicks, H. (1935) *The Prisoner Speaks*. London: Jarrolds.

Wiener, M. (1994) 'The unloved state', *Journal of British Studies*, 33: 283–308.

Wildeblood, P. (1955) *Against the Law*. London: Weidenfeld and Nicolson.

Williams, S. (1959) *Vogues in Villainy*, Columbia, SC: Columbia University Press.

Wines, E. and Dwight, T. (1867, 1973) *Report on the Prisons and Reformatories of the United States and Canada*. Boston: AMS Press.

Wood, S. (1932) *Shades of the Prison House*. London: Williams and Norgate Ltd.

Woodward, L. (1938) *The Age of Reform*. Oxford: Oxford University Press.

Woolf, H. and Tumin, J. (1991) *Prison Disturbances April 1990*. London: HMSO.

Wyatt-Brown, B. (1982) *Southern Honour*. New York: Oxford University Press.

Zimring, F. (1996) 'Populism, democratic government and the decline of expert authority', *Pacific Law Journal*, 28: 243–56.

Zimring, F. and Hawkins, G. (1991) *The Scale of Imprisonment*. Chicago: Chicago University Press.

Index